CHERNOBYL ROULETTE

ALSO BY SERHII PLOKHY

The Russo-Ukrainian War: The Return of History

Atoms and Ashes: A Global History of Nuclear Disasters

The Frontline: Essays on Ukraine's Past and Present

Nuclear Folly: A History of the Cuban Missile Crisis

Forgotten Bastards of the Eastern Front:
An Untold Story of World War II

Chernobyl: The History of a Nuclear Catastrophe

Lost Kingdom: The Quest for Empire and the Making of the Russian Nation

The Man with the Poison Gun: A Cold War Spy Story

The Gates of Europe: A History of Ukraine

The Last Empire: The Final Days of the Soviet Union

The Cossack Myth: History and Nationhood in the Age of Empires

Yalta: The Price of Peace

Ukraine and Russia: Representations of the Past

The Origins of the Slavic Nations:
Premodern Identities in Russia, Ukraine, and Belarus

Unmaking Imperial Russia:
Mykhailo Hrushevsky and the Writing of Ukrainian History

Tsars and Cossacks: A Study in Iconography

The Cossacks and Religion in Early Modern Ukraine

CHERNOBYL ROULETTE

WAR IN THE NUCLEAR
DISASTER ZONE

———

Serhii Plokhy

W. W. NORTON & COMPANY

Independent Publishers Since 1923

For information about permission to reproduce selections from this book,
write to Permissions, W. W. Norton & Company, Inc., 500 Fifth Avenue,
New York, NY 10110

For information about special discounts for bulk purchases, please contact
W. W. Norton Special Sales at specialsales@wwnorton.com or 800-233-4830

Manufacturing by Sheridan
Production manager: Anna Oler

Library of Congress Cataloging-in-Publication Data Available

ISBN 978-1-324-07941-5

W. W. Norton & Company, Inc.
500 Fifth Avenue, New York, N.Y. 10110
www.wwnorton.com

W. W. Norton & Company Ltd.
15 Carlisle Street, London W1D 3BS

1 2 3 4 5 6 7 8 9 0

To the men and women of the Exclusion Zone

CONTENTS

The Russo-Ukrainian War (2022)

POLAND

BELARUS

Homiel

Pinsk

Rivne

Chernobyl

Kyiv Res.

Lutsk

Rivne

Dnieper R.

Khmelnytskyi

Zhytomyr

Kyiv

Lviv

UKRAINE

Ternopil

Khmelnytskyi

SLOVAKIA

Ivano-Frankivsk

Dniester R.

Vinnytsya

Uman

Uzhgorod

HUNGARY

Chernivtsi

MOLDOVA

Chişinău

ROMANIA

Tiraspol

Odesa

Izmail

Danube R.

BULGARIA

Vistula R.

☼ Capital
● City or town
☢ Nuclear power plant (active)
☢ Nuclear power plant (decommissioned)
● Russian-controlled location
● Ukrainian-controlled location
   Russian-controlled territory gained since
   February 24, 2022
   Russian-controlled territory as of
   February 24, 2022
   Territory regained by Ukrainian forces
── Line of contact before February 24, 2022
── International boundary
/// Annexed formally by Russia as of
   September 30, 2022

Chernihiv

Konotop

Sumy

Kursk

RUSSIA

Voronezh

Belgorod

Kharkiv

Kremenchuk Res.

Poltava

Izyum

Siverodonetsk

Cherkasy

Kremenchuk

Kramatorsk

DONBAS

Luhansk

Kropyvnytskyi

Dnipro

Pavlohrad

Horlivka

Donetsk

Kryvyi Rih

Zaporizhia

Kakhovka Res.

Zaporizhia

Rostov

Don R.

Mariupol

South Ukraine

Mykolaiv

Nova Kakhovka

Melitopol

Berdyansk

Kherson

Henichesk

Sea of Azov

CRIMEA

Kerch

Kerch Strait

Krasnodar

Simferopol

Novorossiysk

Sevastopol

Black Sea

0   50   100 mi

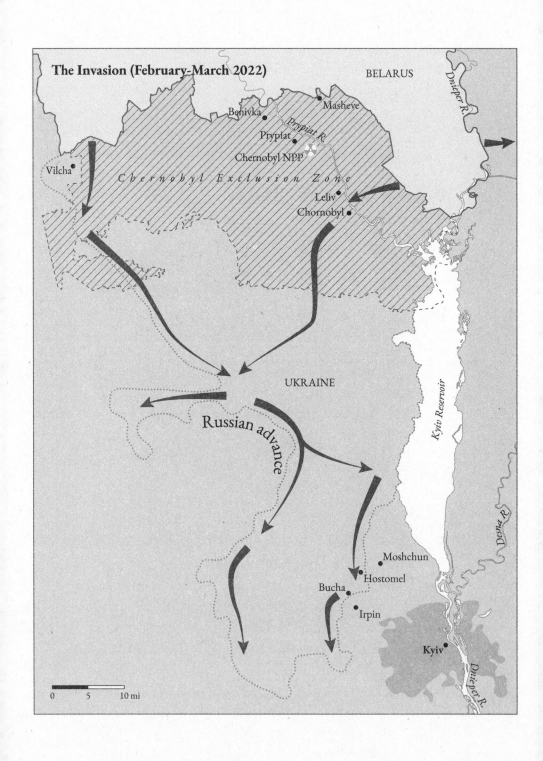

The Invasion (February–March 2022)

BELARUS

Dnieper R.

Bonivka

Masheve

Prypiat R.

Prypiat

Chernobyl NPP

Vilcha

Chernobyl Exclusion Zone

Leliv

Chornobyl

UKRAINE

Kyiv Reservoir

Russian advance

Desna R.

Moshchun

Hostomel

Bucha

Irpin

Kyiv

Dnieper R.

0   5   10 mi

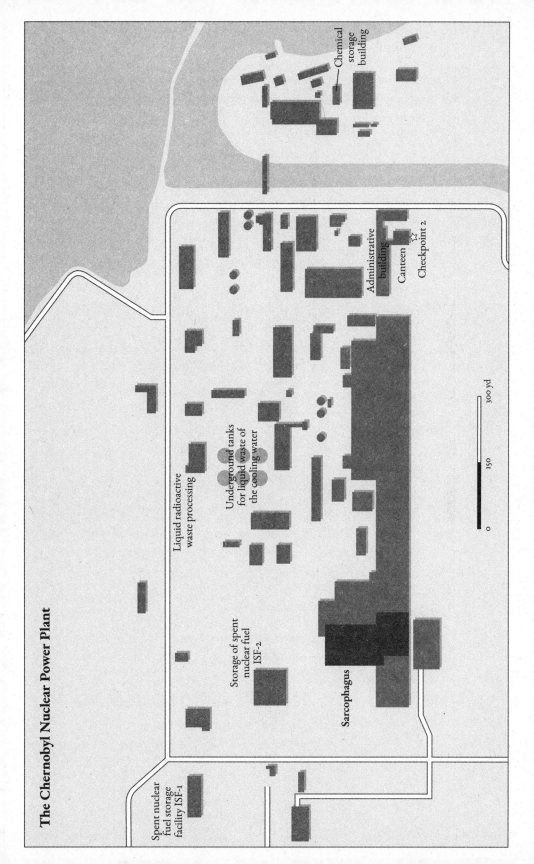

The Chernobyl Nuclear Power Plant

Chemical storage building

Administrative building

Canteen

Checkpoint 2

Liquid radioactive waste processing

Underground tanks for liquid waste of the cooling water

Storage of spent nuclear fuel ISF-2

Sarcophagus

Spent nuclear fuel storage facility ISF-1

0   150   300 yd

NOTE ON TRANSLITERATION

The Chernobyl nuclear disaster of 1986 entered the annals of world history under the Russian spelling of the name of the Ukrainian town of Chornobyl, which gave its name to the power plant. This reflected the tsarist and Soviet-era policy of russifying non-Russian toponyms. Since Ukraine became independent in 1991, the Ukrainian spelling of the town's name has become the norm in Ukraine. The same applies to the spelling of Ukrainian toponyms in general, such as "Kyiv" rather than the Russian "Kiev" for the Ukrainian capital, "Prypiat" rather than "Pripiat," and "Slavutych" rather than "Slavutich." The tendency to switch from Russian to Ukrainian forms not only in Ukraine itself but throughout the world intensified with the start of the Russo-Ukrainian War in 2014 and particularly after Russia's all-out invasion in 2022. The official name of the Chernobyl nuclear power plant is today "Chornobyl NPP," and the leading tour operator in the exclusion zone changed its spelling from the Chernobyl Tour to the Chornobyl Tour.

In this book, which draws parallels between the disaster of 1986 and the Russian occupation of the site in 2022, I use "Chernobyl," established in the English literature of the subject, in reference to the 1986 accident, the plant itself, and the exclusion zone around it. I use "Chornobyl" when referring to the town of Chornobyl and the official names of Ukrainian institutions and organizations whose names are derived from the name of the town. I regard this mixed usage not only as a reflection of certain present-day realities but also as a way of encouraging a worldwide transition from the Russian to the Ukrainian spelling of the name of the city associated with the largest nuclear disaster in history. Ukraine's strong resistance to the Russian invasion, documented in this book, ensured that the city of Chornobyl and the nuclear site remained Ukrainian and that the country maintained its identity, culture, and language, including the Ukrainian spelling of its toponyms.

PREFACE

On the afternoon of February 24, 2022, a column of Russian armored vehicles led by a tank and followed by paddy wagons of internal troops called the Russian Guard (*Rosgvardiia*) approached the main checkpoint of the Chernobyl nuclear power plant in northern Ukraine. The tank pointed its gun at the plant's administration building. Two Russian officers, a general and a colonel, disembarked from their vehicles and approached the defenders of the building, saying that they were under Russian government orders to take control of it. If resisted, they were prepared to unleash a "meat grinder," said one of the officers. The commanders of the Ukrainian National Guard unit that was protecting the Chernobyl site decided to lay down their weapons so as not to endanger the site and to avoid another nuclear disaster. The Russian occupation of the Chornobyl plant had begun. It would last a long thirty-five days.

Like the first Chernobyl crisis, of 1986, that of 2022 took almost everyone by surprise and proved no less dramatic. The Ukrainian government had only limited capacity to help the station's personnel, who became hostages of the Russian military. The international community managed little more than issuing expressions of concern. At the headquarters of the International Atomic Energy Agency in Vienna, the industry's supreme international authority, there were no protocols for operating a nuclear power plant under military attack. Although the Russian Federation was a member of the IAEA, the agency was not prepared to demand that Moscow end its aggression and withdraw its troops from nuclear sites. The Ukrainian personnel at the Chernobyl plant found themselves pretty much on their own.

This book is about the men and women of the Chernobyl nuclear site and the town of Chornobyl who found themselves under occupation on February 24, 2022, the first day of Russia's all-out invasion of Ukraine. The Ukrainian personnel of the plant numbered close to 300, including its operators, firefighters, and members of the National Guard unit. The guardsmen were taken prisoner, while the operational staff became hostages. On the evening of February 23, they arrived at the plant, expecting to work for a twelve-hour period or, in the parlance of the industry, a graveyard shift. Instead, they would spend weeks working at gunpoint in the cramped quarters of their offices, with no change of clothing, medication, or hygienic supplies. They had to make life-or-death decisions on cooperation or resistance, knowing that little if any help would come from outside.

How long would the occupation last? Given the disparity of forces, was it prudent to cooperate with the occupiers or, on the contrary, to escape from the station or engage in sabotage? If they chose the latter course, what would happen to them, the station, and its environs? Might there be another nuclear accident, and was it their responsibility to prevent it, or should they fight the occupying forces with every means at their disposal? Those were the questions preoccupying the Chernobyl personnel. They answered those questions individually day by day, trying to balance loyalty to their families, their homeland, and innocent civilians in Ukraine and beyond who would suffer the consequences of a nuclear accident should it occur. The choices they made helped to save the world from another Chernobyl disaster.

Thirty-five days into occupation, a successful counteroffensive by the Ukrainian armed forces changed the situation in the Chornobyl region, driving the Russians out of northern Ukraine and liberating the station's personnel. A much more dangerous situation developed at the Zaporizhia nuclear power plant in southern Ukraine, the largest such facility in Europe. There the Ukrainian defenders refused to surrender and opened fire on a Russian military column approaching the station on the night of March 3, 2022. The attackers returned fire, shelling the station, setting a training center ablaze, and hitting the plant's administration building as well as the area around the spent-fuel facility. Once in control of the station, the Russians used it as cover to terrorize the neighboring Ukrainian town with artillery fire.

At this writing, the Zaporizhia plant remains under Russian control, and Ukrainian military intelligence claims that the occupiers have mined the facility in preparation for an act of nuclear terrorism. We must face up to a new reality: there has already been warfare at two nuclear sites, and others are vulnerable. There are 440 such sites around the globe today, and there will probably be many more in the future. Russia's aggression against Ukraine is unlikely to be the last war in human history. Thus, the story of the men and women of Chernobyl told in this book may be something more than recent history. Most likely it is also a warning for the future.

1

COUNTDOWN

On January 18, 2022, Yaroslav Yemelianenko, a thirty-nine-year-old founder and CEO of Chornobyl Tour, the zone's largest tour operator, announced on his Facebook page that a drive to recruit new guides for that year's tourist season in the Chernobyl exclusion zone had begun. "On the eve of the new season we are increasing our staff and seeking reliable, responsible people enamored of our subject who speak foreign languages and have a natural flair for multitasking," read Yemelianenko's post. Although the COVID pandemic had put a stop to tourism in the Chernobyl zone, all but killing his business, Yemelianenko was working hard with his fellow tour operators to "revitalize" the zone as Ukraine's prime tourist destination.[1]

Yemelianenko prepared for the 2022 tourist season with enthusiasm and hope, pretty much ignoring the warning signals from all over the world. But he could not ignore the news that reached him on Monday, January 24, six days after he announced the drive to hire new employees. It came from Washington, where President Joseph Biden had spent a good part of the day in teleconferences with world leaders, discussing the chances that Russia would invade Ukraine. On the previous day, the US Department of State had issued an advisory recommending that American citizens not travel to Ukraine, ordering the evacuation of family members of the US Embassy staff in Kyiv and advising American citizens to leave the country—all owing to "the continued threat of Russian military action."[2]

For Yemelianenko, this was a major setback, but not an outright disaster. "Ukraine has found itself in the level 4 advisory 'do not travel' because of the risk of Russian attack and the spread of COVID," he posted on his Facebook page on January 24. "For tourism, this means the suspension of activity for an indefinite period. Unfortunately, that will entail stopping the development of projects and the 'hibernation' of organizations. That's a Monday for you. We are prepared for various scenarios of further development. But for now, let's hold on and prepare for the season." Yemelianenko was not giving up. Not yet. He was still awaiting a flood of visitors in the zone. There would be a lot of them, but they would not come on tourist visas and not use the services of Yemelianenko's agency.[3]

———

President Biden learned of a potential Russian attack on Ukraine on a sunny October morning in 2021, when his chief military commander, General Mark A. Milley, the chairman of the Joint Chiefs of Staff, showed up in the Oval Office with a host of aides.

Also present were Vice-President Kamala Harris, National Security Advisor Jake Sullivan, Secretary of State Antony Blinken, Defense Secretary Lloyd Austin, and the heads of the US intelligence agencies. Biden and Harris were seated in front of the fireplace, while the others took seats around the coffee table. Before Milley began his presentation, his aides placed a set of maps before the participants. They covered the territories of Russia, Ukraine, and Belarus, showing the positions of Russian forces on the eastern borders of Ukraine. Milley told the president that the intelligence available to him and the heads of other government agencies suggested Russian preparations for an all-out attack on Ukraine.

"We assess that they plan to conduct a significant strategic attack on Ukraine from multiple directions simultaneously," General Milley told the president. The maps were there to indicate those directions. Russia had massed troops in its western lands along Ukraine's eastern border and in the Crimea, annexed in 2014. But according to Milley, the Russian General Staff was preparing to attack Ukraine not only from the east, in the Donets Basin (Donbas), where the Russians had created the two puppet "people's republics" of Donetsk and Luhansk in 2014, or from the south, where they had long dreamed of creating a "land corridor" from those "republics" to the occupied in 2014 Crimea, but also from the north, toward the Ukrainian capital, Kyiv.

Milley told the president that the Russians planned to take Kyiv in three or four days, attacking it in winter, when the soil was hard enough to allow the movement of tanks and heavy equipment. President Volodymyr Zelensky of Ukraine would be removed or even killed, and a pro-Russian government would be installed in Kyiv. To achieve that goal, Russian troops would move toward the Ukrainian capital not only from their own territory but also from Belarus, proceeding between the Chernobyl exclusion zone and the Prypiat River marshes. According to Milley's map, the Chernobyl nuclear power plant and the exclusion zone were on the path of the main Russian thrust toward Kyiv, but the map suggested that the Russians would bypass the zone. That appeared to be the most plausible scenario. Why would anyone of sound mind send troops into a nuclear disaster zone?[4]

————

President Zelensky was warned about the Russian plans to attack Ukraine by Secretary of State Blinken in early November 2021. The conversation took place in Glasgow, where they were attending the international climate summit. Zelensky was skeptical: the Americans were not disclosing either their sources of information or the details of what they had learned from them.

When senior officials in the US State Department had advised Zelensky's chief of staff, Andrii Yermak, and the Ukrainian minister of foreign affairs, Dmytro Kuleba, to prepare for a Russian attack and start "digging trenches," no specifics were given on what that meant and where to start digging. Zelensky took the position, at least publicly, that what the United States and the West had warned him about was just another in a long sequence of threats from Russia, with which, as Zelensky pointed out more than once, Ukraine had been at war since 2014.[5]

In his address to the Glasgow summit, Zelensky warned the world about the two "eco-bombs" left by the Russian aggression of 2014 against Ukraine: the Crimea, which had been militarized by the occupiers, and the occupied parts of the Donbas, which had been turned into an ecological disaster zone. Zelensky focused, however, on Chernobyl to underline the global nature of ecological disasters. He then used the example of the return of wildlife to the zone to suggest that the best way of helping to preserve nature was to leave it alone and stop causing further damage.

"In our time disaster, wherever it may occur, affects absolutely everyone," argued Zelensky. "This is proved by the explosion at the Chernobyl Atomic Energy Station, which caused suffering not only in Ukraine but in dozens of countries. This tragedy also shows us another truth: the most effective measure for reviving the environment is noninterference by human beings. In Chernobyl, nature is reviving much more quickly than expected. It seems to be suggesting: people, the best way to help is not to interfere."[6]

Ever since the release of the HBO *Chernobyl* series, the office of the president of Ukraine had been working hard with Ukrainian tour operators to launch a "revitalization" of the Chernobyl zone and turn it into the country's primary tourist destination. What Zelensky heard from Blinken suggested more disasters—political, economic, social, human, ecological. He did not want to believe what the American was saying. But even the US administration did not believe at the time that the invasion would take place through the Chernobyl zone. That seemed unimaginable.[7]

———

The Chernobyl exclusion zone became a news item soon after the Ukrainian president's return from the Glasgow summit, but not because of the warnings that Zelensky had received from Blinken. On November 11, Ukrainian officials announced the deployment of additional border guards to the Ukrainian-Belarusian border, including the exclusion zone. The deployment was a response to the actions of Aliaksandr Lukashenka, the autocratic ruler of Belarus, with which Ukraine shared the Chernobyl exclusion zone created after the nuclear disaster of 1986.[8]

The post-Soviet ruler longest in office, dubbed the last European dictator, Lukashenka had assumed power in Belarus in 1994 and held on to it with the help of brute force unleashed against dissidents by his security forces. When in August 2020 the Belarusian people rebelled against yet another of the many falsified presidential elections, Lukashenka resorted to force once again and turned to his Russian counterpart, Vladimir Putin, for help. He received enough assistance from Moscow to suppress the protests and stay in power. In return, he gave the Russian military and security forces free access to his ostensibly independent country.

After the Lukashenka regime forced a Ryanair flight en route from Athens to Vilnius, with a Belarusian opposition activist on board, to land on Belarusian territory, the European Union responded with sanctions. Lukashenka, with the apparent backing of Putin, then created a humanitarian crisis. Thousands of migrants from the Middle East were flown to Belarus and taken to the border with the EU. On November 8, 2021, several hundred Iraqi Kurds were escorted to the Polish border by the Belarusian security services. They threw stones at the border guards and tried to break into Poland near the Bruzgi-Kuźnica crossing, causing the Poles to respond with tear gas and close the crossing.[9]

On November 11, the UN Security Council discussed the growing migration crisis on the Belarusian-Polish border. By that time, 32,000 attempts to cross the EU border illegally had been registered. The Estonian ambassador to the United Nations, Sven Jürgenson, declared: "We condemn the orchestrated instrumentalization of human beings whose lives and well-being have been put in danger for political purposes by Belarus, with the objective of destabilizing neighboring countries and the European Union's external border and diverting attention away from its own increasing human rights violations." Jürgenson's position was shared by seven members of the UN Security Council. The rest of the Council members, Russia in particular, refused to condemn the actions of the Belarusian strongman.[10]

The Ukrainians had no doubt that the real culprit behind the crisis was not Lukashenka but Putin. "As long as the European Union keeps closing its eyes to Moscow's role in the current crisis, it will continue," wrote a leading Ukrainian online newspaper, *Ukrainian Truth*, on the eve of the UN Security Council meeting. The Ukrainian government announced its own measures to defend the country's border on the day of the UN Council meeting. The morning of that day, the Ukrainian interior minister, Denys Monastyrsky, declared the start of Operation Polisia, named after the marshy region along the Ukrainian-Belarusian border. Monastyrsky personally inspected parts of the border and committed to reinforce it with 3,000 members of the National Guard, 3,500 border guards, and 2,000 policemen, equipped with fifteen helicopters. He also promised to allocate 17 million Ukrainian hryvnias, or close to US $650,000, to establish new observation points on the border that passed through the Chernobyl exclusion zone.[11]

The deployment of new troops began on November 23. The first deputy interior minister, Yevhen Yenin, personally visited the Chernobyl zone to observe the maneuvers of the national guardsmen, border guards, and police stationed in the area. A video of Yenin's visit was released to the media. The Chernobyl zone, accounting for 34 kilometers (21 miles) of the more than 1,000-kilometer- (622-mile-) long Ukrainian-Belarusian border, was home to one border crossing, located north of a settlement called Vilcha. Because the area was highly contaminated, the quarters of the Ukrainian border guards were located a few kilometers away from Vilcha in a village called Mlachivka.

Guards were first stationed there in 2014, when the Russo-Ukrainian War began and Russia annexed the Crimea. In November 2021, with the migration crisis reaching its peak on the Belarusian-EU border, Ukrainian border guards in Mlachivka received new equipment, most notably the Ukrainian-made Cougar armored personnel carrier. Reinforcements were more than timely, but the potential intruders whom the Ukrainian border guards would soon have to face were not Middle Eastern migrants but regular Russian troops.[12]

———

Russian troops began arriving in Belarus and moving south toward the Ukrainian border on January 17, 2022. The Belarusians announced their arrival on the following day. A good many of the troops came from the Russian Far East. They included units of the 5th, 29th, 35th, and 36th Combined Arms Armies of the Eastern Military District. The troops spread all along the Ukrainian border. The 36th Motor-Rifle Brigade from the Transbaikal region and the 155th Naval Infantry Brigade from Vladivostok went to Brest in western Belarus, while the 38th Motor-Rifle Brigade went to Mazyr in eastern Belarus. So did the 37th Motor-Rifle Brigade from Buriatia, which arrived in Rechytsa, across the border from the Chernobyl nuclear power plant and the ghost town of Prypiat.[13]

The reason given for the influx of close to 30,000 Russian troops was preparation for joint military exercises with Belarus, "Union Resolve 2022," to be launched on February 10. "These should be normal exercises to work out a certain plan for confronting these forces: in the west the Baltics and Poland, and in the south—Ukraine," Lukashenka told the media. US State Department officials were skeptical about the allegedly routine nature of the exercises. One senior official suggested that Lukashenka might not even have been informed by the Russians of what they were up to. "I think what we should be concerned about is not whether it increases the intent [to attack Kyiv], but whether or not it increases the capability and their ability to launch that invasion of Ukraine with an intent to topple the government," the official told the media on January 18.[14]

The next day, Secretary Blinken visited President Zelensky in Kyiv with fresh intelligence to warn him about the coming Russian invasion of Ukraine and a direct attack on Kyiv. Blinken urged Zelensky to consider how he could "ensure continuity of government operations depending on what happens." Zelensky believed that the Americans wanted him out of Kyiv "to just end things faster." He told Blinken that he was not leaving the capital and would not announce a general mobilization so as to avoid sowing panic and sending the already struggling economy into a tailspin. But there was no indication that Zelensky was getting the capital ready for defense or making preparations to fend off a possible Russian attack from Belarus. The Ukrainian president appeared to be in denial.[15]

On January 22, 2022, the *New York Times* published an article written by its Kyiv bureau chief, Andrew E. Kramer, from the Chernobyl exclusion zone. Kramer suggested something that appeared to be obvious yet unthinkable: the Chernobyl zone might become a battlefield of the new war that everyone was so concerned about. "While most of the attention around a potential invasion by Russia is focused on troop buildups and daily hostilities in the east, the shortest route from Russia to Ukraine's capital, Kyiv, is from the north," wrote Kramer. He added: "And it passes through the isolated zone around the Chernobyl power plant, where the meltdown of a reactor in 1986 caused the worst nuclear disaster in history."[16]

Kramer's suggestion that there might be an attack on the Chernobyl zone was met with disbelief on the part of locals. "How can this be?" mused Ivan Kovalchuk, a Ukrainian firefighter who had taken part in cleanup operations after the 1986 accident. "We liquidated the [consequences of the] accident together. For them to do this to us now just makes me feel sorry for [those] people." Others were frightened of possible warfare in the zone: as the worker Oleksii Pryshchepa, interviewed by Kramer, suggested, it made no sense for the Ukrainian armed forces to fight in the contaminated area. "It's a wasteland, no crop will ever grow here," Pryshchepa told the reporter. In his opinion it was far more rational to establish Ukrainian defensive lines south of the zone and give it up in case of Russian attack.

Kramer also encountered Ukrainian border guards in the zone. They seemed determined to protect the border no matter what. "It doesn't matter if it is contaminated or nobody lives here," said Lieutenant Colonel Yurii Shakhraichuk of the Ukrainian border guard service. "It is our territory, our country, and we must defend it." "Ukrainian soldiers, Kalashnikov rifles slung over their shoulders, patrolled through a silent, snowy forest, passing homes so long abandoned that vines twirl through the broken windows," wrote Kramer. They were led on their patrol by local policemen who knew the area and helped the border guards avoid the most dangerously contaminated areas. But the troops that Kramer saw in the zone had been deployed there as monitors responding to the migration crisis on the Belarusian border and had no capacity to withstand a major ground attack.[17]

———

The Ukrainians were caught between denial of the coming aggression and determination to resist it. Which would prevail once an invasion began was not entirely clear. The government itself vacillated as to the appropriate response: whether to warn people about the likelihood of a coming war or pretend to conduct business as usual. In public, Ukrainian government officials put up a brave face; privately, they prepared for a possible invasion. The Chernobyl zone became the site where the government tried to merge the two strategies—prepare the country for war without saying so.

On February 3, the Ukrainian defense minister, Oleksii Reznikov, assured his countrymen that there was no threat from Belarus. "We expect no provocations from Belarus; we have no basis for hostility, as we consider it friendly," said the minister. But even as Reznikov was making his statement, something strange was happening in the Chernobyl exclusion zone. A tour group heading toward the zone was blocked from entering it on the grounds that officials had been called with a warning of a mine planted at one of the facilities. Such calls had increased in Ukraine since January and were classified as part of hostile Russian information operations, but this time it was not clear whether that was the reason for closing the zone. On the previous day, the authorities announced that the Ukrainian National Guard would conduct exercises in the zone.[18]

On February 4, representatives of the diplomatic corps and the Western media who had flooded into Kyiv amid increased concerns about the coming Russian invasion were invited to witness the announced maneuvers of the Ukrainian National Guard in the zone. The ghost town of Prypiat became the main theater of the urban warfare game. A drone flew over the heads of reporters, issuing a message that was supposed to prevent panic but was quite capable of causing it. "The enemy is in town," went the prerecorded message. "You must stay inside. Please close all windows. Take all your documents. Warn the neighbors. Be cautious. Do not panic."[19]

An armored personnel carrier drove down what looked like a tree-lined alley but had once been a street in Prypiat. The soldiers, dressed in mottled-white winter camouflage, used the carrier as cover and then took their positions, ready to fire at enemy snipers hiding in apartment buildings along the street. Another group of soldiers opened fire at the upper floors of an apartment building. Firefighters extinguished the blaze in one of the apartments, while a group of "civilians" was escorted from that building to a parked bus that drove them away. The sound of automatic fire was accompanied by bursts of mortar shells as the Ukrainian special forces "stormed" one of the buildings.[20]

In attendance were Minister of Defense Oleksii Reznikov and Minister of Interior (with authority over the National Guard) Denys Monastyrsky. Once the exercises involving the army, National Guard, and personnel from the Ministry of Emergency Situations were over, the two ministers addressed the press. "These are the ruins of the Soviet empire," Reznikov told the journalists, pointing to the Soviet insignia on the wall of one of the buildings. "We will ensure that the Russian empire does not come back to our borders," he continued. He added, with reference to the Russian annexation of the Crimea in 2014: "Russian citizens came and occupied our territory, but there will be no repeat."[21]

The publicity that accompanied the drill left no doubt that the exercises were meant to send a message to the Russians, the citizens of Ukraine, and the world at large: the Ukrainians were ready to fight. Prypiat was chosen as the location for the exercises not because it was the most convenient place to train the military—police with Geiger counters had to go in first to ensure that the soldiers could enter the city safely—but because Prypiat, known to the world at large thanks to the Chernobyl accident, attracted the global attention that the Ukrainian authorities were seeking at the moment. Prypiat also fit the bill because it was close to the capital, making it relatively easy to bring in not only the media but also members of the diplomatic corps who remained in Kyiv.

But in Ukraine the exercises unexpectedly proved to be a public-relations disaster. The live ammunition used by the military left marks on the buildings of Prypiat that the tour operators and their supporters had been working hard to protect. It turned out that the building at which the soldiers had fired was the one in which the firefighter Volodymyr Pravyk, one of the heroes of the 1986 Chernobyl saga, used to live. Plans were under way to turn the building and Pravyk's apartment into a museum, but now the walls had been damaged not by Russian but by Ukrainian soldiers. The tour operators and environmentalists protested publicly and privately, appealing to Zelensky's administration. Their concerns were heard. Lala Tarapakina, an adviser to the minister of environment and an active supporter of the "revitalization" of the Chernobyl zone project, assured the public through her Facebook account that the State Agency of Ukraine for Exclusion Zone Management would block any future attempts to conduct military exercises in the zone. It was supposed to stay military free.[22]

———

As the Ukrainian protectors of historical heritage and the environment did their best to keep the Ukrainian armed forces out of the zone, the Russian army on the Belarusian side of the border prepared to enter it. On February 13, Russian troops launched their joint exercises with the Belarusian army near Ukraine's northern border. The Ukrainian president and government put up a brave face. On the day the exercises began, Volodymyr Zelensky asserted that the military situation had not changed much since the start of Russia's aggression against Ukraine eight years earlier. He spoke of psychological pressure applied by Moscow rather than a real threat of war, adding: "We see nothing new in this. As for the risks, there are risks, and they have not ended since 2014."[23]

It was wishful thinking at best. New threats were emerging daily, and some of them pointed to the Chernobyl zone as a corridor from Belarus toward Kyiv. On February 16, world media published satellite photos of a pontoon bridge installed by the Russian military across the Prypiat River a mere four kilometers (2.5 miles) from the Ukrainian border on the Belarusian side of the exclusion zone. Two days later Olha Vasylevska-Smahliuk, a Ukrainian parliamentary deputy from a constituency bordering on the exclusion zone, confronted Prime Minister Denys Shmyhal in a question period. "My electors, who live in the zone of voluntary resettlement, have been disturbed by photographs of a pontoon bridge crossing the Prypiat River from the side of the Belarusian border," she said. She then posed her question: "What [measures] concretely, point by point, Mr. Prime Minister, have you taken in case of a possible offensive against Ukrainian territory from the direction of the Chernobyl [zone]?"[24]

Shmyhal referred the question to the defense minister, Oleksii

Reznikov, who assured the deputy that his ministry was in touch with the Belarusian military with regard to the bridge. "We have raised the question of this pontoon bridge, this pontoon crossing, and received a reply, an assurance that this is part of the training, and that it will soon be taken down," Reznikov told parliament. He continued: "Our law enforcement agencies, which ensure security and order in the exclusion zone of the Chernobyl Nuclear Power Station, believe me, are absolutely taking care, and know everything, and are observing everything, and are prepared for any scenarios whatever."[25]

The Ukrainian authorities however decided to close the Chernobyl zone to tourists and other visitors from February 20 to March 20, 2022. A statement issued by the State Agency of Ukraine for Exclusion Zone Management stated that this decision was being adopted as part of "prophylactic measures in reaction to extraordinary situations of a natural and man-made nature." The Ukrainian decision to close the zone came not a day too early. On February 20, the day the restrictions went into effect, the Belarusian government declared that the Russo-Belarusian maneuvers scheduled for ten days, from February 10 to February 20, would be extended indefinitely.[26]

For President Biden and his advisers, this was a clear sign that the information they had first obtained in October 2021 about a Russian invasion from Belarus was genuine. "Everything we are seeing suggests that this is dead serious, that we are on the brink of an invasion," Antony Blinken told the media that day. American agencies published news obtained from the US intelligence community that the Russian military had been ordered to proceed with the invasion of Ukraine, and that commanders on the ground were making specific plans for maneuvers in their sectors of the battlefield. Although the media was silent on that, one of those sectors was the Chernobyl exclusion zone.[27]

2

EXCLUSION ZONE

I n the early hours of April 26, 1986, an accident at reactor no. 4 at the Chernobyl nuclear power plant in northern Ukraine, then part of the USSR, opened a new page in the history of the nuclear industry and a new era in the history of the region—the detonation of a chain reaction that contributed to the disintegration of the USSR.

The Chernobyl nuclear disaster was man-made. Although it had features in common with nuclear disasters elsewhere, the explosion revealed the surprising recklessness with which the Soviet government and its military and scientific elites treated the dangers of managing nuclear energy. The facility that exploded at Chernobyl was a Soviet-made RBMK, or high-power channel reactor. It could enrich uranium and produce plutonium for nuclear bombs as easily as it could produce electricity. The peculiarities and weaknesses of its design were kept secret even from its operators, which was one of the key reasons for the accident. Pressed to fulfill their production quotas and knowing nothing about the inherent dangers of the reactor, the operators would often cut corners, ignoring regulations and instructions in order to meet their targets.

On April 26 they cut one corner too many. A massive explosion blasted one thousand tons of the reactor's "lead" into the air, contaminating huge swaths of the territory of Ukraine, Belarus, Russia, and parts of Western Europe. The first to leave their homes were the families of the plant's operators—close to 50,000 residents of the city of Prypiat, located a few miles away from the troubled facility. They were evacuated because the authorities expected another, even more powerful, blast to follow the first two. That did not happen, but it soon became clear that no one could return to Prypiat or the neighboring towns and villages for permanent residence. The Chernobyl exclusion zone was born.

At first the zone was 10 kilometers (6.2 miles) in diameter, then 30 kilometers (19 miles). Later it would be extended to 2,600 square kilometers or 1,000 square miles on the Ukrainian side of the border alone. In neighboring Belarus, the Polesie radioecological preserve covered a territory roughly half that size. The zone ceased to be circular in shape as the authorities struggled to include the most contaminated areas around the nuclear plant. In drawing the new boundary, they followed wind directions during the first weeks after the explosion: radioactive particles were spread by winds and deposited into the soil by spring showers.[1]

The town of Chornobyl, as opposed to the ghost town of Prypiat that was abandoned in 1986, served as a logistical hub for all operations in the zone conducted by the numerous organizations involved in managing it. Chief among them were the government agency called "Chornobyl Nuclear Power Plant," which managed the devastated power station, the State Agency of Ukraine for Exclusion Zone Management, and the Chornobyl Radiation and Ecological Biosphere Reserve, charged with the study and preservation of the zone's unique ecological system. Last but not least, Chornobyl and the zone in general became a base for tourist firms, whose facilities were located in the town.[2]

The hub of activity in the zone had always been the nuclear power plant: decades after the accident and years after the shutdown of the last functioning reactor in 2000, it still needed plenty of work and supervision. The government agency running it was charged with decommissioning the three shut-down reactors and operating the confinement structure over reactor no. 4, damaged in 1986. The agency's headquarters were located in the company town of Slavutych, built in 1986 approximately 45 kilometers or 28 miles east of the plant to house its personnel and liquidators of the accident. Initially the agency employed more than 5,600 managers, scientists, engineers, and workers. Their key preoccupation was the safety of the damaged reactor no. 4.[3]

In 1992, the year after the dissolution of the USSR, the Ukrainian government held a competition for the construction of a new confinement structure over reactor no. 4. The original one, built within half a year after the April 1986 disaster, was considered temporary from the outset, had major structural problems, and did not fully prevent the continuing release of radiation into the atmosphere. The construction of the original safe confinement, or what was referred to as the "sarcophagus," had been a Soviet project; the design and building of the new one would become an international one. Not unexpectedly, it turned out be a much lengthier undertaking. The Soviet sarcophagus was designed in a few weeks, and construction took only 206 days. The international project took more than a quarter of a century from its inception to completion—approximately the maximum life span of the Soviet confinement designed back in 1986.[4]

The construction of the new confinement was begun in 2007 by the French Novarka Consortium, which included Vinci Construction Grands Projets and Bouygues Construction. It took Novarka twelve years to complete the work, the delay being caused largely by the higher than originally estimated levels of radiation in and around the old shelter. The money, 1.5 billion euros for the construction of the arch itself and 2.2 billion euros for the project as a whole, including the assembly of numerous systems designed to monitor and control radiation levels, was provided mostly by international donors, mainly members of the G7 (the world's largest democratic economies). Altogether, the governments of forty-five countries contributed to the project, and more than 10,000 engineers and construction laborers, half of them from Ukraine, worked on it. They built the largest movable structure in the world, 843 feet long (about the size of twelve soccer fields) and weighing 36,000 tons. The shelter was constructed next to the damaged reactor and then "sledded" over it. Its expected life span was 100 years.[5]

A successful operating test of the new shelter was conducted in April 2019, thirty-three years after the accident. Tourist visits to the newly built shelter were allowed in July of that year, a few months after the release of the HBO/Sky miniseries on Chernobyl. The new shelter deprived tour guides of one of the most impressive tricks they had performed in front of astonished visitors. Standing in front of the old shelter, they would show tourists a dosimeter that would beep because of the higher than natural background levels of radiation around the shelter. Then a guide would place the dosimeter behind the granite monument to the cleanup workers, known as "liquidators," erected next to the shelter, and it would stop beeping. Now, with the construction of the new shelter, dosimeters would remain silent in front of the monument or behind it. The level of radiation around the shelter had fallen by a factor of ten.[6]

The completion of the new shelter significantly reduced the number of people coming to work in the Chernobyl exclusion zone, but many were still needed to keep it from presenting a threat to the world. As spent nuclear fuel was removed from the three undamaged reactors, a task completed in 2016, the agency's staff was further reduced. Altogether, 2,000 people did various jobs in the zone in 2019, and about 2,500 in early 2022. They operated the new $1.7-billion confinement structure over reactor no. 4, which went into service in 2019, maintained storage facilities for the spent fuel removed from the Chernobyl and other Ukrainian reactors, and monitored radioactivity levels in the zone.[7]

Radioactive processes in the heart of the damaged reactor were far from over. In May 2021, a few weeks after the world marked the thirty-fifth anniversary of the accident, global media reported on the "awakening" of reactor no. 4. Engineers detected a spike in the number of neutrons in underground room 305/2, full of radioactive debris that included uranium and zirconium. An increase had first been detected in 2017, suggesting that the original fission reaction was continuing in that room. It might stop on its own or keep going, which would make another accident more likely. Scientists believed that any new radiation would be contained by the new shelter but would further complicate the ultimate cleanup of the reactor and the removal of 200 tons of highly radioactive waste, including fuel remaining in the reactor after the explosion. According to the best-case scenario, that task would take another fifty years to complete.[8]

The spent fuel from the other Chernobyl reactors was stored on-site, presenting another problem to be dealt with by the staff of the nuclear plant. In 2020, an American company called Holtec completed the roughly twenty-year-long construction of a new off-site facility for spent nuclear fuel from the long-decommissioned Chernobyl reactors. It was estimated at the time that eight years would be required to move 21,000 fuel assemblies to the facility from temporary storage at the site of the Chernobyl nuclear power plant. The new complex was supposed to be safe for 100 years.

Another Chernobyl project that began about the same time was the construction of a facility capable of processing and storing spent fuel from other nuclear power plants. Ukraine had fifteen reactors responsible for roughly half the nation's electricity production. Before the start of the Russo-Ukrainian War in 2014, which led to the annexation of the Crimea and the de facto loss of the Donbas region in eastern Ukraine, all spent nuclear fuel from Ukrainian reactors was sent to Russia at an annual expense of $200 million, but the Ukrainian government was now looking to the Chernobyl zone for storage of its nuclear waste.[9]

––––––––

Most of those who worked in the Chernobyl zone lived in the city of Slavutych. Born of the emergency caused by the Chernobyl accident of

1986, Slavutych had been intended to serve as a new Prypiat, replacing the city depopulated by radiation as the new home of the operators of the Chernobyl reactors that were still running and of personnel involved in managing the consequences of the disaster.

The city planners had chosen the site for Slavutych at the intersection of railway lines and highways in the pine forests on the left bank of the Dnieper, where there was relatively little radiation fallout. The railway line connected Slavutych with the Chernobyl nuclear power plant. It cut through Belarus, but that was of no importance: the railway bridge across the Dnieper, which connected the power plant with the new city, was already in place, and a mere 20 kilometers of Belarusian territory were no obstacle. The administrative borders of Soviet republics did not mean much at the time, and railway lines crossed them as easily as interstate highways traverse multiple American states today. It would be a different story after the collapse of the USSR and the emergence of international borders in the region.

Construction began in December 1986, the month following the completion of work on the sarcophagus covering reactor no. 4. Construction workers from various Soviet republics worked in shifts of fifteen days and lived in cruise ships moored on the Dnieper (Dnipro) River approximately 10 kilometers (6 miles) from the construction site. The city came into existence thanks to the efforts of several Soviet republics. Eight of them pooled their resources to build a model city, leaving their marks on the architecture of the districts they constructed, named after the capitals of the republics and regions from which the construction crews had come. Almost the entire geography of the former Soviet Union was represented in Slavutych, with districts named for Baku, Yerevan, Vilnius, capitals of other republics, and three districts named for the Russian cities of Moscow, Leningrad, and Belgorod.[10]

For the first year, the city still under construction was known as Nerafa after its railway station, which had been named for a local ravine, but in 1987 the Ukrainian authorities renamed it Slavutych, one of the Ukrainian names for the nearby Dnieper, Ukraine's largest river. "The Dnieper is known there as the Slavuta, or glorious river," wrote the Polish author Marcin Paszkowski in his 1615 account, *Acts of the Turks and the Clashes of the Cossacks with the Tatars*. The names "Slavuta" and "Slavutych" became popular in the nineteenth and twentieth centuries, both were considered to have been derived from the word *slava* (glory). Thus, the name of the new city resonated closely not only with that of the largest Ukrainian river but also with the promise of future glory.[11]

The first occupants of the new apartment buildings moved into the city in March 1988. The original plan envisioned a city of some 22,000 dwellers, potentially increasing to 30,000. The first citizens of Slavutych had formerly resided in Prypiat: altogether, about 19,000 citizens of Prypiat and cleanup workers would eventually move to the new city. Even the piano for the local palace of culture was brought there from Prypiat. The city grew. In 1989, its second full year of existence, it counted more than 11,000 citizens, increasing to 27,000 by the mid-1990s. Then, with the shutdown of the last functioning Chernobyl reactor in 2000, more than 6,000 people—plant operators and their families—left the city. Its population eventually settled at 25,000.[12]

Slavutych, which had welcomed its first citizens slightly more than three years before the Soviet collapse, became the youngest city in Ukraine and the last to be built in the USSR. It was a Soviet city not only in date of birth but also in ethnic composition. Many of its citizens came from Russia and other republics during the last years of the Soviet Union's existence. It was multiethnic, with representatives of forty-nine Soviet nationalities calling it home. Russians constituted 30 percent of the population in 2001, compared to 6 percent in the Kyiv region. Slavutych, with its ethnically mixed Soviet-era population and districts bearing the names of capitals of Soviet republics as well as the two Russian capitals, remained in many ways a Soviet city, the symbol of a bygone era, its citizens figuring as bearers of Soviet identity and nostalgia.[13]

It became a sad irony that in February 2022, Slavutych, the last

Soviet city, found itself at the center of the battle between Russia and Ukraine, the two largest Soviet republics and founding members of the USSR. In the war between the much stronger Russia and the much weaker Ukraine, the city would choose the Ukrainian side.[14]

———

On February 16, 2022, Yurii Fomichev, the forty-five-year-old mayor of Slavutych, called a meeting of the city council to discuss a plan of action in case of what he described as an "emergency situation." As he delivered his address, Fomichev wore a white surgical mask with a blue-and-yellow flag embroidered on it: COVID was very much an issue, with 900 cases registered in the city at the time. The emergency Fomichev had in mind, however, was not the COVID epidemic but the possibility of warfare.[15]

American and British intelligence services had identified February 16, the day of the Slavutych council meeting, as the possible date of a Russian attack. President Zelensky declared February 16 Unity Day, seeking to calm the nerves of his citizens and those of foreign investors, who were leaving the country along with the staff of Western embassies. By that time, the latter had moved from Kyiv to Central European countries adjacent to Ukraine. Zelensky's declaration did not stop the foreigners but worked when it came to his own people.[16]

"Everyone was awaiting [February 16]; now it has arrived, and life is going on," Fomichev told the members of the city council, which was broadcast by the local television station. He spoke in an assured, almost fatherly manner, but without patronizing his listeners. "Stay calm, don't spread panic, don't shout that the skies are closed to travel because there will be war tomorrow—that is a fake news that we received two days ago." He then noted what many in Ukraine considered their main reason for optimism—the imminent support of Western allies. "A most powerful coalition has been formed: only the blind do not see it," said Fomichev before instructing his listeners to beware of misinformation.

"You have to think critically and use common sense against political subversion," continued the mayor. "There are fake reports that politicians' families have gone abroad, including the mayor of Slavutych."

Fomichev's purpose was not only to calm frayed nerves but also to convince his fellow citizens that he and the city council were doing everything in their power to prepare for a possible state of emergency, including an invasion. He assured his viewers that civic officials had consulted with the administration of the Chernobyl nuclear power plant and the local hospital, prepared a supply of diesel fuel to power the generators in case electricity was shut off, and identified alternative routes to bring new shifts of engineers and operators from Slavutych, where the personnel of the Chernobyl plant lived, to the plant itself. In closing, Fomichev informed his fellow citizens that the city was getting ready to defend itself by forming a territorial defense unit—a Slavutych company of a battalion headquartered in the town of Ivankiv, north of Kyiv.[17]

Fomichev called on the citizens not only to avoid yielding to panic but also not to overreact by trying to form unsupervised military units. Veterans of the war in the Donbas, which Russia had attacked in 2014, had already organized courses to train civilians in the use of small arms. The task of defending Slavutych would fall mainly to the Ukrainian armed forces, explained Fomichev's first deputy, Viktor Shevchenko, and the territorial defense unit was to hold the city until they arrived. Fomichev told the council that his team was working hard to provide the defense unit with everything necessary, from buildings to supplies, but added that no one was about to dig trenches and occupy them. Like President Zelensky in Kyiv, Fomichev was trying to find a middle ground between realization of the danger and panic.[18]

3

INVASION

Volodymyr Zelensky surprised everyone when, ignoring the threats of his foes and the warnings of his friends, he left his country on February 19, 2022, to pay a visit to the annual Munich security conference, where the looming war in Ukraine was the central item on the agenda.

A few days earlier he had been warned by Director William Burns of the Central Intelligence Agency that a Russian attack was imminent and would include the landing of Russian paratroopers at Hostomel Airport, north of Kyiv, located on one of the highways leading from the Ukrainian capital to Chernobyl. Burns also told the Ukrainian president that he had to consider his personal security. Some in Munich assumed that Zelensky had finally taken the warning seriously and decided to do what the Western embassies had done a week or so earlier—leave Kyiv and Ukraine. Some leaders of states participating in the conference suggested that he should set up a shadow government-in-exile either in Poland or in the United Kingdom.[1]

Zelensky denied such suggestions. Instead, he delivered by far the most powerful presentation of the security forum. He reminded the Western powers of the obligations they had assumed when Ukraine joined the nonproliferation treaty as a non-nuclear state, only to put up no resistance when Russia attacked Ukraine in 2014. "Ukraine has received security guarantees for abandoning the world's third[-largest] nuclear capability," Zelensky told the gathering, referring to the Budapest Memorandum of 1994, which documented the obligations assumed by major powers in return for Ukraine's renunciation of the nuclear arsenal that it inherited from the USSR. "We don't have that weapon. We also have no security. We also do not have part of the territory of our state that is larger in area than Switzerland, the Netherlands, or Belgium. And most importantly—we don't have millions of our citizens. We don't have all this. Therefore, we have something. The right to demand a shift from a policy of appeasement to ensuring security and peace guarantees."

The word "appeasement," pronounced at a conference held in Munich, drew a direct parallel between the West's failure to stop Hitler on the eve of World War II and its inability to stop Putin on the verge of a war that everyone expected to start in a day or two. Zelensky demanded consultations between the parties to the Budapest Memorandum and threatened, if his request was not met, as similar requests had been ignored on numerous occasions, to consider the document void. "Ukraine," stated Zelensky, "will have every right to believe that the Budapest Memorandum is not working, and all the package decisions of 1994 are in doubt." Was he suggesting that Ukraine had a right to acquire nuclear weapons? He never said so, but the Russian authorities would weaponize that interpretation of his remarks in the propaganda war that had been unleashed immediately after the end of the conference.[2]

On February 21, in a speech recognizing the "independence" of the Donetsk and Luhansk "people's republics," the two puppet states created by Russia on Ukrainian territory, and de facto declaring Russia's war on Ukraine, Putin stated that Ukraine not only wanted nuclear weapons but could actually obtain them. "There have already been declarations to the effect that Ukraine is preparing to produce its own nuclear weapons, and that is no empty bravado. Ukraine actually has all the Soviet nuclear technologies and means of delivering such weapons," Putin said. He then proceeded, in the same statement, to make a case for the coming Russian aggression: "With the appearance of weapons of mass destruction in Ukraine, the situation in the world and in Europe will change in cardinal fashion particularly for us, for Russia. We cannot fail to react to that real danger."[3]

Putin claimed that Russians and Ukrainians were one and the same people, denying Ukraine's right to exist as a distinct nation and an independent state. He accused the Ukrainian government of grabbing historically Russian lands and trying to eradicate Russian identity and language in those territories. He was determined to liberate not only the Russians of Ukraine but also the Ukrainians themselves, especially the Russian-speaking ones, from alleged Nazis and nationalists in their government. Those were the declared goals of the imminent war. But now Putin had also found a nuclear pretext to launch that war.[4]

Two days after Putin's speech, on February 23, the Russian news agency RIA Novosti published an article referring to discussions in the Ukrainian media and claiming that Ukraine could build a nuclear bomb by enriching the irradiated materials available at the Chernobyl plant. The nonexistent Ukrainian nuclear threat thus became one of the last-minute justifications of Russia's coming attack on Ukraine, and Chernobyl its most unexpected kernel.[5]

———

February 21, the day on which Putin accused Ukraine of trying to annihilate Russians and the Russian language and of having plans and capabilities to build a nuclear bomb, was a festive occasion in Slavutych schools, where teachers and students marked the national day of the Ukrainian language. The director of the local school stated that the city was multiethnic in composition but located on old Ukrainian land, that of Chernihiv. The local television station declared Ukrainian one of the world's three most melodious languages. A student wearing an embroidered Ukrainian shirt suggested in front of the camera that without language there would be no people and no nation, adding that it was the day of "our Ukraine." All that was stated in the predominantly Russian-speaking city, but in this case language served more as a marker of identity than a means of communication, and it was the nation as a whole that was under threat from the rumored invasion.[6]

The attitudes of the citizens of Slavutych toward language and identity had undergone a major transformation with the outbreak of the Russo-Ukrainian War in 2014. The city's mayor, Yurii Fomichev, elected in 2015, became a symbol of that change. An ethnic Ukrainian bearing a Russian surname, Fomichev had been born in a middle-size Ukrainian village less than 20 kilometers (12 miles) from the Southern Ukrainian nuclear power plant. He had graduated from high school with a gold medal, studied in Kyiv, and then moved to Slavutych, where he became president of a construction company.

In 2010, he was elected to the city council as a deputy representing the party of the incumbent president, Viktor Yanukovych. Party membership gave Fomichev access to the highest echelons of government in Kyiv, an all-important prerequisite for running the city effectively: like all Ukrainian cities at the time, it depended on central sources of funding. The start of the Maidan protests and the Revolution of Dignity in Ukraine in 2013–14 changed the political scene in Ukraine in general and Slavutych in particular. The incumbent mayor of Slavutych, Volodymyr Udovychenko, abandoned Yanukovych's party immediately after the Maidan protests began in Kyiv in December 2013.[7]

Then came the annexation of the Crimea and the war in the Donbas. Many citizens of Slavutych volunteered to join the Ukrainian army in order to fight against Russian troops and the insurgency in the Donbas, incited and supported by Russia. Father Ioann Shepynda, the priest of St. Illia Ukrainian Orthodox Church (Moscow Patriarchate), noted a difference in the attitude of his parishioners. If before 2014 many had considered him a Ukrainian nationalist because he came from western Ukraine and spoke Ukrainian, after 2014 some began referring to him as pro-Russian because of his allegiance to the Moscow Patriarchate.[8]

In February 2022, Fomichev was fully supported by the vast majority of the citizens of Slavutych when he took a clearly pro-Ukrainian stand, mobilizing the city's resources to protect it from a looming attack by Russia—for many of those citizens their ancestral homeland and even place of birth. On February 23, the eve of the invasion, Fomichev used his regular television appearance to prepare his viewers for the defense of their city. Fomichev informed them about the meeting of city mayors that he had attended a few days earlier. Called by Oleksii Danilov, the secretary of the Ukrainian Security Council, it had dealt with the formation of territorial defense units.

"I call on all those prepared to defend their home town: enlist!" said the mayor. Fomichev informed his audience that more than a thousand citizens had already undergone military training in the use of small arms. "You can enlist in the territorial defense company, sign a contract, and reserve your place," he continued. People were needed to man checkpoints at entrances to the city and guard the television station and administrative buildings. There were plans to call in reservists and form additional volunteer units if the Slavutych territorial defense company needed assistance. Beyond that, Fomichev contacted the commanders of the Ukrainian armed forces and the National Guard unit protecting the Chernobyl nuclear power plant to involve them in the defense of the city.

Fomichev still sounded confident and reassuring, but what he said left no doubt that the situation was deteriorating. As in the past, he called on his citizens not to panic, but first and foremost he was eager to inform and mobilize them.[9]

————

Russian troops began to cross the Ukrainian borders early in the morning of February 24, 2022, as Vladimir Putin declared the start of a "special military operation" on Russian television. As he called on the Ukrainian military to surrender, he made a veiled threat of the use of weapons of mass destruction against the West. "Anyone who might try to interfere with us or, all the more, create threats to our country, to our people, should know that Russia's answer will be immediate and will present you with consequences such as you have never yet encountered in your history," declared Putin. "We are prepared for any development of events. All necessary decisions in that regard have been taken."[10]

Russian armies moved into Ukraine in several directions simultaneously, just as suggested earlier by American intelligence. One group of military formations broke out of the Crimea and attacked the Ukrainian south, while other units launched an offensive in the Donbas, aiming at the city of Mariupol. In the northeast, the Russians attacked Ukraine's second-largest city, Kharkiv, while two groups of armed forces moved toward the capital, Kyiv. One of them advanced from Russian territory through the city of Chernihiv, approaching the capital from the east, while the other, comprising some 30,000 troops, moved out of Belarus to approach Kyiv from the northwest.

"Tomorrow you are going to Ukraine to fuck up some shit," a Russian commander told Corporal Nikita Chabin, a twenty-seven-year-old soldier in a unit posted on the Belarusian- Ukrainian border. The "shit" happened to be radioactive. That task force moved not only between the Chernobyl exclusion zone and the Prypiat marshes to the west of it but also through the exclusion zone itself. There were nineteen battalion-strength tactical groups altogether, or close to 15,000 troops, crossing the Ukrainian border from the region of Homel, northeast of the Chernobyl exclusion zone. Nine battalion-strength tactical groups, consisting of up to 8,000 officers and soldiers, began advancing from Belarus toward Kyiv, departing from their positions northwest of the exclusion zone.[11]

The Russian movement toward the border began a few hours after midnight. The 35th Russian Combined Arms Army began the assault west of the Chernobyl exclusion zone. The 104th paratrooper assault regiment from Pskov, reinforced by units of riot police and rapid-response police from the Russian city of Belgorod, was ordered to start moving from a military testing ground in Belarus northwest of the exclusion zone toward the Ukrainian border at 1:33 a.m. Their column of eighty-two vehicles, more than 4 kilometers (2½ miles) in length, proceeded at the head of a much longer column of Russian troops numbering altogether 495 vehicles and extending as long as 25 kilometers (15.5 miles). At 3:15 a.m. the column had to cross the Prypiat River via a pontoon bridge; forty-five minutes later it approached the Belarusian-Ukrainian border, heading from there to Prypiat and Chernobyl. Its ultimate destination was Kyiv.[12]

The 36th Russian Combined Arms Army along with other troops moved into the Chernobyl zone from a narrow corridor of Belarusian territory that extended into Ukraine between Slavutych and Prypiat. Colonel D. Yershov, who commanded one of the columns, began his advance toward the border from positions near the Belarusian village of Krasnoe, located a few dozen kilometers west of Slavutych. They began their advance at 5:00 a.m., crossing the border at about 7:30 p.m. on the same day. The column proceeded through the Chernobyl exclusion zone during the night but got stuck near the village of Cherevach, as the Ukrainian armed forces had partly destroyed a bridge across the Uzh River near the village. It took the unit four hours, until midday on February 25, to cross the river. At that point, the unit was still in the Chernobyl exclusion zone.[13]

The Russian columns moving from the areas northwest of the zone entered it through the Vilcha checkpoint. The pontoon bridge across the Prypiat River, which had been spotted northwest of Vilcha a few days earlier, was removed by the Russians. But they had built a new one roughly in the same area by February 24, and dozens of armored vehicles and trucks were spotted crossing it toward Ukrainian territory. The Ukrainian border guards accepted battle, but the Russians attacked their positions at their base in Mlachivka with Grad multiple rocket launcher systems. According to information released by the Ukrainian border guard directorate around 6:30 a.m., the Ukrainian guards retreated while coordinating their actions with the armed forces and national guard.[14]

The troops moving to the northeast of the zone started their march near the Belarusian town of Komaryn, located on the narrow tongue of

Belarusian territory between Slavutych and Prypiat. As they headed for Chernobyl, columns of military vehicles passed through the abandoned village of Benivka, deep inside the "western trace" of the highly contaminated area polluted by Chernobyl fallout in 1986. The dust raised by the passing tanks, armored personnel vehicles, pieces of artillery, and heavy machinery sent the readings of dosimeters in the area six to eight times higher than usual. Readings were particularly high in the village of Masheve, on the border with Belarus, exceeding the norm tenfold.[15]

———

Yaroslav Yemelianenko, the founder of Chornobyl Tour, watched the movement of Russian troops across the Chernobyl zone in real time from his Kyiv apartment. The images of Russian tanks and armored personal vehicles came from camera installed near Chornobyl Tour property in the zone.

Yemelianenko had spent the previous day in the exclusion zone. An Israeli television crew filmed him for a report on Ukrainian readiness to repel the possible Russian attack. The camera operators asked Yemelianenko and one of the Chornobyl Tour's female employees to climb onto a Soviet-era armored personnel vehicle, or BTR, in order to demonstrate their resolve and that of their people to fight back. They complied with the request. The armored personnel vehicle belonged to the company, an artifact of the 1980s, when similar vehicles were used by Soviet troops for radiological control of the terrain. It was parked near the booth of the Chornobyl Tour information center next to checkpoint Dytiatky, which was located at the gates of the exclusion zone on the road from Kyiv to Chornobyl. The Chornobyl Tour booth was monitored with the help of a battery-powered video camera that also covered the checkpoint and the adjoining highway.[16]

That camera would become Yemelianenko's eyes on the day of the invasion. He woke to the sound of sirens and explosions of Russian missiles targeting the city. His first move was to get in touch with his family members, establish where members of his staff were located, and decide what to do next. Yemelianenko checked the video camera in the zone. Everything seemed to be in order: no movement whatever was registered around the Dytiatky checkpoint. On his Facebook page, Yemelianenko posted: "All quiet in the direction of Chernobyl. I'm watching it constantly. Not driving anywhere. Not withdrawing any cash; not waiting in line for gas. Staying home. In Kyiv. The first day is always psychically the most difficult, so nothing unnecessary should be done. We are being reliably protected by the UAF [Ukrainian Armed Forces] on our territory." Responding to a friend's comment that she had heard explosions from the direction of Chernobyl, Yemelianenko wrote: "I am watching the direction from Dytiatky: everything is calm. Camera refreshes every second."[17]

In another part of Kyiv, Kateryna Aslamova, the Chornobyl Tour guide coordinator, was also monitoring the Dytiatky checkpoint camera from her apartment. To her, as to Yemelianenko, everything seemed to be in order: the Ukrainian guards were manning the checkpoint and performing their usual duties. She noticed that one of them was feeding a dog. But then the Ukrainian guards disappeared. Sometime afterward, Aslamova saw a column of military vehicles emblazoned with the letter V arriving. Soldiers got out of the vehicles and began removing the Ukrainian flag flying over the checkpoint. There was no longer any doubt that they were Russian troops. Yemelianenko saw the same picture on his monitor. He and Aslamova, now in contact with each other, began counting the vehicles.

"And so we sat and counted: 1, 2, 3, 10, 40, 100, 200. . . . We began to get the impression that there would be no end to these vehicles," recalled Yemelianenko. "For example, some of the pictures appeared to be freeze-frames, but they were videos. The Russian vehicles halted because they could not proceed. The whole highway lane for traffic heading toward Kyiv, as far as the town of Ivankiv, was jammed with their vehicles." They passed on the information recorded by their cameras to the Ukrainian security services and the military.[18]

Yemelianenko kept updating his Facebook page for most of the day but wrote nothing more about his camera and the story it was telling.

At 1:58 p.m. he updated an earlier post: "There is news that in order to stop the adversary, the bridge across the Vuzh River at Cherevach has been destroyed." The next update came at 2:19 p.m.: "Russian forces that broke through to Vilcha have been driven back to the border." At 5:21 p.m. came the last post of the day: "There is news of an attempt to seize the Chernobyl atomic energy station." Yemelianenko added: "I'm not updating the post, as the situation is changing constantly." It was changing indeed, but only for the worse.[19]

It was soon after 4:00 p.m. that Anton Herashchenko, an adviser to the interior minister, informed a global audience through his Telegram and Facebook accounts that Russian troops had entered the exclusion zone from Belarus, and there was fighting in the zone itself. "The National Guardsmen, who guard the collectors of unsafe nuclear radioactive waste, are fighting hard," wrote Herashchenko. He added: "If the invaders' artillery hits and ruins/damages the collectors of nuclear waste, radioactive nuclear dust may be spread over the territory of Ukraine, Belarus, and the countries of the EU!"[20]

Later in the day, President Zelensky tweeted: "Russian occupying forces are attempting to seize the Chernobyl AES. Our boys are giving their lives so that the tragedy of '86 is not repeated. I have informed Premier Magdalena Andersson of Sweden about this. This is a declaration of war on Europe as a whole." The information turned out to be mistaken. By the time Herashchenko and Zelensky posted about the Russian attempt to capture the station, it was already under Russian control—the guardsmen had laid down their weapons.[21]

4

———

HOLDUP

It was sometime after 4:00 a.m. on February 24 that Valentyn Heiko, the fifty-nine-year-old foreman of the night shift at the Chernobyl nuclear power station, received a telephone call from the station's facility in the abandoned city of Prypiat. A veteran of the Chernobyl zone—he had begun working at the plant back in 1987, soon after the nuclear accident—Heiko was on the phlegmatic side, calm and considerate, not easily thrown off balance. He had survived many emergency situations at the plant, but this one was unique.

The caller told Heiko that shots had been heard near the city, and a battle was being waged near the Vilcha border-crossing checkpoint, just outside the exclusion zone. "It all happened very suddenly, you know, like at the beginning of World War II," remembered Heiko. More calls followed, now from people at the station itself. "Personnel are reporting that a cannonade can be heard beyond the Prypiat River," Oleksii Shelestii, the chief electrical engineer of the shift, told Heiko over the phone. "Yes, we're aware of it; the roar has been going on for some time," responded Heiko. "We're keeping calm for the time being."[1]

Closer to 6:00 a.m. came more disturbing news: the regional authorities had announced the evacuation of civilians from the area, in particular Chernobyl and Dytiatky, the location of the checkpoint at the entrance to the zone. From Slavutych came the news that the Russians were already in the abandoned village of Paryshiv, across the Prypiat River from Chornobyl, and it was only a matter of time before they would reach the station. Heiko admitted later that at the time, "It was not clear what to do; there was no protocol in case of war." The engineers and operators at the plant who monitored radiation levels, temperature, humidity, and other parameters of the confinement structure over reactor no. 4 and the pools of spent fuel in the exclusion zone were all civilians. In theory, they were supposed to be evacuated as well. But what would happen to the plant and radiation levels if there was no one to ensure their safety?[2]

Their instructions prohibited them from leaving their positions and workstations. Heiko began preparing to evacuate nonessential staff. But the others would have to stay. Later he would consider anyone who left among the key personnel a traitor. But he took a different view of the 169 officers and soldiers of the Ukrainian National Guard at the station. Given the impending encirclement and occupation of the Chernobyl plant, they would have to leave. He called their commanders and told them: "We are alone here, so I know that [the Russians] will come here, and there is no help for that. I therefore recommend, while time remains, that you take all your servicemen and cross the bridge across the Prypiat in the direction of Belarus. You have weapons. You have subordinates. You know best what to do afterwards." But the national guardsmen, like Heiko's crew, could not simply abandon the nuclear power plant and flee. They stayed.[3]

Heiko called his wife in Slavutych to tell her that the war had begun. Soon after 8:00 a.m. he used the loudspeaker system to proclaim a state of accident readiness at the plant and order that searchlights lighting up the station be switched off. Heiko informed the personnel that military action had begun and asked everyone to follow his orders. "Sounds of bombardment were heard immediately; planes were roaring overhead. We were asked to go to the shelter," recalled Liudmyla Kozak, a physical safety engineer at the station. Oleksii Shelestii, who had been among the first to inform Heiko of the start of military action, stayed in his office. "I remained at my workplace: I have no right to leave it," he recalled later. "I cannot even go for lunch or supper unless the head of shift at the station takes my place. I am responsible for controlling electricity supply parameters at the Chernobyl AES."[4]

More than 100 people involved in nonessential tasks gathered in the anti-radiation shelter of the administration building in preparation for a possible evacuation. There was no panic, as no one expected trouble at the station. Staff members, especially women, were thinking instead about loved ones who were either serving in the Ukrainian armed forces or might be called up for duty. But tension gradually increased. In the basement and outside it, more than 300 people, who apart from the operators and engineers included about 80 firefighters and close to 170 national guardsmen, waited for their fate to be decided by developments pretty much beyond their control, and many began to feel the pressure. Liudmyla Mykhalenko, the plant's paramedic, recalled that "girls began coming to me. Their reaction was situational, that is, they were upset, distressed, or had high blood pressure; understandably, they were all suffering shock and stress."[5]

A regular twelve-hour shift (9:00 a.m. to 9:00 p.m.) would normally arrive to replace a night shift like the one Heiko was running at the time. Most of those on duty lived in Slavutych, 45 kilometers east of Prypiat by railway, and more than 70 kilometers by road. Those working the shift would arrive by rail after crossing the Dnieper River and passing through Belarusian territory. None of that had been a problem in 1986, but it had become a problem now. With Belarus being Russia's ally in the war against Ukraine, and the bridge across the Dnieper a strategic target for the warring armies, it was no longer clear whether the night shift could safely leave the station to be replaced by the day shift. Heiko called station headquarters in Slavutych to discuss the situation.

In Slavutych the workers of the day shift were gathered at the railway station by 7:00 a.m., waiting for the commuter train to arrive. It never came, and by 8:00 a.m. it was clear that the shift would be going nowhere. Engineers and workers passing through Belarusian territory might well become hostages. In the weeks leading up to the invasion that had been a risk for the national guardsmen, who also traveled to the station through Belarusian territory, but now it became a real concern for civilians as well. Heiko and his superiors decided that his shift should stay, presumably for another day or two. The evacuation of nonessential staff would be canceled as well: the roads were full of advancing Russian forces that cut off escape routes toward both Slavutych and Kyiv.[6]

The citizens of Slavutych learned from a television announcement by Mayor Fomichev that Heiko's shift would not be coming home. The mayor had been awakened that morning by a telephone call from his son, a student at one of the Kyiv universities. The son told his father to start gathering his belongings. In disbelief, Fomichev called his other son, also in Kyiv, and learned from him that the Ukrainian capital was under missile attack. By 6:00 a.m. Fomichev and his aides were in the mayor's office. "We believed in common sense; unfortunately, common sense did not prevail in this instance," the mayor told his viewers in the course of his usual television appearance. He asked citizens to be vigilant, seek shelter in basements, and have documents, food, and clothing ready in case of a need to evacuate. He added that for safety reasons the rotation of shifts at the Chernobyl nuclear power plant would have to be postponed.[7]

At the station, some workers climbed onto the roof of the mechanical plant of the arch, the new containment structure over the damaged reactor no. 4, to assess the situation. "Our first impression was that we had seen airplanes, but then we understood that those had been two rockets launched from the Belarusian side," recalled Viacheslav Yakushev, an engineer at the arch's radiation safety department. The workers, aware that Russia's all-out war on Ukraine had begun, were already following the news on Ukrainian media and Telegram channels. The station's security officers and members of the National Guard unit were on high alert, expecting Russian troops to show up at any moment.[8]

But the first to appear at the checkpoint were four unarmed young men. The soldiers of the National Guard met them, pointing their automatic rifles at the intruders. "Stalkers," as illegal visitors to the zone were called at Chernobyl, were nothing new there. In fact, one of the tasks of the National Guard unit at the plant was to keep the facilities safe from them. But that had been before the war: now, who could tell a stalker from a Russian saboteur? "Guys, put your stuff down, raise your hands, and we'll approach you one by one. We'll find out who you are," the soldiers told the intruders. The search produced cell phones, a drone, GoPro cameras, and knives. The story they told the guardsmen was as bizarre as it was normal for the Chernobyl zone.

The four men, all Ukrainians, had spent the night of February 23 in a sixteen-floor apartment building in the abandoned city of Prypiat. They had come to the zone from two industrial cities in southern Ukraine, Zaporizhia and Dnipro, in order to walk a tightrope stretched between two such sixteen-story buildings at the height of 60 meters (197 feet) and film their exploit. A few years earlier two of them, Kostiantyn Karnoza and Stanislav Paniuta, had received a certificate confirming their record: walking a tightrope barefoot at the height of 94 meters (308 feet). Now they wanted to test their skills in the zone. They had made their way there, illegally bypassing checkpoints, on February 21, and were preparing to install wire for the walk.

On the morning of February 24 the four were having an early breakfast when they heard artillery fire. They immediately went onto the balcony, saw jets flying above them, and heard the explosions of rocket artillery shells. Karnoza, Paniuta, and their two friends left the building where they had spent the night and headed toward the closest checkpoint in Prypiat, only to see the taillights of a car leaving the checkpoint. They then walked to the checkpoint of the nuclear power plant. The guardsmen, having listened to their story, took away their equipment and cell phones and locked them in a basement.[9]

The Chernobyl plant operators had spotted a column of Russian troops approaching the station late in the afternoon of February 24. Mykhailo Makhyna, a shift electrician, called Heiko to break the news. He could not discern whose vehicles were approaching, "ours" or "theirs." But Heiko had no doubt that they were Russian, as there were no Ukrainian troops in the area.[10]

A column of Russian military vehicles approached the checkpoint of the Chernobyl plant shortly after 2:00 p.m. Fifty-two-year-old Colonel Andrei Frolenkov commanded a special unit of the Russian Guard charged with taking over the plant. This was a secondary task: the main mission of Russian troops entering the Chernobyl zone from a different direction was to pass it as quickly as possible and head toward Kyiv.

Several units of the Russian Guard, former interior troops of the Russian Federation now under the overall command of Putin's former bodyguard, Viktor Zolotov, had entered the Chernobyl nuclear zone from Belarus. Among them was an elite unit of the Chechen interior forces, the 141st Mechanized Infantry Regiment, named after Akhmat Kadyrov, the father of the Chechen strongman Ramzan Kadyrov. Its commander was thirty-five-year-old General Magomed Tushaev, who was personally close to Kadyrov. The regiment began its march toward Ukraine in the Russian city of Smolensk and proceeded from there to Belarus. After crossing the border and reaching northern Ukrainian cities, first Prypiat and then Chernobyl, soldiers of the regiment made a video that they posted on social media. The regiment then proceeded toward Kyiv.[11]

The same route from Russia through Belarus to Ukraine via the Chernobyl exclusion zone was followed by other Russian Guard units, including a rapid-response unit of riot police from the Kemerovo region of western Siberia under the command of Colonel Konstantin Ogii. One of his subordinates, Captain Yevgenii Spiridonov, of a special-purpose police detachment from the Russian city of Novokuznetsk, later testified that he had joined Ogii's group in early February in the town of Sofrino, where they underwent training. They were then moved to Smolensk, where they joined other Russian Guard units, the Tushaev regiment in particular. The commanders took away the soldiers' cell phones, and soon the troops were moved to the Homel region in Belarus, where they arrived on February 22 and camped in tents.

On February 24, with the start of the missile bombardment of Ukraine, Ogii, Spiridonov, and their unit were trucked from Belarus across the Ukrainian border. The Ukrainian checkpoint where they crossed the border had been completely destroyed by Russian artillery; the corpses of Ukrainian border guards still lay on the ground. Spiridonov's unit proceeded first to Prypiat and then to Chernobyl. There the commanders set a new task: the unit was to march toward Kyiv and enter the city. The same command was given to a special-purpose unit of Russian Guards from Khakasia in southern Siberia. That unit started its movement toward the Ukrainian border from a base established at the Smolensk airport but headed toward Chornobyl from the Belarusian city of Bragin.

The first echelon of Russian troops, consisting of Russian paratroopers, Chechen fighters, and Russian Guards, rushed toward Kyiv from Chernobyl, only to be ambushed by the Ukrainian troops and all but destroyed on the approaches to the Ukrainian capital. On February 25, they encountered stiff resistance near Hostomel, the site of a strategic airport and a de facto suburb of Kyiv. The Russian Guards were decimated. Spiridonov was wounded but survived, ending up in Ukrainian captivity on February 26, the third day of the war. His unit suffered the greatest casualties of all. Both Ogii and Tushaev were first thought to have been killed but survived the destruction of their forces. Ogii emerged on foot from encirclement and reestablished contact with his commanders in early March. A few weeks later, Tushaev recorded a video disproving earlier reports of his death. Although the commanders survived, many of their soldiers did not.[12]

Colonel Frolenkov proved much luckier than Tushaev, Ogii, Spiridonov, and their men. For him, Prypiat became the final destination of his mission, not just a transit point toward the killing fields around Kyiv. Before the invasion, Frolenkov had been deputy commander of the rapid-response unit of the police (OMON) regiment of the Briansk region of Russia and had served in the Russian Guards. He therefore had more experience of dealing with riots and disturbances than with enemy soldiers. Although he did not expect much fighting at Chernobyl, he approached the power station with his force at full strength. Altogether 100 officers, some of them representing the armed forces and others the Russian Guards, arrived at the station in a column led by a tank, which was followed by an infantry fighting vehicle (BMP), an armored personnel carrier, and a number of trucks that turned out to be prison transport vans. They had an old map, lost their way, and arrived later than planned.

Frolenkov remembered that as he and his column were passing checkpoint no. 2 of the Chernobyl power plant, a Ukrainian guardsman emerged from the building and fired at the column. Frolenkov was the only one who recalled that episode, raising questions as to whether anyone had indeed fired at the column, or if he simply used that story as an excuse to attack the plant. "I ordered two storm groups to penetrate the territory of the plant and start cleaning it up," recalled Frolenkov. The groups knew the layout of the plant very well. Frolenkov later admitted that a year before the invasion he and his people had conducted military exercises at the Kursk nuclear power plant in Russia, which was almost identical to the Chernobyl station. The Briansk region had become the most contaminated part of Russia after the Chernobyl accident, and Frolenkov's officers were psychologically ready to deal with radiation.[13]

As a group of nine commandos began to cross the perimeter of the plant, breaking the locks of checkpoint no. 2, Frolenkov ordered the tank and armored vehicles to proceed to the plant's main checkpoint and aim their guns at the administration building, to which the Ukrainian guardsmen retreated from the perimeter of the station. "We turned our cannons toward that building," recalled Frolenkov. "Three vehicles, i.e., the BMP in which I was riding, a tank to the right of me and, farther right, a BTR [armored personnel carrier], all their cannons pointed that way." But Frolenkov was not yet ready to attack the building. At its windows he saw Ukrainian guardsmen with automatic rifles taking their positions. They had been given live ammunition sometime around 3:00 a.m., shortly before the Russians crossed the border, and were now ready to fight.[14]

The Ukrainian stand took Frolenkov by surprise. He had expected a much smaller and more agreeable detachment of Ukrainian troops guarding the plant. "As it happened, our preliminary data about the site did not correspond to what I saw on arrival," he explained later. Indeed, the number of Ukrainian guardsmen at the plant had been increased a week before the Russian aggression out of concern that the regular rotation of shifts across the Belarusian border could become impossible. So two shifts were stationed at the plant at the same time. Either Russian intelligence did not know about the presence of another shift, or the information was never passed on to Frolenkov. He estimated that 80 percent of his men might die in battle. "Understanding that delay at this point might threaten irrevocable consequences of some kind, that is, we might simply be shot to pieces, I immediately jumped off the vehicle, raised my hands, and proceeded to the checkpoint," recalled Frolenkov a few weeks later.[15]

As he was heading toward the entrance of the building, he passed a newly installed monument to Oleksandr Lelechenko, the operator of the plant who sacrificed his life preventing the spread of fire during the 1986 accident. Frolenkov had no clue what the monument meant, and what he was getting into. The spirit of Lelechenko, who ran from the hospital bed to join his friends dealing with the consequences of the accident, was still very much alive among the new crop of the plant operators.[16]

———

Valerii Semenov, a senior engineer in charge of the physical security of the Chernobyl facility, spotted Frolenkov and his column approaching one of the station's checkpoints around quarter past two. He was monitoring the power station by means of closed-circuit television screens in front of him, up to thirty altogether, when he noticed a gray blur on one of them—a cloud of dust moving toward the station from the border with Belarus. The dust cloud, which soon turned into a column of five armored trucks and about eight prison transport vans led by armored military vehicles, passed by the fence of the station.

Semenov could hardly believe his eyes. "Somehow I expected in my soul that they would not seize it," he recalled later. "We understand perfectly that our subunit works in a field such that we expected and knew that according to legislation it would be an act of nuclear terrorism. Therefore we pushed that thought as far as possible from our minds." But all his doubts vanished as soon as another camera showed the column arriving. He then saw Russian soldiers in black uniforms disembarking from the tank and the armored vehicles, and then commandos trying to break through the security perimeter of the plant at checkpoint no. 2. Semenov alerted the Ukrainian guardsmen, who took up positions inside the administration building. They told the staff that they were ready to fight.[17]

Semenov then dialed the shift foreman, Valentyn Heiko, under whom he had cut his teeth as a young engineer at the plant back in the 1990s and with whom he had worked ever since. Semenov reported the arrival of the convoy and an attempt by nine Russians to break through the security gate. "Yes, I can see them through the window," responded Heiko. "They are pointing their guns at me." Semenov checked the camera again and realized that the Russians had sent two negotiators. He could see a number of Ukrainian national guardsman exiting the building and stopping some eight meters (twenty-six feet) away from the Russians. They began to talk, but Semenov could not hear them. After some time, the Ukrainian guardsman opened the entrance and invited the Russians inside. The negotiations continued. Semenov reported to Heiko that the Russians were already inside the station, and negotiations were underway. Heiko asked him to check what was going on and, if necessary, to invite the intruders into his office.[18]

Semenov rushed to the main turnstile of the administration building, where he found Russian officers engaged in conversation with

Ukrainian guardsmen. The latter had already agreed to lay down their weapons. Frolenkov remembered that the negotiations did not last long. He told the Ukrainian guardsmen that they had been surrounded by a huge army and "they will perish if they give battle." According to his recollection, Frolenkov promised the Ukrainian guards "protection of their lives and spoke earnestly that it was our common duty to keep the nuclear facility inviolable; that it was our common duty not to permit a repetition of the catastrophe of 1986."

The Ukrainian guardsmen recalled the conversation differently. Frolenkov had allegedly told them: "If you don't want to have a meat grinder here, lay down your weapons." The Ukrainians knew that not only Frolenkov's detachment confronted them. By the afternoon of February 24, they were already deep in the rear of the Russian forces that had passed the station on their way to Kyiv, and thus were facing the whole Russian army. The arrival of the tank was a clear sign of what kind of equipment the Russians could bring up next to deal with the lightly armed Ukrainian unit. "Armed resistance appeared futile: the Russian army was plowing through Chernobyl—hundreds of vehicles and thousands of soldiers," a Ukrainian journalist later wrote. But no less important was the Ukrainian soldiers' concern for the safety of the nuclear installation, carried out according to a prohibition established in UN treaties on conducting military actions on the premises of nuclear facilities.[19]

The Ukrainians decided to lay down their arms, opening themselves to accusations of cowardice and treason. The decision to surrender was made by the commander of the unit, Colonel Yurii Pindak. "The commander of the battalion of the Ukrainian National Guard was on the spot with his fighters. He exchanged glances with them and gave his consent—we shall surrender; the time it all took was about five minutes maximum," recalled Frolenkov. It is not clear whom Pindak consulted before making his decision, but one official to whom he spoke that morning advised him to "spare your people." The official was Valentyn Viter, an officer of the Ukrainian security service who had been seconded to the plant as deputy director for security. On the day of the invasion he was in Kyiv and would later be arrested on a charge of abandoning his post and on suspicion of spying for the enemy.[20]

According to Frolenkov, he soon took control of the whole station: "After that, it was my patrols that went into service. It took half an hour to bring the station completely under control." The station personnel accepted the laying down of weapons by the Ukrainian National Guard unit as an act informed by safety considerations. But many of the guardsmen were upset by what had happened: they were prepared to fight and felt guilty about being unable to perform their duties. Zoia Yerashova, a staff member at the plant, who spent most of the day in the bomb shelter, recalled that at some point "one of our military men [went down to the basement], simply fell to his knees, and apologized to all, all the mothers and daughters, fathers and sons, and said, 'Excuse us; we could not protect you.'"[21]

———

On Heiko's orders, Valerii Semenov invited the Russian commanders to the shift foreman's office. The tense negotiations about the future of the station had begun. Heiko recalled that there were two Russian officers, three commanders of the Ukrainian National Guard, and a civilian whose name he never revealed. The Russians were Colonel Frolenkov and General Sergei Burakov. The Ukrainian officers included the commander of the National Guard unit, Colonel Yurii Pindak, and a representative of the regional National Guard headquarters.[22]

Heiko introduced himself: "I am the shift supervisor and represent the state of Ukraine here." He asked who the Russian "guests" were and the purpose of their visit. The Russians introduced themselves and declared that the Chernobyl power plant was now behind the Russian lines. They had to protect it against a possible terrorist act that might be blamed on the Russian Federation. Heiko recalled that the first demand voiced by the Russians was to turn in members of the "Right Sector" and "Banderites," meaning Ukrainian nationalists or national activists.

"Do you have criteria whereby you determine who the 'Right Sector' and 'Banderites' are?" Heiko asked the Russians, who were surprised by his question. "If there are no criteria, then start with me," continued Heiko. The general and the colonel looked at each other and smiled but said nothing.

Heiko seemed calm and unintimidated by the presence and posture of the Russian military at the plant. He had experienced a somewhat similar situation at the beginning of his career, when the military were involved in cleanup operations at the plant after the 1986 accident. He had little respect for military commanders who were prepared to send their men to the most dangerous areas of the plant, sometimes to their death. Besides, no matter how powerful the military were, at the nuclear power plant they were not and could not be in charge. The rules were established by the scientists and engineers. Safety rules in the zone of the nuclear disaster were obligatory for all, and the military were subject to them like anyone else. The plant personnel, under Heiko's authority, were there to enforce those rules.[23]

Heiko established himself in a position of power when, according to Semenov, he told the officers that "they were not merely in an atomic station but in a post-accident atomic station. Since they were invaders on foreign soil, they should observe both Ukrainian legislation concerning presence on the territory of a restricted zone and our rules about the regulation of the Chernobyl atomic power station. Should they remain on station territory, they were not to interfere with or venture into any facilities." Heiko told the Russian officers that they were taking over a highly contaminated territory, and it was his obligation, no matter who they were, to instruct them, like any other visitors, on safety regulations. He began enumerating the restrictions on movement between the zones of the plant—a necessity for radiation checks—prohibitions on walking along nondesignated paths in the zone adjacent to the plant, and prohibitions on eating or drinking in areas not designated for those purposes. He invited them to study the instructions and manuals and observe them for their own safety.[24]

Power in the relations between occupiers and occupied was slowly shifting to Heiko. The Russians who had come into his office feeling that they were in control now felt trapped, hostages in the place they had allegedly conquered. Semenov, who was present throughout the hours-long procedure, noticed that General Burakov's cheek kept twitching from tension. Heiko emerged in the moment of crisis as the unquestioned leader of his staff and a master negotiator who managed to turn weakness into strength. "In war, many questions are decided on the spot. The shift supervisor at the station, Valentyn Heiko (whom everyone called simply "Valia"), turned out to be a very tough and steadfast man," recalled Kostiantyn Karnoza, one of the four stalkers who had found safe refuge at the station after the start of the Russian invasion. "He established relations with the occupiers such that either they would behave decently or be up shit creek. That is why they did not touch us or any of the workers."[25]

Frolenkov was clearly taken aback by Heiko's behavior but could do little to rein him in. He later recalled that during negotiations, Heiko "dictated his conditions" and did not hide his feelings. He allegedly told the Russians: "Even though I detest you, I swore before the International Atomic Energy Agency that I would maintain nuclear security." Frolenkov took those words as an insult to himself and to Russia but, according to his own testimony, endured them in order to achieve his main goal of ensuring the safety of the nuclear power plant. In negotiations that went on for close to three hours—not a few minutes suggested by Frolenkov—Heiko insisted that operational control of the plant remain in the hands of his staff and that they be free to move around the station so long as their movements were reported to the occupiers ahead of time.[26]

Semenov later explained that this was done for the safety of the personnel to prevent the possibility of the Russian soldiers firing at them. The Russian soldiers were allowed into the administration building, but Semenov insisted that they could not freely move around the plant, that arms would be prohibited in operational areas, and that the Russians would be kept away from the defunct power blocks, including the damaged block no. 4. Access to those facilities would require a pass issued by Heiko and Semenov. They issued 170 such passes overall, with only 15 permitting access to zones with nuclear waste. But the main point was that passes were issued by Heiko and Semenov, not by the Russian occupiers. Heiko remained in control. "We achieved our negotiation goals. They were living with us under our rules," recalled Heiko.[27]

Last but not least, Heiko convinced the Russians to allow the Ukrainian national guardsmen to take charge of the checkpoints inside the station. "Those occupiers," recalled Heiko, "had insufficient manpower to carry out those functions. And in the process of negotiation agreement was reached that our National Guard—unarmed, to be sure—would take responsibility for safeguarding the plant, making sure that no one entered it." The Russians, who by now had fully succumbed to Heiko's logic, agreed: they had captured a dangerous nuclear site, and if they were to survive, they would have to accommodate his wishes.[28]

———

Before the end of the day, the Russians took over part of the plant's administration building, claiming the fourth floor of the complex, which would subsequently be designated mostly for officers—close to 150 personnel would be housed there in the following weeks. The soldiers, whose numbers would eventually grow to a thousand, turned the sanitary checkpoint into their quarters.[29]

Sometime in the evening, Semenov recalled that the four stalkers were still being held in the basement of the administration building. By now, with Russian occupation of the plant a fait accompli, the stalkers, whether potential saboteurs or not, presented no danger. One of them, Maksym Kibets, recalled Semenov showing up in their room around 9:00 p.m. "Guys, there's been a 'change' of administration: Russian troops entered the plant at 4:00 p.m.," Semenov told the "saboteurs." "A column of tanks has come in; that's why the plant is occupied!"

The stalkers were shocked. "We went up to the second floor, the door opened, and a fairly short Buriat appeared before us, holding a submachine gun of about his stature," recalled Kibets. "Once again, we went nuts. We entered the toilet. There were containers of arms and ammunition strewn about the floor and Russian soldiers lying around. That is, they were resting." According to the stalkers, the Russians were brainwashed, looking for Nazis and NATO bases, but at that moment they were not hostile toward the personnel or the stalkers. "Guys, you just wait three days. Your people will hoist white flags, and it will all be over!" said one of the occupiers to the stalkers.[30]

The laying down of weapons by the Ukrainian guardsmen at Chernobyl was hailed as a major success by the Russian media, a result of the heroism and cool demeanor of Frolenkov, who made over 170 Ukrainian guardsmen (according to the Ukrainian count, there were 169 officers and soldiers) surrender when confronted by a unit of only 100. Frolenkov would soon acquire hero status in Russia and give numerous interviews presenting his version of events at the Chernobyl plant. In none of them would he mention that he was not the only Russian officer who participated in the negotiations. Frolenkov never mentioned General Burakov in public. Like Frolenkov, Burakov was awarded the gold star of Hero of Russia for his role in taking over the Chernobyl nuclear power plant, but unlike Frolenkov, he remained in the shadows.[31]

The fifty-one-year-old Burakov was one year younger than Frolenkov, but he not only looked older—he had lost all his hair long before his arrival in Chernobyl—but also had a much more impressive service record. Burakov began his military career during the first Russo-Chechen War, in which he served as an interpreter in the paratroop unit of the Russian armed forces and received the Order of Courage. He later commanded the special-purpose forces of the Russian Guards before becoming first deputy commander of those forces at the time of the February 24 invasion. Burakov's presence suggested that the operation to capture the Chernobyl plant was planned at the highest level of the Russian Guards command and supervised by one of the top generals of the Russian internal forces, whose commander reported directly to Vladimir Putin.[32]

Burakov may have deliberately avoided the spotlight to hide behind his subordinate, Colonel Frolenkov, as he knew quite well that what he was doing at the Chernobyl nuclear power plant was nothing short of a war crime. Heiko had told him so on one occasion at least. "I told Burakov," recalled Heiko, "that you understand that you have broken all the laws not of the State of Ukraine but of the whole world. And you have taken over nuclear premises. Generally speaking, that already constitutes what is known by all standards as nuclear terrorism." Burakov allegedly cast a glance at Frolenkov, who was present during the conversation, and they both smiled. "They understood it perfectly well," continued Heiko. "All that they did, they understood completely." Both Burakov and Frolenkov would end up on the European Union sanctions list for their role in the occupation of the Chernobyl nuclear plant.[3]

5

INTERNATIONAL CRISIS

The news about the emerging crisis at Chernobyl first reached the International Atomic Energy Agency, located in the Vienna International Center, at 6:41 a.m. on February 24. It was 7:41 a.m. in Kyiv. Russian troops were already in the Chernobyl exclusion zone. Valentyn Heiko was about to declare a state of accident readiness.[1]

As morning turned into day and day into evening, there was more disturbing news from Ukraine, landing on the desk of the IAEA emergency response manager. The source was the State Nuclear Regulatory Inspectorate of Ukraine, a body created four years after the Chernobyl nuclear disaster and located in Kyiv. For a few months in 2017 the inspectorate was headed by Borys Stoliarchuk, one of the four operators who had been on duty on April 24, 1986, when reactor no. 4 of the Chernobyl nuclear power plant exploded. Since December 2021 it had been headed by Oleh Korikov, a fifty-one-year-old nuclear engineer and manager who had started his career at the Zaporizhia nuclear power station and had decades of experience in the industry.

About 5:00 p.m. on February 24, Korikov and his colleagues in the inspectorate learned that all facilities at the Chernobyl plant, including the arch, the confinement structure over the damaged reactor no. 4, and the other three reactors had been taken over by military forces "without insignia." The Ukrainian National Guard unit on-site had been disarmed. As of 5:30 p.m., no damage had been done to the site, and there had been no victims of the takeover among the personnel, but at 8:30 p.m. the directorate of the Chernobyl nuclear power plant had lost control of the station. Korikov immediately told the IAEA what had happened. The military takeover of the station was a direct violation of the additional protocol to the 1949 Geneva Conventions on the protection of civilians in wartime.[2]

That evening, the IAEA issued the first in what would be a long sequence of statements on the situation in Ukraine in the name of the IAEA director general, Rafael Mariano Grossi. The sixty-one-year-old Grossi assumed his position in December 2019. A distinguished Argentinian diplomat, Grossi had worked on nuclear issues in his country's ministry of foreign affairs and served as deputy secretary general of the IAEA in 2010–13. Despite his considerable experience with the bureaucracy and politics of the organization, little had prepared him to deal with the nuclear crisis now unfolding in Ukraine. It had nothing to do with Iran and the proliferation of the nuclear arms—the top priorities of the IAEA in previous years. Instead, the new crisis blurred the line between nuclear industry, or atoms for peace, and nuclear weapons, or atoms for war that the IAEA had been created to police.[3]

Russia's aggression turned the site of the world's worst nuclear disaster into an instrument of war. No state, especially a member of IAEA (as was the case with Russia), had previously attacked and seized a nuclear power plant. Grossi was entering uncharted waters. In the statement he expressed "grave concern" over the developments in Ukraine and appealed "for maximum restraint to avoid any action that may put the country's nuclear facilities at risk." He reminded his global audience of the decision made by the IAEA General Conference in 2009, which stated that "any armed attack on and threat against nuclear facilities devoted to peaceful purposes constitutes a violation of the principles of the United Nations Charter, international law and the Statute of the Agency."[4]

Rafael Grossi and Oleh Korikov had their first telephone conversation about the new Chernobyl crisis on the second day of the war, February 25. According to the press release issued by the Ukrainian inspectorate, Korikov "informed the head of the IAEA about the unprecedented challenges facing Ukraine in connection with the Russian Federation's assault." He told Grossi that "the Russian forces' military seizure of the Chernobyl NPP and the exclusion zone makes it impossible to carry out completely the responsibilities according to the Convention on Nuclear Security." Korikov demanded action. "Ukraine counts on the active support of the IAEA and other international organizations and the exercise of measures of influence on the aggressor nation," he told Grossi. Grossi promised nothing of the sort. According to the Ukrainian press release, he thanked the Ukrainian inspectors for maintaining contact with the IAEA, praised them for providing reliable information, and stated that Ukraine had fulfilled all its international obligations despite difficult circumstances.[5]

Ukrainian readers of the inspectorate's press release, made public on its Facebook page, were appalled. "Thanks? And that's it?" commented Yurii Haiduk from Netishyn, a company town of the Khmelnytskyi nuclear power plant in northwestern Ukraine. He then added in desperation: "Not even an expression of profound concern?" Oksana Kazymyrska from Varash, a company town of the Rivne nuclear power plant in the same region of Ukraine, was even more upset. "Just so! Mr. Grossi is merely concerned, but everything is under their control," she wrote. "It leaves the impression that the management of the IAEA and of the WANO [World Association of Nuclear Operators] consider that this confrontation and the war in Ukraine will not affect the nuclear sphere in any way, so that 'peace, friendship, and chewing gum' will continue as usual. Not even any comments with regard to Moscow."[6]

Later that day the IAEA issued Grossi's next statement on the situation in Ukraine. The major issue was the sudden spike in radiation levels within the zone. Grossi tried to calm the nerves of the global community. He accepted the Ukrainian interpretation that they were being caused "by heavy military vehicles stirring up soil still contaminated from the 1986 accident." He also provided readings from the automated monitoring system: levels had increased "up to 9.46 microSieverts per hour." According to Grossi, those levels were low, remaining within the "operational range" of the exclusion zone, "and therefore do not pose any danger to the public." As before, Grossi's statement made no reference to Russia, mentioning "unidentified armed forces" instead.[7]

———

Grossi's reference to "unidentified armed forces" was technically correct, as the Russians wore no insignia identifying them as citizens of the Russian Federation. This was similar to Russian policy during the annexation of the Crimea in 2014, when the invaders became known as "little green men" because of the color of their uniforms. The "no insignia" reference had also appeared in the Ukrainian report on which Grossi based his statement. But by now everyone knew who the occupiers were.

The Ukrainian Nuclear Regulatory Inspectorate immediately got into trouble after posting its statement on February 24. "Correct the mistake in the statement, replacing the phrase 'armed forces without insignia' with 'armed forces of the rf [Russian Federation],'"[8] wrote Oleksandr Lavrenchuk, an employee of the Rivne nuclear power plant in western Ukraine, on the Facebook page of the Ukrainian nuclear inspectorate. "Call things by their right names," concluded Lavrenchuk. The press department of the Ukrainian inspectorate swiftly corrected itself. In a Facebook post dated February 25 it quoted the acting director of the Chernobyl nuclear plant, Valerii Seida, who declared that all the facilities had been taken over by "armed forces of the Russian Federation." It would take not hours or days but weeks for the IAEA to adopt a similar position.[9]

Sticking to the notion that the Chernobyl site had been taken over by "unidentified" armed men, Grossi and the drafters of his statements seemed undisturbed by the possibility that they were dealing with free-

wheeling terrorists and made no effort to call on them to identify themselves and their goals. Like everyone else, they knew that Chernobyl
had been captured by Russia, one of the most influential members of
their own organization. Anatolii Nosovsky, the director of the Institute of Nuclear Safety of the National Academy of Sciences of Ukraine,
explained Grossi's silence as follows: first, Russia was a major donor to
the IAEA, and, second, one of Grossi's six deputy director generals was
Mikhail Chudakov, a veteran of the Russian nuclear industry. "They
merely expressed concern. They ought to condemn the Russian aggression. They ought to call Russia nuclear terrorists. They did nothing,"
Nosovsky told a Western reporter.[10]

Russia was indeed a major force in the IAEA. Its contribution to the
Agency's coffers amounted to more than $8 million, while Ukraine's
was less than a quarter million. And there were additional projects that
Russia was expected to fund through the IAEA. Chudakov, besides
being deputy director general of the IAEA, was in charge of its all-
important department of nuclear energy, overseeing its expansion into
new markets—a top priority of Rosatom, the Russian nuclear energy
monopoly, which was trying to increase its share of the nuclear construction market in the Global South. In 2022, Rosatom began construction
of a nuclear reactor in Egypt, continued its nuclear reactor construction
projects in Hungary and Turkey, and made inroads into Myanmar and
Uganda. Before moving to Vienna in 2015, Chudakov had served as
director of a Russian nuclear power plant and deputy director general
of RosEnergoAtom, the operational branch of Rosatom.[11]

The conflict of interest that was obvious to anyone who looked at
Chudakov's background and his responsibilities at the IAEA was largely
ignored by governments and media alike. It was only the outbreak of
the Russo-Ukrainian War and Rosatom's involvement in the takeover
of the Chernobyl nuclear plant that attracted global attention to Grossi's
deputy. In mid-March, Greenpeace demanded that the IAEA remove
Chudakov from his post, arguing that he could not have assumed such
a high-profile office without the support of "Putin's government." In
April the Swiss energy counselor Simonetta Sommaruga wrote to

Grossi, asking that Chudakov be excluded from any business deal-ings with Ukraine and limited in his access to classified information. Switzerland, wrote Sommaruga, wanted to ensure that the Ukrainian government and IAEA would exchange security information "on the basis of confidence and without any possibility of political influence." Chudakov remained in his position, and no reduction of his duties or restrictions on his access to information were reported by the IAEA.[12]

With Grossi refusing not only to condemn but even to mention the Russian Federation in any statements attributed directly to him and the IAEA, the European Nuclear Safety Regulators Group (ENSREG), which represented the EU countries, took on the task of formulating a public response to the Russian attack on Chernobyl.

On February 27 the group held an extraordinary teleconference to which IAEA representatives were invited. Unlike the World Association of Nuclear Operators, ENSREG did not have either Russia or Ukraine as a member and could take a position not impeded by the interests of Moscow or Kyiv. That is exactly what participants in the teleconfer-ence did when they issued a statement siding with the previous opinion of the European Council and condemning "in the strongest possible terms the Russian Federation's unprovoked and unjustified military aggression against Ukraine." They urged "the Russian Federation to immediately cease unlawful activities." The statement continued, "For-eign military forces must leave the site and permit unhindered regular access of knowledgeable staff of the licensee and the national regulator in order to ensure the continuing safe operation of the site." The group wanted Russia to stop its activities within the internationally recog-nized borders of Ukraine and leave the Chernobyl nuclear power plant. The IAEA issued no similar declaration.[13]

———

While Grossi and the IAEA avoided any direct reference to Russia and its military, the Russians claimed responsibility for their action in the most public way possible. The news was delivered by TASS, Russia's leading news agency, on the afternoon of February 25. On the evening of February 26, the third day of the all-out war, Russian television channels carried a report from the Chernobyl nuclear plant featuring an interview with a Russian military officer who wore no insignia except the St. George ribbon on his upper chest—the marker used by Russian troops in Ukraine back in 2014. The camera showed images of disarmed and clearly depressed Ukrainian guardsmen and Ukrainian personnel dressed in white uniforms.[14]

The television anchor stated that the plant had been taken over by the Russian military to avoid provocations by Ukrainian nationalists and protect the lives of millions of people from the consequences of another nuclear catastrophe. The Russian television journalist Irina Kuksenkova, who reported from the Chernobyl plant, gave some details about its capture. It was allegedly the work of the Russian paratroopers who had now joined Ukrainian guardsmen in protecting the plant. She elaborated on the claim that the plant had been taken under Russian control as a precaution against its seizure by Ukrainian nationalists. If that were to happen, said Kuksenkova, the scope of the tragedy would be difficult to imagine, and its consequences would be catastrophic not only for Ukraine but also for Belarus and Russia.[15]

On February 28, a few days after Russia admitted its takeover of the Chernobyl plant in its television broadcasts, the Prypiat region entered the news for a reason not directly related to the plant. The first Russo-Ukrainian negotiations since the start of all-out hostilities began that day at an undisclosed location near the Prypiat River close to the Ukrainian-Belarusian border. Some believed that the meeting was taking place in or close to the Chernobyl exclusion zone. The location was a matter of public controversy and utmost secrecy.[16]

The Russian delegation, led by Putin's adviser Vladimir Medinsky, who served as chairman of the Russian government commission on historical education and was at least partly responsible for Putin's own historical views and pronouncements, arrived in the Belarusian city of Homel on the same day as the public announcement of the negotiations. But the Ukrainians were in no hurry to go to Homel, which is located northeast of the Chernobyl exclusion zone. With the Russians attacking Ukraine, and Chernobyl in particular, from Belarusian territory, the Ukrainian government considered that country inappropriate for negotiations.

Zelensky's spokesman Serhii Nykyforov also questioned the security guarantees provided to the Ukrainian delegation by the Belarusian strongman, Aliaksandr Lukashenka. Nykyforov, speaking ostensibly on behalf of Zelensky, proposed that the Russians meet the Ukrainian delegation in any other country or city, including Baku, Istanbul, Warsaw, or Vienna. The Russians refused, insisting on Belarus. The Ukrainians, for their part, refused to come to Homel and proposed negotiations on the Ukrainian-Belarusian border.[17]

Eventually the two sides agreed on an undisclosed location by the Prypiat River known to the media only as the "fisherman's house." Journalists soon discerned that the "fisherman" in question was none other than Lukashenka, and the negotiations took place in his residence near the village of Liaskavichi, the administrative center of Prypiat National Park, located approximately 100 kilometers (62 miles) west of the Polesie radioecological preserve, the Belarusian part of the Chernobyl exclusion zone.[18]

At the Chernobyl nuclear power plant, Valentyn Heiko and his colleagues followed the news with particular attention, if not anxiety. They convinced the occupiers that they had to have Ukrainian radio on constantly in order to be aware of any official warning that might affect the safety of the plant. To the disappointment of many, the five-hour-long negotiations in Belarus produced scant results. The Russians, declaring that their objective was the demilitarization and denazification of Ukraine, did not get very far, while the Ukrainians, led by defense minister Oleksii Reznikov, who claimed that their objective was a cease-fire and an end to hostilities, also achieved little. That little was an agreement to resume talks.[19]

Fighting continued, and people at the Chernobyl nuclear station saw Russian jets flying over the zone and Russian troops moving through it, all in the direction of Kyiv. But contrary to what the Russians had hoped for, Kyiv did not fall in three days. Russian troops moving south from Chernobyl encountered stiff Ukrainian resistance on the approaches to the Ukrainian capital. On February 27, the Ukrainian media reported on a battle in the town of Bucha, located on the highway leading from Chornobyl toward Kyiv. Ukrainian artillery fire destroyed a column of armored vehicles moving through the streets of Bucha, incinerating up to 100 units of military equipment.[20]

On the following day, the mayor of Bucha, Anatolii Fedoruk, posted a video showing the remains of Russian armored vehicles on one of the city streets. The Ukrainian banner flew over Bucha once again, and electricity was restored a few days later. But that was not the end of the story. Bucha would soon become the site of one of the worst massacres of the war.[21]

————

After the first few days of the occupation, Valentyn Heiko and his shift at the Chernobyl plant realized that they would not be replaced anytime soon. They began turning their offices and workplaces into combined work-sleep areas. Conditions were difficult during the day because of the occupiers, who limited and controlled movement around the plant; they were also an obtrusive presence at night. But the most depressing aspect of the occupation was the operators' seemingly endless shift.

A press release issued by the administration of the plant in Slavu-tych decried the situation. It read: "A shift at the Chernobyl Nuclear Power Plant lasts twelve hours. Throughout that time the personnel are constantly at their workplaces (at a control board, at a computer, using equipment, and the like). At present, the Chernobyl personnel who find themselves on the premises of the occupied station are begin-ning their twelfth shift, that is, they have actually spent almost 144 hours at their workplaces."[22]

On February 28, the acting director of the plant, Valerii Seida, and its top managers met in Slavutych with relatives of those on duty at Chernobyl in an attempt to reassure and calm them. Valentyn Heiko joined the meeting by telephone. He described the takeover of February 24 and assured family members that their loved ones were safe. He had managed to reach an agreement with the occupiers that they would not interfere in the work of the personnel. According to the press release issued by headquarters, Seida "assured the relatives that no one was threatening the personnel; people were at their workplaces carrying out their appointed tasks. It was impossible to change shifts under wartime conditions, although rotation scenarios were actively being developed and discussed." The relatives were advised to use telephone landlines in order to reach their loved ones, as mobile communications were not working.[23]

On March 1, the landlines between Slavutych and the Chernobyl plant were used to pass on greetings as well as information. On that day Valentyn Heiko, the man in charge of the troubled station, was turning sixty. There was no hope that he might spend the day with his family, but the event was duly noted. At the plant, Heiko employed the internal communication system to keep up the tradition of greeting people whose birthday fell on a day when they were on shift. On March 1, as was the ritual at 1:00 p.m., Heiko's voice was heard on the plant's loudspeaker system. He announced that it was his own birthday, saying "briefly that he hoped never to celebrate a special occasion under such conditions and wished everyone peace of the spirit," recalled one of the engineers.[24]

The Ukrainian Nuclear Inspectorate under Oleh Korikov posted birthday greetings to Heiko on its Facebook page. "Valentyn Oleksandrovych Heiko, the shift supervisor at the Chernobyl AES State Specialized Enterprise, has now been holding the security of nuclear facilities at the station, occupied by the Russian military, in his hands for six days," read the post. "He cannot pass on his shift or leave his post; he remains at his workplace just as his colleagues did during the greatest nuclear accident in 1986."[25]

The birthday greetings touched on matters of loyalty and betrayal, heroism and cowardice. Heiko was praised for remaining at his post during the occupation instead of being blamed for helping the occupiers. It was an act of heroism equivalent to that of the operators and firefighters who had overcome the nuclear disaster in 1986. Both were hostages of the situation: indeed, the author of the post referred to those on duty as hostages and called on the Russian military to "return home."

Heiko's colleagues in Kyiv wished him strength to "endure this challenge and come home safe and sound." Eager to lend moral support to Heiko and his crew, they affirmed that he was a hero not only in their eyes but also in those of the international community. "We believe in your endurance, professional intuition, and dedication to putting safety first, no matter what 'dramatic situation' may arise. You are the pride of the whole professional community not only in Ukraine," went the post. "In the course of this week, all duty officers of the IAEA Incident and Emergency Center have learned your name, and you are the one from whom they obtain credible information about the state of security at the nuclear facilities of the Chernobyl AES."[26]

———

The officers of the IAEA Incident and Emergency Center did indeed know Heiko's name by heart. They were the first to receive reports about the occupation of the Chernobyl plant and maintained constant contact with the State Nuclear Regulatory Inspectorate of Ukraine, providing information for the daily statements issued by the Secretariat of the IAEA on behalf of Rafael Grossi. In the statement issued on March 1, Heiko's birthday, Grossi expressed "deep admiration and sincere gratitude for the tireless work, vigilance and bravery of the personnel operating the nuclear power plants, other nuclear facilities, and the staff of the regulator." He continued: "We can all be very thankful for their determined and courageous efforts to ensure continued nuclear safety and security."[27]

Those were important words, but the Ukrainians were not satisfied with Grossi's verbal support. On the day he issued his statement, Grossi received a letter from Oleh Korikov, requesting the IAEA "to provide immediate assistance in coordinating activities in relation to the safety of the Chernobyl NPP and other nuclear facilities." Grossi responded by promising to hold "consultations and maintain contacts in order to address this request." The consultations he had in mind included an emergency meeting of the IAEA board of governors that Poland and Canada had asked him to call on behalf of Ukraine on February 26, the third day of the Russian aggression. The thirty-five-member board, which included Russia, convened for a two-day meeting on March 2, one week after the takeover of Chernobyl.[28]

Addressing the members of the board, Grossi acknowledged that "Russian forces have taken control of all facilities of the State Specialized Enterprise Chernobyl Nuclear Power Plant, located within the Exclusion Zone," and that the "Russian Federation's military operation" had caused a "conflict" with "safety, security and safeguards implications." But he did his best to downplay the consequences of the Russian occupation of Chernobyl. "No casualties or destruction at the industrial site were reported," stated Grossi. "While increased levels of radiation were initially measured at the site, likely due to the movement of heavy military vehicles disturbing the soil, the IAEA assessed that they remained low enough not to pose a hazard to the public."

Grossi presented a list of seven requirements needed to ensure the safety of nuclear sites in Ukraine. They included radiation monitoring of the sites, the availability of offsite sources of electricity, and the ability of staff to function "free of undue pressure." He stressed: "It is of utmost importance that the staff working at the Specialized Enterprise Chernobyl Nuclear Power Plant are able to do their job safely and effectively, and that their personal wellbeing is guaranteed by those who have taken control." To the disappointment of many board members, Grossi failed either to condemn the actions of the Russian occupiers or demand, or even suggest, their withdrawal.[29]

On March 3, as the IAEA board prepared to vote on a resolution concerning the Russian takeover of Chernobyl, Oleh Korikov together with the Ukrainian minister of energy, Herman Halushchenko, and the head of the state nuclear energy corporation, Petro Kotin, published an appeal to the IAEA calling the Russian takeover of the Chernobyl plant an act of nuclear terrorism. The Ukrainian officials stated that the personnel of the Chernobyl plant had been subjected to psychological pressure by being forced to work seven days in succession without a break. They demanded that the IAEA apply "peer pressure" on the Russian Federation and activate its Incident and Emergency Center to deal with the threat of a nuclear accident at Chernobyl. The center's staff was placed "on call," but full response mode was not activated by the IAEA leadership. The Ukrainians also wanted the IAEA to deny Russia access to the intellectual and material resources of the IAEA and break all relations with Russian citizens employed by the IAEA and other UN bodies dealing with nuclear energy.[30]

The IAEA board was not prepared to go so far. Nevertheless, in spite of Grossi's reluctance to call a spade a spade, it adopted a resolution by majority vote that "deplored . . . the Russian Federation's actions in Ukraine, including forcefully seizing control of nuclear facilities" and called on Russia "to immediately cease all actions against, and at, the Chernobyl Nuclear Power Plant and any other nuclear facility in Ukraine." Twenty-six members voted in favor, while Russia and China voted against. Russia's representative at the IAEA, Mikhail Ulianov, suggested that the resolution included "intentional politically motivated lies and mistakes." Five members of the board—India, Pakistan, South Africa, Senegal, and Vietnam—abstained.[31]

The Ukrainians, on whose behalf the emergency meeting was convened, had clearly hoped for more. Their appeal to the IAEA did not concern the Chernobyl plant alone and was meant to stop similar action against Ukraine's four other nuclear power plants, comprising fifteen reactors. The Ukrainians wanted the IAEA to help establish a 30-kilometer (19-mile) no-fighting zone around their country's nuclear sites and to appeal to NATO to police the no-fighting and access denial zones around such facilities. Of particular concern was the rapidly worsening situation around the Zaporizhia nuclear power plant in southern Ukraine. By March 3, the Russian army had all but surrounded the Zaporizhia station, the largest nuclear power facility in Europe, running six 1,000 megawatts electric (Mwe) reactors. What had happened at Chernobyl was beginning to look like a prelude to a much more dangerous situation at Zaporizhia.[32]

6

GOD'S GRACE

Petro Kotin, CEO of Enerhoatom, the company that ran the Ukrainian nuclear power plants, first approached Rafael Grossi with a request to help him establish a 30-kilometer (19-mile) no-fighting zone around the plants on February 28, 2022, the fourth day of the war.[1]

On the previous day, Russian troops had appeared at the approaches to Enerhodar, the city that housed the Zaporizhia nuclear plant. Like the Chernobyl plant, the one in Zaporizhia turned out to be directly in the path of the Russian incursion. In the case of Chernobyl, the Russians moved from Belarus through the Chernobyl exclusion zone toward Kyiv. As for the Zaporizhia plant, the Russian troops who broke out of the Crimea tried to make their way to the regional capital of Zaporizhia, 120 kilometers (75 miles) northeast of the plant, and farther north to the city of Dnipro (formerly Dnipropetrovsk). Zaporizhia, with a population of more than 700,000, and Dnipro, with close to a million inhabitants, were among the main Russian targets in mainland Ukraine.

If in northern Ukraine the Russian troops were slowed down by forested areas and an abundance of rivers, in the Pontic steppes of the Ukrainian south they moved easily along the highways, with no major natural obstacles to stop their advance. On the first day of the war the Russians captured the city of Nova Kakhovka, 150 kilometers (93 miles) down the Dnieper River from Enerhodar. The city was located on the shores of the Kakhovka Sea, a huge reservoir created by blocking the free flow of Dnieper water with the dam of the Kakhovka hydroelectric power station. The reservoir was the source of water for the Zaporizhia station. On the morning of February 25, Russian troops approached Melitopol, a city of 150,000 and a major transportation hub known as the "gates of the Crimea." Now they could easily reach Enerhodar, located about 100 kilometers (62 miles) northwest of Melitopol.[2]

The situation was considered worrisome enough for the management of the Zaporizhia nuclear plant to shut down two of its six operating reactors. Under threat was also the station's spent nuclear fuel facility, including 174 dry casks to store the fuel. It became operational in 2001, making Zaporizhia the first Ukrainian nuclear power plant fully independent of the Rosatom structures in Ukraine. At that time spent fuel from other Ukrainian nuclear power stations was shipped to Russia for treatment and storage. In January 2021, slightly more than a year before the Russian invasion, the Zaporizhia plant reached its full production capacity, made possible by the installation of an additional power line linking the station with the national electricity grid.[3]

Like Chernobyl, the Zaporizhia plant had a town to house its workers. In the case of Chernobyl it was the city of Prypiat, while Zaporizhia's satellite community was Enerhodar, meaning "gift of energy." It was located 6 kilometers (4 miles) from the plant. Enerhodar was a new town originally built for the construction workers and operators of the Zaporizhia thermal power station, the largest in Ukraine, constructed before the nuclear station. The city was born in 1970; the construction of the nuclear power station began in 1980. It replaced Chernobyl as the largest nuclear power plant in Ukraine soon after the Chernobyl catastrophe of 1986. At that time the station had two VVER-

1000 pressurized light water reactors, generating 950 MWe of electricity each. The third reactor, of similar design and equal capacity, was launched in 1987, the fourth in 1988, and the fifth in 1989. The sixth and last reactor went into service in 1995, four years after the proclamation of Ukrainian independence.[4]

Of Enerhodar's 53,000 citizens, 12,000 were employed at the nuclear power plant, and another thousand at the thermal one. As in Prypiat and then in Slavutych, the population of Enerhodar was multi-ethnic, with many families tracing their roots back to Russia and other republics of the former USSR. In 2001, ethnic Ukrainians constituted 57 percent of the population and ethnic Russians close to 40 percent, but almost 62 percent of the citizens of Enerhodar considered Russian their "mother tongue," while only 38 percent claimed Ukrainian. The city was predominantly Russian-speaking, as the "native language" marker indicated the individual's ethnic identity rather than his or her language preference.[5]

In 2014, when the Russo-Ukrainian War began, politics in the Enerhodar city council were dominated by members of President Viktor Yanukovych's Party of Regions. The mayor, Pavlo Muzyka, and the largest faction in the city council belonged to that party. After Yanukovych fled Ukraine, Muzyka and his allies made their political home in a new party, the "Oppositional Platform—For Life," organized by former backers of the Party of Regions and associated with Ukraine's most notorious pro-Russian politician and personal friend of Vladimir Putin, Viktor Medvedchuk.[6]

But the elections of 2020 ended the monopoly of the former Yanukovych allies, bringing to the mayor's office a thirty-five-year-old nuclear engineer and novice politician named Dmytro Orlov. He gained twice the number of votes cast for his main competitor, Pavlo Muzyka, who had been criticized for increasing his salary by more than 60 percent in less than three years and earning more than the mayor of Kyiv, Vitalii Klychko. Muzyka was gone. The proponents of Medvedchuk and his pro-Russian policies were still in the council, but now in a minority. Neither the city council nor most of the population wanted Russian troops in their city. They would soon let the world know where they stood.[7]

———

General Igor Konashenkov, a spokesperson of the Russian Ministry of Defense, announced the capture of Enerhodar on February 28, the fourth day of the war. It was wishful thinking at best: a column of Russian armored vehicles had indeed approached Enerhodar but turned back after being confronted by many of its citizens, who blocked the entrance with barricades made of used tires and told the Russians to go home. The Russian commanders, apparently surprised not to have been welcomed, were at a loss and turned back.[8]

They did not go far. On March 1, the Ukrainian interior ministry reported the movement of a column of ninety vehicles near the village of Dniprovka, 12 kilometers (7 miles) south of Enerhodar. The Russian commanders unsuccessfully approached the city officials to negotiate the surrender of Enerhodar. Dmytro Orlov, the city's young mayor, rejected the Russian threats and inducements to surrender. In his own words, he was determined to demonstrate to them that "Enerhodar is Ukraine; everything is calm and normal in Enerhodar, and occupiers are not expected here. Judging by the reaction of those representatives of occupation 'authority' and those who contacted them for conditional negotiations, they understood that they were not awaited here."[9]

Orlov also rejected a Russian officer's request to let his troops take selfies against the background of the nuclear power plant to prove to their commanders that they had accomplished the task and captured the city and the plant. The Russian officers were indeed under enormous pressure from their commanders, as the station had been declared under their control two days earlier. Orlov recognized that it was a trick: once admitted, the Russian military would never leave. He refused permission.[10]

The city council formed a Defense Council, and all city institutions and services went into emergency mode. The authorities declared the city under siege. The citizens, mobilized by means of social media, rallied to stand by their council and help defend the city. On March 2, as a Russian column once again approached Enerhodar, a call went out on social media for volunteers to gather at the entrance. "On the [city] telegram channel there was a notification that we were gathering by the checkpoint, and anyone wishing to come could do so," recalled a citizen who had agreed to talk to a Ukrainian journalist that day on condition of anonymity. To protect her privacy, she was called "Alena."[11]

"Of course, my daughter and I had already shown up there at 9:00 a.m.," recalled Alena. "There were a great many people. . . . It couldn't really be said that we were afraid, because there was some hope, after all, that such a mass of like-minded people could hold them [the Russians] off and show them that there was nothing for them to do here, and no one was awaiting them." It turned out to be a false alarm. No Russian column showed up at the gates of the city. Mayor Orlov asked people to go home and come back at 2:00 p.m. They followed his advice. "And the second time there were even more people," recalled Alena. She was impressed by the level of patriotism demonstrated by her fellow citizens: "There was such pride in our city that people were not sitting around or expecting something but taking action."[12]

Drone photos taken that day showed a long stretch of highway leading toward the city filled with thousands of people, mostly men but women as well, carrying Ukrainian blue-and-yellow flags. Photos taken on the ground show improved fortifications: the barricade of tires had been reinforced with garbage trucks blocking the entrance to the city. A poster on the approaches to the city read: "Russian military vessel, go fuck yourself!" Those were the words addressed to the Russian naval cruiser *Moskva* by the outgunned and outnumbered Ukrainian defenders of Snake Island in the Black Sea on the first day of the war. It was the response of a Ukrainian border guard to the Russian appeal to surrender. The phrase went viral on Ukrainian social networks and media, becoming a symbol of Ukrainian resilience. The Russians failed to reach the city gates because their column had been stopped by another group of protesters near the village of Vodiane, east of Enerhodar. Two protesters were injured after Russian soldiers threw light-and-noise grenades into the crowd.[13]

On March 3, a Russian column once again approached Enerhodar. This time they had orders to shoot and began shelling the checkpoint at the entrance to the city. Alena was putting on warm clothing as she prepared to respond to Orlov's appeal on social media to come to the checkpoint when new information came from the mayor: "There is firing at the checkpoint, and tanks have approached." Orlov urged citizens to stay home. He kept his citizens informed through social media about developments at the checkpoint. "An enemy column of more than 100 heavy vehicles is approaching the city. Clear the streets immediately. Stay away from windows. Don't use elevators!" Orlov advised his fellow citizens. He assured them that the self-defense unit was there to protect them: "Our boys are resisting and doing all they can to stop the enemy from getting through." That ended the nonviolent stage of the city's defense. "And then it all started," Alena recalled later.[14]

Alena remained at home but could not stay away from the window. "We could see from our window at the entrance to the building that something was burning, probably tires at the checkpoint, and we heard shooting. Sirens wailed nonstop," she told a journalist later. "Then dusk fell, and news came that [the Russians] were approaching the nuclear power station. And we can see the station from our balcony. So we saw the whole battle. And that was when it became frightening." The Ukrainian guardsmen whose main task was to protect the Zaporizhia nuclear power plant now picked up their weapons to do their job.[15]

———

The battle for the nuclear plant began around 11:30 p.m. on March 3 as a column consisting of two tanks and ten armored personnel carriers with a searchlight on began advancing toward the power station along the facility's service road. The Ukrainian guardsmen were ready. They knew what had happened at Chernobyl and were not prepared to surrender. Someone fired an anti-tank missile, hitting one of the tanks. But the remaining vehicles continued their advance, opening fire in the direction of the plant's main administration building and its training facility.

The battle for the station could be viewed in real time on its YouTube channel, as one of the engineers had livestreamed the security camera footage the moment the Russian advance began. In the administration building the acting director of the plant, Ihor Murashov, watched the footage with his colleagues. "We thought that they would block us but would have enough sense not to shoot," recalled Murashov. "But they started shooting chaotically, sparks flew from their bullets, which struck the power lines." It felt dreadful. "We're all living people; it was terrifying indeed," recalled Murashov. "We saw them shooting at the building in which we found ourselves at the time; we saw smoke rising and thought, among other possibilities, that we might simply burn up." Murashov and his colleagues were also concerned about the safety of the reactors. "The thought that a nuclear catastrophe might take place was there."[16]

The Russians fired rocket-propelled grenades indiscriminately at the administration building, and the training center was on fire. The operators began the lengthy process of shutting down still-working reactor by reducing its power level. The public address system transmitted a message to the attackers: "Stop shooting at a dangerous nuclear facility. Stop shooting immediately! You are threatening the security of the whole world!" It had no effect. Apart from the administration building and the training center, Russian fire damaged the building of reactor no. 1 and hit the power transformer of unit no. 6, and some shells landed in the area of the spent-fuel facility, the pride of the plant and one of its most dangerous areas.[17]

"All that took place at the Chernobyl nuclear plant and in our plant does not correspond to any logic," commented Mayor Orlov later. "I cannot imagine what was in the head of the individual who gave orders to fire on the nuclear station and even to enter the city." According to Ukrainian investigators, the order to storm the city and the station was given by Major General Aleksei Dombrovsky, a senior officer in the Russian Guards, the same subdivision of the Russian armed forces to which General Burakov and Colonel Frolenkov, the commanders of the Russian takeover of Chernobyl, belonged.[18]

The Russian troops captured the Zaporizhia plant by 2:30 a.m., when reinforcements arrived. Three Ukrainian defenders were killed. The Russian losses, if any, remained unknown. The battle was over, but not the danger of an accident. The Russians had no firefighters of their own to extinguish the blaze in the training facility and would not allow the Ukrainians to do so until 5:00 a.m. The Ukrainian crews extinguished the fire by 6:20 a.m. The worst had been avoided, but it was a terrifyingly close call.[19]

Edwin Lyman, the director of nuclear power safety at the Union of Concerned Scientists, envisioned the possibility of another nuclear accident. "If the firefight had damaged more of the plant's critical subsystems and the nuclear engineers on-site hadn't been able to reach emergency backups," he observed later, "the situation could have turned dire. In a couple of hours, you have core damage starting and a situation that is potentially irreversible." Lyman referred to the possibility of another Fukushima, while Tom Bielefeld, a nuclear security expert based in Germany, called the shooting a "near miss" and an act of "dangerous idiocy."[20]

On the next day, March 4, the Russian Ministry of Defense announced that the Zaporizhia nuclear power plant was under Russian control. To explain what had happened the previous night at the station, of which they had allegedly been in charge since February 28, the ministry officials came up with a bizarre story. According to them, the Russians had had to deal with a "monstrous provocation" by the Ukrainians. A Ukrainian reconnaissance and sabotage group had penetrated the training complex, from which it opened automatic fire at the Russian Guards patrol. "The firing points of the Ukrainian diversionists were destroyed by small-arms fire," read the ministry's press release. It made no mention of the Russian tank and missile volleys at the station and its facilities. The training complex had allegedly been set ablaze by the retreating Ukrainian commandos.[21]

————

The YouTube footage of the Russian takeover of the Zaporizhia nuclear plant went viral almost in real time, alerting not only the Ukrainian government but the world at large to the Russian attack on the largest nuclear station in Europe. The realization that the war in Ukraine had already gone nuclear, threatening radioactive contamination of people and the environment, was largely missed by the world after the takeover of Chernobyl. Now the situation was different. Footage of the battle involving charging tanks and firing missile launchers at the nuclear site was there for everyone to see. The danger of a major nuclear accident could not be ignored anymore.

As the battle for the station was going on, the Ukrainian minister of foreign affairs, Dmytro Kuleba, tweeted about the dangers of the attack on the Zaporizhia plant, saying that fire had already broken out. "If it blows up, it will be 10 times larger than Chernobyl!" Kuleba demanded that "the Russians must IMMEDIATELY cease fire and allow firefighters to establish a security zone!" Before night's end, Zelensky addressed the world through his Telegram channel. "Europe should wake up," declared the Ukrainian president. "Europe's largest atomic station is on fire right now. Russian tanks are firing on atomic blocs. These are tanks equipped with thermal imagers, so they know what they are shooting at. They prepared for this. I am addressing all those . . . who know the word Chernobyl. Russia wants to repeat that and is already doing so, but multiplied by 6."[22]

The State Nuclear Regulatory Inspectorate of Ukraine kept the public aware of what was happening almost in real time on its website. "Shooting at the grounds of the Zaporizhia Atomic Energy Station by the military forces of the Russian Federation began approximately at 1:00 a.m., causing fires on its territory," read one of the real-time posts.

The inspectorate informed the public that at the time of the attack, only one of the six reactors was operational: two had been shut down earlier, one more was undergoing planned repairs, and two were shut down and disconnected from the grid as a result of the attack. The remaining unit, no. 4, provided the electricity needed for the functioning of the station as well as to avoid the meltdown of the reactors that had been taken out of service. Fortunately, the units were not compromised.

Readers of the inspectorate's website, most of them associated with the nuclear industry, were uncharacteristically silent when it came to offering technical advice. They simply hoped and prayed for a miracle. "Lord, forgive us and have mercy on us sinners. Queen of Heaven, cover the skies above Ukraine with your Veil. All Heavenly Powers, protect us from the hostile adversary," commented Zoia Koval from Varash, the site of the Rivne nuclear power plant. "Angels of God, protect the AES; all heavenly powers, help the defending warriors. Hold on, our people," wrote Nadiia Ratushna from the city of Bila Tserkva, south of Kyiv. "Lord God, have mercy on us sinners and give wisdom to Putin," added Mykola Kuryk, a Ukrainian from Slovakia. Natalia Saltysh from Hlukhiv, a former Cossack capital in northeastern Ukraine on the Russian border, tried to talk sense to the Russians: "They do not even understand that a radioactive Cloud, following the windrose, will descend on the Kuban region, Rostov oblast, and Krasnodar krai."[23]

In Israel, the seventy-five-year-old former chief engineer of the Chernobyl nuclear plant, Nikolai Steinberg, could not sleep. He sat down to write an appeal to the world and to his colleagues in Ukraine. He began: "I, Nikolai Steinberg, chief engineer of the Chernobyl Atomic Energy Station from May 1986 to March 1987, know what a nuclear catastrophe is not from textbooks, not from newspaper articles, and not from political statements." He had a solid reputation and broad contacts among nuclear professionals all over the former Soviet Union, as well as significant name recognition and a following among the general public because of his participation in numerous documentaries that flooded television screens after the release of the Sky/HBO blockbuster *Chernobyl*.

First and foremost, Steinberg addressed his fellow nuclear engineers and scientists. "What more does that bastard [Putin] have to do for the world to realize that it is not global warming that will kill everyone? He is being collegially supported by 'peaceable' atomic scientists—not one of the leaders of Russian atomic energy has condemned the criminal acts of their Führer or even expressed concern about the consequences of such a flagrant criminal act! Base cowards! And where are you, atomic scientists of the world? Hiding your heads under your wings, like ostriches? You know better than anyone else that nuclear tragedy is not local! The time for political correctness is over." Steinberg also attacked German leaders for replacing nuclear energy with Russian gas and French leaders for failing to react. His appeal was published the same day on numerous "nuclear" sites in Ukraine.[24]

Although Steinberg did not mention the IAEA by name, his reference to the world nuclear community was directed first and foremost toward that organization. The IAEA, for its part, saw it as its main task to calm the nerves of the international community before alerting it to the dangers of the situation. The organization's Twitter account informed followers that radiation levels at the plant had not changed, and that Director General Grossi was in communication with the Ukrainian government. He was appealing for a halt to the use of force and warning of the serious danger that reactors might be hit. In the press release issued by the IAEA that day, Grossi was quoted as saying that he was "extremely concerned about the situation at the Zaporizhia NPP and what happened there during the night." Once again, it was not clear to whom Grossi's appeal was addressed. Russia was not mentioned, and Grossi seemed to be in touch with the Ukrainians alone.[25]

The attack on the Zaporizhia plant triggered an emergency meeting of the UN Security Council. Grossi joined the session by video link from a plane headed for Iran, which he had long planned to visit. He reported to the council that he had finally put the IAEA Incident and Emergency Center in full response mode but never explained why the takeover of Chernobyl a few days earlier had not produced a similar reaction. Grossi also spoke of plans to send an IAEA mission to Ukraine in order to assess and ensure the security of the reactors. While he decried the fact that "armed forces are in charge of the site," he failed once again to say whose armed forces they were. Grossi still could not bring himself to pronounce the word "Russia," giving the impression that his appeals were addressed to both sides.[26]

Not everyone at the UN Security Council meeting shared Grossi's apprehension. While another senior UN official, Under-Secretary General Rosemary DiCarlo, also managed to brief the council on developments at Zaporizhia without referring to "Russia" and "Russians," Ambassador Linda Thomas-Greenfield of the United States clearly had no problem in calling a spade a spade. "Russia's attack last night put Europe's largest nuclear power plant at grave risk," she stated. "It was incredibly reckless and dangerous and threatened the safety of civilians across Russia, Ukraine, and Europe. . . . By the grace of God, the world narrowly averted a nuclear catastrophe last night." She was echoed by the French ambassador, Nicolas de Rivière, who declared: "Russia must immediately cease its illegal and dangerous activities in order to restore the control of the Ukrainian authorities over all nuclear facilities."[27]

As expected, the Russian ambassador to the UN, Vassily Nebenzia, prevented the Security Council from adopting a resolution condemning the actions of the Russian army at the Zaporizhia plant. He admitted that Russian troops had taken control, but accused the Ukrainians of causing the fire and stressed that there had been no radioactive leaks. "In the course of negotiations with the leadership of the Zaporizhia AES, agreement was reached about its being taken under military protection," declared Nebenzia, using more or less the same language as that employed by Russian officials in relation to the takeover of the Chernobyl nuclear plant ten days earlier.[28]

The UN and its institutions proved incapable of stopping or reversing the Russian takeover of the Zaporizhia plant, as they had been unable to stop the takeover of Chernobyl or mitigate the situation there in any way. Ukraine and the people of Enerhodar were pretty much left to their own devices.

The Russian occupation of the Zaporizhia plant began with the disarming of its defenders. According to Russian sources, the members of the Ukrainian National Guard unit protecting the plant, altogether 250 officers and soldiers, including 50 women, had laid down their weapons and, after signing a document guaranteeing their nonparticipation in future hostilities, were allowed to leave the plant. They had fought back and, for the time being at least, were being treated better by the Russians than their counterparts in Chernobyl, who had not fought. The Russian guardsmen bragged to the media about having seized a large cache of weapons, some of them NATO models.[29]

"The administrative offices and the passage to the station are under the control of the occupiers," reported the Kyiv-based headquarters of Enerhoatom. "Station personnel are continuing to work in the energy blocks, ensuring the stable operation of the nuclear technology." The Russians did not immediately interfere with the work of the station personnel or the city administration. Enerhoatom remained in charge of operations. The Ukrainian flag continued to fly over the city administration building, but Russians manned the checkpoint at the entrance to the city. For the time being, they stayed away from the city streets. Mayor Orlov posted a video calling on the citizens of Enerhodar not to "provoke" the Russian military, as they might open fire on civilians. "There was an SMS from the mayor to the effect that it was better to stay home, as there might be subversive intelligence groups in town," recalled Alena, who was still in the city during the first weeks after the Russian occupation.[30]

The "interregnum" or, rather, dual authority in the city and at the station lasted only a few days. On March 6, the Ukrainian authorities informed the IAEA that the staff of the nuclear power plant had been subordinated to Russian military authority. In the city, the occupiers turned off mobile networks and the internet to make it difficult, if not impossible, for citizens to communicate with one another and the world at large. On March 7, people defiantly showed up en masse at city hall, carrying Ukrainian banners, to mourn the defenders of the power plant who had died in battle with the Russian attackers on the night of March 4. Mayor Orlov posted photos of the funeral with the caption: "Enerhodar says farewell to the heroes who died defending the Zaporizhia AES." The photos showed a priest, two coffins next to a Ukrainian flag, and the flag of the city of Enerhodar, with hundreds filling city hall square to bid farewell to their defenders.[31]

Although the Russians did not interfere with the funeral, changes became apparent in the next few days as they began arresting Ukrainian activists one at a time. On March 19, they kidnapped Orlov's first deputy, Ivan Semoidiuk. "Mostly, they took pro-Ukrainian people actively involved in the resistance movement," Orlov commented later. After the abduction of Semoidiuk, Orlov called on the citizens to rally in protest at city hall. Once again, they showed up en masse: more than 1,500 people gathered in less than an hour and protested under Ukrainian banners. This time, the Russians hurled light-and-noise grenades at the protesters.[32]

Once again, Alena was among the protesters. "As we walked down the avenue, we heard the cries of the crowd and automatic fire," she recalled. "We turned and went back. We were told that someone had been caught and that they were trying to shove him into a car. The crowd surged to beat them back. Then one of them jumped out with a submachine gun and started firing into the air. The crowd was not frightened and did not disperse; on the contrary, people ran toward the car. I thought that they would overturn it. They quickly squeezed into the car and said that the individual had been released, and apparently no one had been taken away. And they drove off to their base." The Ukrainians celebrated a victory. It turned out to be the last one.[33]

On April 2, almost a month into the occupation, the citizens of Enerhodar gathered with Ukrainian flags at the square near the Suchasnyk (Contemporary) cinema theater, still decorated with a poster featuring the Ukrainian flag and coat of arms. It was a show of defiance rather than a political rally with specific goals and demands. Russian guardsmen were nearby observing the gathering, not interfering at first with what was going on. They changed tactics once the protesters began to leave the scene after the rally, deciding that it was time to strike and prevent any more demonstrations in the city.

"People began to disperse, and we stood talking," recalled Alena, who attended the rally with her young daughter. "I looked and saw their vehicles increasing in number. Then they started coming up to us and saying, 'Disperse, gatherings are forbidden!' The crowd began to get angry and asked, 'Why? We're not bothering anyone, not doing anything, just standing and talking.' Naturally, some people lost their temper and started shouting. And then someone in the crowd shouted, 'Why can't we? You freed us, after all!' The answer was, 'Who told you that you were freed? The city has been occupied by troops of the Russian Federation.'"[34]

As Alena was leaving the rally, she suddenly heard behind her the sounds of exploding light-and-noise grenades. She remembered her thought at the time: "We won't run; we are walking. . . ." Photos shot on that day show smoke rising from the explosions, and videos capture the sound of automatic fire in the background. People now started to run. Four participants in the rally were wounded and ended up in the local hospital. According to the Ukrainian authorities, the order to use live ammunition to disperse the rally was given by General Valerii Vasiliev, the commander of the Russian radiological, chemical, and biological defense units, who had replaced the captor of the city, General Aleksei Dombrovsky, as the top Russian officer in Enerhodar sometime in late March.[35]

The Ukrainians never charged Vasiliev but they charged Dombrovsky with giving the order to storm the Zaporizhia plant. The forty-seven-year-old Dombrovsky had served as deputy commander of Russian Guard troops in the Krasnodar region of southern Russia. He apparently had no experience of dealing with nuclear sites. But many of his subordinates did, as was the case with Major Muradkhan Akhmedkhanov, who had led a Russian Guard battalion in Dagestan and had previously been responsible for the security of the Leningrad nuclear power plant. Colonel Aleksei Reshetnev had commanded a regiment protecting a munitions factory in the Volga region, and Colonel Sergei Dovgan had headed a Russian Guard unit protecting a Rosatom complex in Siberia.[36]

Unlike Colonel Frolenkov, who was awarded the star of the Hero of Russia Order for his role in the takeover of Chernobyl and would become a guest on television programs, General Dombrovsky would disappear from the public eye after his sojourn at the Zaporizhia plant. His handling of the takeover probably was not considered worthy of notice or award. With Dombrovsky gone, most of his subordinates stayed in Enerhodar, turning the operators of the plant and the citizens into hostages akin to those whom the Russians already had at Chernobyl.

7

DIRTY BOMB

One day in early March, Valentyn Heiko, the foreman of the Chernobyl shift, invited his captors, General Sergei Burakov, Colonel Andrei Frolenkov, and another Russian officer, to his office in the administration building of the station. It was around 7:00 a.m. but they came as requested—Heiko had something important to say to the Russians.

The reason for the conversation was a recent report on Ukrainian radio about Vladimir Putin's decision to put Russian strategic forces on high alert as a response to NATO's "aggressive statements." In the United States and around the world, Putin's statement was treated as a nuclear threat. Once Heiko learned about the statement, he gave it the same interpretation. "We now have nothing to lose," Heiko told the Russians. He added that he had been at Chernobyl since 1987 and witnessed many developments at the station, including the cleanup of the nuclear disaster of 1986. "I promise you that you will slowly and certainly die here together with me. I have enough knowledge and skill to ensure that you will remain here with us forever," he said. "Tell your commanders that either they conduct themselves in a civilized manner or there will be another Chernobyl here!"[1]

The message was clear: if the Russians used nuclear weapons against Ukraine, Heiko would unleash Chernobyl radiation to kill the Russians. The Russian officers had no reason to disbelieve Heiko. Frolenkov would later complain on Russian television that the Ukrainian had blackmailed him. Heiko demanded that Russian military operations in Ukraine cease, or he would sabotage the station's three allegedly still active reactors. "He threatened to begin irreversible processes, as he said, that you would be unable to influence, since you do not know how the electrical station is constructed, how it is operated," said Frolenkov, recalling one of his conversations with Heiko.

No reactors were still running at the station—the last of them had been shut down in 2000. But the Russian commanders, who had no knowledge of nuclear reactors or how to control them, believed that there were. Frolenkov learned precious little about the station in the course of his sojourn there. Asked later by a television host whether the three reactors were still active and whether another accident might be thrice as severe as that of 1986, he confirmed that was indeed the case. "I made all possible concessions in return for a promise of nuclear safety," he said, recalling his first encounters with Heiko. "As for his personal insults to me, and insults to Russia—I closed my eyes to that."[2]

In a few days, the alarmed Russians brought their own experts to the station from Rosatom. They were led by a man who introduced himself as Nikolai Nikolaevich. "He said that he was on a business trip here and had brought two or three professors, as he called them," recalled Serhii Dediukhin, an engineer in the station's safety department. He then added: "Well, it was apparent from his bearing, his way of dealing with people, that he was not FSB [Federal Security Service] but straight KGB [Committee for State Security]. That is, it was all gentle, polite, and cultured, but just as unprincipled, with a clearly defined purpose." Nikolai Nikolaevich introduced himself to Heiko as a deputy director at a Moscow institute researching nuclear explosions and offered his help. Heiko believed he was an FSB general.[3]

Nikolai Nikolaevich's surname was Muliukin. He was in fact a former major general of the Ministry of Internal Affairs and deputy director for security of a Rosatom institute involved in the development of uranium depositories and managing nuclear waste. He was eager to engage the Ukrainian personnel, trying to understand the "level of their radicalism" and determine whether they were actually prepared to sabotage the station. Vitalii Popov, one of the Ukrainian engineers, assured him that he was not going to engage with the Russian military, since the Ukrainians had their own military to deal with them, but had come to the station to make sure that the disaster of 1986 would not happen again.[4]

Heiko explained to the "professors" brought by Muliukin that the Chernobyl nuclear station was not a standard one, and the technical processes involved in monitoring such a station were different. "The Russian engineers made an excursion through the production areas and said that they had never dealt with such equipment," recalled the shift's chief nuclear safety engineer, Valerii Semenov. Despite behaving as if they were the actual masters of the plant, the Russians decided to leave the Ukrainian personnel in charge of it. According to rumors that reached the Chernobyl plant headquarters in Slavutych at the time, the representatives of Rosatom told the personnel: "We do not know what to do with this. This is a functioning station with its own systems; we do not want to be responsible for it."[5]

They tried to bribe the Ukrainians by promising them Rosatom salaries. "There were simply proposals that you now understand that it's all over, all over for Ukraine; even if some part of Ukraine survives, no one will guarantee your salary; that's it," recalled Semenov. "But we representatives of Rosatom can compensate you for everything in abundance." Neither he nor the others were interested. There were no takers. General Burakov and Colonel Frolenkov had no choice but to deal with the rebellious Heiko and his crew. Like Muliukin, the Russian commanders were eager to establish good personal relations with the Ukrainian managers.[6]

The Russians asked Valentyn Heiko to call them by their first names while addressing him by first name and patronymic in deference to his position and experience. Heiko considered the top Russian commanders to be members of the "intelligentsia," the Russian educated class, and would later refer to Frolenkov as a smart and honest officer. After what had happened at the Zaporizhia nuclear power plant, he came to appreciate the fact that Burakov and Frolenkov had not opened fire on the station. Heiko had a son working at Zaporizhia, and one of his relatives served there in the Ukrainian National Guard unit, so he had firsthand information from Enerhodar. He was convinced that Ramzan Kadyrov's Chechen fighters had opened fire on the station, a perception based on the fact that many Russian Guard units that occupied the city and the station came from the North Caucasus. "Russians in the regular army are, in general, more or less people you can talk to. But those [the Kadyrov men] are frostbitten and have to be put in their place [killed] right away."[7]

Heiko tried to use the relationship he had developed with the senior Russian officers to influence their behavior. He appealed to their sense of honor as officers. "Andrei, tell me, you're an officer, you took an oath to that Putin of yours or whomever else," said Heiko, recalling one of his conversations with Frolenkov. "And you violated it. How? You are the Russian Guard. According to your law, your constitution, you are forbidden to take part in any activities beyond the borders of your state. So tell me, as an officer, that you violated it. Can you tell me anything?" Frolenkov had no answer. On the second day of the occupation he allowed Heiko to take the Ukrainian national flag that the Russians had removed from the flagpole in front of the station's main building. But eventually Frolenkov stopped coming to Heiko's office for private conversations. "He had evidently realized that future talks might not end as he wished," recalled Heiko.[8]

———

Apart from possible sabotage by the Ukrainian staff, the Russian military at Chernobyl had another major concern that became something of an obsession: they believed that there was a secret nuclear weapons program housed in the Chernobyl exclusion zone and looked for sites of American laboratories allegedly working on the production of Ukrainian nuclear weapons. In effect, they fell victim to their own propaganda.

During the first week of March, as the world was still recovering from the shock of watching images of the battle waged by the Russian troops on the site of the Zaporizhia plant, the Russian government launched what is known in US intelligence parlance as a psyop, or psychological operation. Its purpose was to justify the Russian takeover of the Chernobyl and Zaporizhia nuclear power plants by claiming that both, especially the one in Chernobyl, were involved in a Ukrainian attempt to produce nuclear weapons. That subject had first been introduced in the run-up to the war by the Russian media, but after the international scandal caused by the military takeover of Zaporizhia, it was revived with new force.

The first salvo in the new media campaign was fired by Interfax, the allegedly independent Russian news agency, which on March 6 published an article based on an interview with an unidentified "informed source in one of the competent agencies of the Russian Federation." Given the history of the Russian use of the term "competent agencies" in reference to the KGB and its successors, as well as the interviewee's reference to information coming from the SVR, the Russian Foreign Intelligence Service, this material was very probably planted by the Russian intelligence agencies.

The Interfax source accused Ukraine of running a secret program called "Nuclear Ukraine" since the 1990s and attempting to acquire the requisite weapons-grade uranium and plutonium. "The zone of the Chernobyl atomic energy station should be noted particularly as a site for the development of nuclear weapons," suggested an unnamed interviewee, linking the "Project Nuclear Ukraine" with the Russian occupation of the Chernobyl nuclear site. "It was precisely there," continued the interviewee, "that work on production of a 'dirty bomb' and on the extraction of plutonium was carried out. The heightened background radiation that was natural in the Chernobyl zone concealed the conduct of such activities."

The Interfax article suggested that in order to conceal preparations for the acquisition of nuclear weapons from the rest of the world, the Ukrainian authorities ordered the destruction or transfer of all documentation related to the project from the academic institutions in Kharkiv and Kyiv to Lviv. But some of the documentation allegedly remained at the Zaporizhia plant. "To all appearances, the armed encounters with Ukrainian diversionary intelligence groups on the administrative premises adjacent to the nuclear power station pertained to that very circumstance," suggested the Interfax source. He stuck to the official story of the Russian occupation of Zaporizhia NPP, according to which the station was already under Russian control on February 28, and what happened on March 4 was an attack on the Russian troops by Ukrainian commandos, not the other way around. Now there was a motive to explain the alleged Ukrainian attack: it was carried out to cover the tracks of "Project Nuclear Ukraine."[9]

Almost immediately, the bizarre Interfax story about Ukraine's nuclear program and Russia's efforts to stop nuclear proliferation by taking control of Ukrainian nuclear sites was picked up by the rest of Russian state media. Some outlets summarized the story, while others added commentary from in-house and outside experts. The editors of Channel One television asked Igor Korotchenko for comment. A propagandist rather than a journalist specializing in military affairs, Korotchenko would end up next month on the sanctions lists of the United Kingdom and a number of EU countries for his promotion of the Russian war on Ukraine. He suggested that initially the Ukrainians had worked on the production of a "dirty bomb," but after Zelensky took power they switched to the project of building a conventional nuclear bomb and tried to develop a "full cycle" of the production of nuclear warheads.[10]

Another Channel One expert, Andrei Koshkin, chair of the department of political and social sciences at Plekhanov Russian University of Economics, added more details to the story told by Interfax. According to him, the Chernobyl nuclear plant had been used for the development of the Ukrainian nuclear project because operations there "aroused no suspicions from anyone and, all the more, [were conducted at the plant] in order not to attract the attention of the IAEA." To be sure, Koshkin had no idea that the Chernobyl zone was continuously monitored by the IAEA: anyone wanting to conceal anything from the agency would have stayed as far away from Chernobyl as possible. Other outlets added their own insights. Interviewed by *Izvestiia*, a former member of the UN Commission on Biological and Chemical Weapons, Igor Nikulin, claimed that if Russia had not initiated a "peace enforcement" operation, Ukraine would have become a nuclear power within a few months. Intervention was therefore a necessity and came not a moment too soon.[11]

It fell to the Russian military in the Chernobyl zone to prove their propaganda right and find American plutonium and Ukrainian "full cycle" production of either dirty or conventional nuclear bombs in the exclusion zone. After all the plant's buildings had been checked with no result, the Russian officers turned their view toward the mounds erected over the site of the burial of radioactive debris after the 1986 disaster. "They had notions of opening the mounds with an excavator to take a look at what was inside," recalled Semenov. He tried to dissuade the occupiers from exposing radioactive debris and putting everyone in danger of contamination. "I told them: are you in your right mind at all?" The idea was eventually abandoned. The Russians realized that they would be digging their own radioactive grave.[12]

The search for nuclear arms and chemical and biological laboratories was conducted by General Aleksei Rtishchev, who commanded the directorate of troops engaged in the radiological, chemical, and biological defense of the Siberian military district. Heiko met the Russian actions with complete disbelief, which he did not conceal from the commanding officers. "You don't know anything," Rtishchev once told him. "I've found ten laboratories." Heiko had had enough. "You know, Aleksei," responded Heiko, addressing Rtishchev by his first name, "Maybe you found something or other. But here, at the Chernobyl atomic energy station, there are concretely no such laboratories. So it would be better if we agreed not to raise the issue again." The Russians kept searching. "They kept looking for something at least, but they had to find it," recalled Heiko.[13]

———

As relations between Heiko and the Russian commanders remained strained, forty-six-year-old Valerii Semenov emerged as the key person managing daily relations between occupiers and occupied at the Chernobyl plant.

Semenov was generally very good at dealing with people. In 2020, he was elected to the Slavutych city council, where he represented a reformist party called Voice and led by the popular Ukrainian singer Sviatoslav Vakarchuk. An ethnic Russian born in Russia, Semenov had come to Chernobyl as a teenager. That background made him an ideal interpreter between the two worlds, one represented by soldiers from his old homeland and the other of the people who had shaped him as a personality. Semenov spoke predominantly if not exclusively Russian, but his language displayed his complex background: some words, sounds, and intonations came from roots in the Volga region, while others linked him to Ukraine and its northern dialects. Some of Semenov's colleagues doubted whether he was indeed on their side; as a go-between he inevitably ended up under the suspicion of both the occupiers and the occupied.[14]

Semenov divided the occupiers into two categories: the relatively reasonable majority of Russian officers and soldiers and the minority, approximately a third of the occupiers, whom he called *uporotye*, or "obsessed." "Those among them who were adequate," recalled Semenov, used to ask him daily: "Valerii, what's happening at the negotiations? When are we going home? What are we doing here?" Semenov noted that "they had a constant lack of information. . . . They asked that the television be turned on for them so that at least some information might come through. And in the morning and evening they watched our News. I don't know how much of it they understood."

When it came to the "obsessed," Semenov told a journalist: "You can't convince them of anything, and it's impossible even to converse with them; they only stick to their own." As he recalled, "In answer to the question 'Why have you come?' some of them answered with an open heart, 'We have come to free you from the radicals.' Some had come to free [us] from oppression of the Slavic faith." Semenov added: "That is how propaganda affects them, and they repeated it word for word."[15]

According to Semenov, "their senior commanders, the colonels and generals, were 200 percent polite. And that was so unpleasant, although it was clearly apparent that they found it difficult to say those things. Their facial expressions showed it; their cheekbones worked when they said that very politely. Probably the greatest kick for me was that they were obliged to act that way. I was simply stunned by their psychological preparation; how they may have been trained to deal with us."

The senior officers were apparently under orders not to exacerbate the already tense situation at the station, given the global attention fixed on Chernobyl. They also realized that their own health depended on those, like Semenov, who knew how to manage radiation and could easily put them in harm's way.[16]

Semenov had to deal with a succession of Russian military commanders. General Sergei Burakov, in charge of the takeover of the plant on February 24, stayed there until March 6 and was then replaced by General Oleg Yakushev. General Aleksei Rtishchev was at the site through a good part of March. The Ukrainian investigative reporter Dmytro Fionik suggested, on the basis of his interviews with Ukrainian law enforcement officials and witnesses, that in the course of the occupation there were five Russian generals on the premises. The Russians used the Chernobyl zone as a base to supply the Kyiv front with arms, ammunition, and food, as well as to send their wounded back to the Russian bases in Belarus.[17]

The troops belonged to different branches of the Russian armed forces. The army was represented by the tankmen, mainly Buriats by nationality, who had helped to storm the station. They were eventually replaced by marines. Troops engaged in radiological, chemical, and bacteriological defense constituted the largest military unit at the station. The Russian Guard units included commandos from the Special Rapid Response Unit (SOBR) located near Moscow and the Special-Purpose Police Detachment (OMON) from Briansk. On March 5, Russian Guard units were reinforced by detachments experienced in guarding nuclear power plants in Russia. There was no longer any need for the unarmed Ukrainian guardsmen who had guarded the station's buildings, and they were removed from their posts around the station.[18]

The Russians treated the Chernobyl station as a shield against possible Ukrainian attacks. "The city and the station function precisely as places of shelter and rest," said Heiko, commenting on this Russian tactic. "They understand that no one is going to fire on the city or the station itself. Because those are nuclear sites, so they feel free and easy there, and they can fire from that territory because they know that no one will fire back. That's why they behave in that manner." Serhii Dediukhin agreed with Heiko's assessment: "Even when they installed their systems of radioelectrical combat, they placed them right beside the buildings of the station, hoping that no one would fire at them."[19]

"The Russians used the station as a place of recuperation after battles near the capital," recalled Liudmyla Kozak, a forty-five-year-old engineer in the station's department of physical safety. "They came back here to catch up on sleep, to wash, to eat. They used our showers and slept in our quarters. Food was brought to them from Homel. A field kitchen cooked for them at first; then they took over a floor of our dining hall and ate there."

Semenov recalled that the Russians who had taken over Chernobyl were not prepared for a long war. The Russian officers confided to Semenov: "Valerii, we traveled three days; we were supposed to go into Kyiv from the station and keep your people apart in the government quarter to give a wide berth to your president so that he could come out and sign what we needed; then we would gather and take our leave." Semenov believed that they were telling the truth, indicating that they were completely unprepared for the kind of warfare they would encounter in Ukraine. OMON riot police units such as those Frolenkov had commanded before coming to Chernobyl brought along a whole truckful of plastic shields of the kind used by riot police.[20]

The morale of the Russian army and the Russian Guard troops was low. They drank heavily; according to Semenov, 30 to 50 percent of their household garbage consisted of empty bottles. Soldiers from different units also clashed with one another. "Conflicts among them were very frequent," recalled Liudmyla Kozak. "Someone would steal a notebook, someone else would steal a phone, people came to blows, there was anything you want. Some would get drunk, others would decide who was stronger or smarter." Liudmyla, whose office-turned-living-quarters was on the same floor as the Russian soldiers, did not feel safe. She could only look to senior officers for protection against their drunken subordinates.[21]

The first cases of looting at the station were associated with the drinking problem in the Russian army. "They might stop traffic for half an hour," recalled Semenov. "Then they explained the reason: to open the offices. . . . I think they were looking for alcohol." The Ukrainian personnel locked their quarters and offices but could do little to protect the equipment and facilities outside their quarters. Semenov was especially concerned about the safety of the expensive equipment in the mechanical repair shop. One day he discovered that Russian soldiers had removed the window frame at night to get into the shop. The next night they got in again and broke into the safes. It was a relief to find that they were still looking for alcohol, not for mechanical equipment.[22]

The standard Ukrainian recourse was to report cases of looting to the Russian senior officers. It worked in general, but at first some Russian officers tried to shift responsibility for break-ins to the Ukrainians. Heiko recalled having approached a Russian colonel to tell him that there were break-ins into the offices of the plant's top managers. "You know, it was one of your people who broke in," Heiko told the colonel. He was shocked by the answer: "And why do you think it was my people?" It took Heiko some time to understand what he just heard. He then told the officer: "You know, until the moment of the seizure of the Chernobyl plant and your arrival here, no one stole anything, no one broke into anything."[23]

In mid-March, soon after the Russian commanders gave up hope of finding American nuclear and biological laboratories, they began to fortify their position in and around the station. "The occupiers feared that our people would come to drive them out, so they fortified themselves, made dugouts and trenches, and set up defensive structures," recalled Liudmyla Kozak.[24]

One day Valerii Semenov saw soldiers delivering sandbags to protect firing positions atop the station's buildings. He could not believe his eyes. He approached the commanders: "You're grownups, aren't you? You're building a cupola for protection, for defense. What are you thinking? Our army is going to storm this position, or what? To destroy buildings and cause a radiation disaster, to have our personnel injured in a firefight, if it comes to that? I repeat, are you in your right mind? Our people will approach and surround the place, take positions a kilometer around it. They'll cut off light and water, we'll shit our pants, and you yourselves will either ask for a corridor or ssurrender." This intervention did not have much effect as the Russians were following their orders no matter what.[25]

The Russian commanders had little understanding of the hazards they would encounter in the nuclear exclusion zone and scant concern about the health of their soldiers. Semenov wanted them to check the radiation level of the sand they were bringing to the station. He asked Frolenkov: "Where is the sand from?" The colonel replied: "They're digging it up around here." Semenov exploded: "And has all this been checked with dosimeters? Are you in your right mind at all? You're bringing in dirt [radioactive particles] from outside, even bringing dirt into the station if you don't know what kind of sand it is." They had to check the radiation levels and continued their work after concluding that the levels were acceptable.[26]

Semenov had no control or influence over what was happening outside the station. There the enlisted men ended up digging trenches in some of the most contaminated areas of the zone, including the huge Red Forest, destroyed by radiation in 1986 and featured in every Chernobyl book and movie. The pine trees growing there had turned ginger brown after being exposed to high levels of radiation, giving a new name to the forest, *Rudyi* in Ukrainian and Ginger or Red in English. Following the disaster of 1986, the Soviets had bulldozed and buried the contaminated pines in long trenches—the trees' mass graves. But the trees that grew in their stead were still deformed and contaminated.

"They chose the Red Forest, because it was near the central road," suggested Liudmyla Kozak later. "They dug it up with their bare hands, filling bags with radioactive sand for their fortifications. They set up a field kitchen in the Red Forest. They slept and ate in the same clothing," recalled Kozak. "We explained: You will die," Kozak told a reporter. "But they replied: We have our orders. No one thought anything out or discussed the purpose. Thoughtless."[27]

Semenov had no explanation for the Russian decision to dig trenches on the edge of the Red Forest, and was shocked by the Russians' disregard for nuclear safety regulations. "I imagined what would happen if they were to strike a particularly important spot. Mainly I followed where they were going and monitored their steps, warning that you may run into something that will leave you an invalid," recalled Semenov. "But they kept trying to stick their noses everywhere, going so far as to say what they simply found interesting." Those were the officers. They showed even less concern for the soldiers.[28]

"The rank-and-file soldiers told me that they had been led to believe it was almost a health spa there. The enlisted personnel did their laundry, hung it all on fences, and it took twenty-four hours to dry," recalled Semenov. But those who had a chance to wash their clothes were the lucky ones. Those who dug trenches in the Red Forest had no chance to do so, since they carried out that task just as the station lost its outside electrical supply, and water could not be delivered to many of the station's facilities. Semenov recalled that "those who dug outside the station were the Russian Guard. For two weeks they went without light and water; the clothes in which they dug were those in which they slept."[29]

For Heiko it was all déjà vu. He remembered scenes from the cleanup after the Chernobyl disaster of 1986, when Soviet generals sent young conscripts to the most dangerous parts of the station with limited protection. Now he recognized the Soviet generals' disregard for human life in the new crop of Russian military commanders. Heiko was trying to appeal to the generals' sense of decency.

He once told General Yakushin: "Oleg, I don't pity you and your colonel. I want the way you came here without firing a shot . . . you would leave without a shot and stay alive." He continued: "You've brought in young people aged 25–30. And if, let's say, because of particular actions of some kind they sustain inner or outer radiation, and you didn't warn them about it and didn't take measures of some kind. Then, I think, you will probably reproach yourself to the end of your life, or not. I don't know."[30]

8

HOSTAGES

On March 9, the commander of the Russian Guard, a member of the Russian Security Council General Viktor Zolotov, declared that his units had assumed control of both the Chernobyl and the Zaporizhia nuclear power plants. The news was reported by Lenta.ru, one of Russia's most popular online resources, owned by Sberbank, Russia's state-owned banking and financial services company. The Lenta.ru reporters added an allegedly exclusive news item from the Russian security services. "A food delivery service for both atomic stations has now been arranged," an unnamed source told the reporters. "The Russian Guard fighters supply food for themselves, the station personnel, and the surrendered security detail of the atomic energy station, since the Ukrainian authorities did not trouble to ensure a supply of food for the station personnel." In fact, it was a mere recycling of the "news" already present in the Russian media.[1]

Leonid Kitrar, a Russian military correspondent and a recipient of the Ministry of Defense medal for his coverage of Russia's war in Syria, was among the first to report from the Chernobyl exclusion zone.

On March 6, the Russian media had released a video in which Kitrar arrived there with a convoy delivering food, allegedly to the operators of the Chernobyl plant and the detained Ukrainian guardsmen. "It's best to make your way to the Chernobyl atomic energy station that way, in a BMP-1 armored car," Kitrar told his viewers from inside the infantry fighting vehicle. "We are driving along the road, and it is not without danger." He then declared that the Ukrainian authorities had abandoned the operators of the plant and the national guardsmen, leaving them without food and supplies. "It falls to the Russian army to deal with those issues," he said. The camera later showed the Russian military unloading packages at the nuclear station. "We brought plenty of food: pasta, buckwheat, stew, condensed milk. . . . The makings of normal food," continued the reporter. The video showed no member of personnel, civilian or military, accepting this "humanitarian assistance." They simply refused to take anything from the occupiers.[2]

Oleksii Shelestii, the shift foreman of the electrical division, recalled that on the day the Russian convoy arrived, Valentyn Heiko called a teleconference of the shift's management and informed his subordinates that the Russians had offered humanitarian assistance. But he maintained that "we do not need humanitarian assistance from the aggressor state; we need nothing." Shelestii recalled that, given their craving for cigarettes, some employees were thinking of accepting "aid" from the Russians, but no one dared to cross Heiko. The Ukrainians refused the Russian offer. "We drove them away with curses, like the Russian naval ship. We hung a chain at the entrance so that they would not return," recalled the Ukrainian engineer Liudmyla Kozak. But the Russians still did what they had come to do. "They filmed a propaganda video showing the purported delivery of humanitarian assistance to their own dining hall, with Rosatom personnel unloading the goods," recalled Semenov.[3]

Russian television featured scenes of Russian military personnel wearing white armbands unloading and bringing food packages into the building. According to Shelestii, they also shot another scene. The propagandists had found uniforms belonging to Novarka, the French company that had built the new confinement structure over reactor no. 4. The French uniform looked quite similar to that worn by the Ukrainian operators but had the word "Novarka" on the back. The Russians dressed their own soldiers in the Novarka uniforms and filmed them accepting the Russian food.[4]

––––––––

Contrary to Russian propaganda statements, there was sufficient basic food available at the Chernobyl plant to supply both the guardsmen detained by the occupiers and the personnel operating the plant for weeks. Those supplies had been delivered to Chernobyl in January to meet the needs of the increased number of guardsmen.

The problem was the lack of kitchen staff. "There were three cooks on staff whose job was to heat and distribute food, not to cook it. But now it became necessary to feed almost three hundred people," recalled Valerii Semenov. The kitchen staff was overwhelmed. "Our cook worked so hard that on the sixth day she simply collapsed," recalled Kozak. "The medics brought her around, gave her an injection, and put her back on her feet. Then they gave her janitresses to assist her, and heavy stockpots were carried by our military personnel." According to Semenov, "It was the stalkers, sitting in the basement until that moment, who saved the situation. They spent 20 days of their imprisonment in the kitchen, learning the culinary art." "We ate every 12 hours," recalled Liudmyla Kozak, "but we had both first and second courses, as well as compote. Even casseroles and pancakes."[5]

The lack of nonfood supplies, including items of personal hygiene, was a major problem from the first days of the occupation. "Many of us had neither toothbrushes nor toothpaste," recalled Shelestii. "That was difficult in the first days. Then we reached out to workers who had remained at home. At first, while the internet was still available, I called [them] and asked what they had in the lockers for personal effects. We broke locks and opened lockers. [We found] notebooks and cigarettes. That was a great help. The use of teapots is allowed at all workplaces, and almost everyone had tea, coffee, and sugar [in his locker]. We also found soap and toothpaste. Of course, we didn't take toothbrushes. We cleaned our teeth with our fingers. Then I remembered that I had toothpaste and a toothbrush at my old workplace in the substation. I asked the engineer, and he passed them to me at lunch."[6]

Most of the personnel being men, shaving emerged as another major problem. Neither shaving cream nor regular soap was available. "There were problems with soap," recalled Shelestii. "Once again, we solved them in collegial fashion. We appealed to other shops. Does anyone have a bit of soap? Yes. Do you need anything in exchange? Tea, if possible. Here you are." Razors were an even greater problem. "There was a small supply—only a few—in the first aid office," recalled Shelestii. He cared little about razors personally, as he already had a beard. Others had no choice but to start growing theirs, and Valerii Semenov was among those who joined the beard club.[7]

The real challenge for smokers was the lack of cigarettes. "We smoked everything," recalled Semenov. "At first, all that people had in their pockets; then everything we found in the lockers." Semenov, who usually smoked two packs daily, knew what he was talking about. The supply from other people's lockers did not last long. Smokers went in search of cigarette butts still lying around. "We have a place where there used to be a smoking room," recalled one of the engineers. "And just imagine, you break off a board and see a huge pile of butts. What luck!!"[8]

———

The appalling conditions in which the Ukrainian personnel lived and worked at the station were the greatest difficulty. "My quarters were 30 square meters in size; two women, two men," recalled Semenov. "That is how we lived for 25 days, working and sleeping in those quarters. On the other side of the wall was a staff of Orcs [Russians]. Their bedroom was next door." Keeping up the morale of the operators-turned-hostages under such circumstances was no easy task. Under normal circumstances, they were supposed to take a twenty-four-hour rest after a twelve-hour shift, but now a new shift began immediately after the previous one. Exhausted and homesick, the staff felt hunted, as they were continuously under surveillance, not free to move around the plant without the permission of the Russian officers and soldiers.[9]

The Russian commanders played a cruel mind game, declaring in public that they were not holding anyone at the station against his will. Colonel Frolenkov stated publicly: "With regard to the station staff and your own military servicemen, we are not keeping anyone here. You may go in all four directions, but if you go beyond 500 meters of the station, I do not guarantee your life." Around the station there were Russian troops fortifying their positions against a possible Ukrainian attack; the roads were full of Russian vehicles heading toward the front or the rear. The road across the Prypiat River to Belarus was also closed: anyone leaving the station and heading that way would be detained by Belarusian border guards and possibly turned over to Russian counter-intelligence. "That is, everyone heard that there was freedom, and not even any of the military were prisoners of war and could go," recalled Semenov. "But the upshot was that going beyond 500 meters might have unforeseeable results."[10]

"People reacted in various ways," recalled Shelestii. "Some succumbed to depression or panic. Others, conversely, tried to pull themselves together." Some considered leaving the station and walking home—more than 30 kilometers (18.5 miles) over forested terrain, across the Dnieper River, and all that in the midst of a war. Valentyn Heiko and the managers tried to do whatever they could to support people morally. Again and again, Heiko told his subordinates: "You came here with me, and we will leave together," suggesting that he would not abandon them.

On March 8, International Women's Day, widely celebrated in post-Soviet countries, including Ukraine, the men at the plant threw an improvised party for their female colleagues. "On March 8 the station's shift supervisor summoned all 17 women," recalled Liudmyla Kozak. "The guys—some soldiers and firefighters—found candies of some kind, coffee, and tea in nightstands. We could hardly keep from crying.

We drank coffee, listened to greetings—our director recorded one of them, and it was transmitted through the public address system. And then they even played a song. We felt like people who are cared for."[11]

The representative of Rosatom, General Muliukin, known to the Ukrainian staff as Nikolai Nikolaevich, tried to use the March 8 holiday to improve his relations with the Ukrainian women—his de facto hostages. Muliukin brought gifts and came to greet the women in Semenov's unit on Women's Day. "They were prepared to do anything in order to gain trust," recalled Semenov. "It was chocolate of some kind for the women on March 8 and almost [proposals] to buy whatever they wanted and bring it back." He then added: "Perhaps some of them even wanted to show that they were also good people and understood everything."[12]

The Russian officers and soldiers whom Semenov called "obsessed" continued their efforts to convince the Ukrainian personnel of the superiority of their way of life, which Russian propaganda called "the Russian World." The problem was that the Ukrainians, most of them university-educated, spoke better Russian than their Russian captors. This was especially true in the case of ethnically non-Russian members of the occupying force. Heiko told one of the Russian generals: "Look, you're explaining things to us here or you want to foist your Russian World on us. And yet you Russians have come here, but you don't know the Russian language." He was referring to an incident involving a Buriat soldier who came to the Ukrainian kitchen staff, asking for a cup of coffee, but the Ukrainian member of the staff who spoke perfect Russian, could not understand what he wanted. "But he doesn't speak Russian," Heiko told the general.[13]

As the Ukrainian personnel suffered from weariness and exhaustion, tensions rose between them and the Russian occupiers. His diplomatic skills aside, Semenov found it difficult to keep his Ukrainian friends and colleagues from openly showing resentment and hostility toward the invaders. It did not go well with the most patriotically minded members of the staff. Semenov's main concern was that his people "would either engage in conflict, in verbal crossfire with the invaders or, even worse, take action of some kind." He tried to talk to people as much as he could, explaining that "we were now collectively, not at all individually, responsible." He also tried to limit contacts between the personnel and the Russians. "It fell to me to take on the maximum burden," recalled Semenov. "To keep [contacts] to a minimum and tell our personnel that if you don't want contacts, then avoid them."[14]

Liudmyla Kozak tried to control her emotions as much as she could, but she was also eager to prove to the Russians and herself that they could not break her. "I had no dealings with those Herods," recalled Kozak. "They warned me twice to wear a white armband on my sleeve. They went around that way, but I did not want to be like them." The Russians told her that if she did not wear the armband, they might simply mistake her for someone else in the dark and shoot her. Kozak then approached a Russian general and asked whether she could wear a medical white cap instead, and he gave permission. She then embroidered her white cap with images of the Ukrainian coat of arms and the national blue-and-yellow flag. She wore the cap for the rest of her stay at the plant. "No one said anything to me," she recalled.[15]

Semenov admitted that he and others used the threat of nuclear irradiation to frighten and manipulate the occupiers. He recalled that those most fearful of radiation were the young conscript soldiers; less susceptible and pretty much immune were Frolenkov's police officers from the Briansk region of Russia, which had been contaminated with fallout from Chernobyl. "Radiophobia is, let's say, not a pleasant thing," he said later. His message to the occupiers was as follows: "We are already emotionally burdened by being confined with us for such a long time in one space, one workplace, two meals per day. But if you go farther and insult someone or force him to do something, then who can guarantee that that person won't turn a valve the wrong way?"[16]

Semenov's colleague Serhii Dediukhin put Russian radiophobia to good use when he heard a Russian soldier saying to him: "I wish we would shoot them all." "Fine," responded Dediukhin. "And in which coffin do you want to be shipped—zinc or lead?" The soldier was puzzled by the reaction and did not know what to say. Dediukhin helped him out: "You'll shoot me and somebody else here. And so you'll end up being shipped not in a zinc coffin but a lead one?" The soldier got the message: back in 1986, Chernobyl firefighters who had sustained enormous doses of radiation were buried in lead coffins to prevent the spread of radiation.[17]

Other staff members found less provocative means of resistance. One staffer on shift, Oleksandr Cherepanov, recalled a scene that he staged with a colleague in front of the Russian guards. "Have you already taken the anti-radiation pills?" he asked. "They're all gone. Now we're screwed," responded Oleksandr's colleague. They made a point of speaking loudly enough for the Russians to hear their voices. There were no such pills, of course, but the operators knew what they were doing and what the risks were, while the Russians did not.[18]

There were also some tragicomic cases of linguistic and cultural misunderstanding. On one occasion, staff members brought clean laundry to the operators. They wore uniforms with the Ukrainian word *Riatuval'nyk* (Rescuer) on the back. The Russians misread it as Russian *Ritual'nik* (Funeral Service Official). According to Kozak, they became hysterical, demanding that the operators explain why they had called a funeral service and whether they had killed anyone.[19]

The Russians in Chernobyl were unable to receive the latest news from the front. "Everything was as it had been in Soviet times," recalled Semenov. "There was a new battle report every day. Their last battle report that I remember was dated March 25. It said that they had damaged or destroyed 1,916 of our tanks." But the Ukrainian government and social media were telling a different story: the Ukrainians were fighting back and driving the Russians away from Kyiv. "We had radio reception points everywhere, so we knew what was going on in Ukraine and throughout the world," Liudmyla Kozak told a journalist. "Radio can't be switched off. The Russians heard everything as well." At first they didn't believe that they were suffering such losses. They began paying attention on the second or third week: "Are they really destroying us so badly? What will I tell the parents of so-and-so, who did not come back from the Kyiv area?"

The Russian officers tried to stop the Ukrainians from listening to the radio, Ukrainian news in particular, but the personnel refused to follow orders. "This is an operational-search communication system, and our rules forbid us to turn it off," said Semenov, recalling the answer given to the Russians. "That is what we cited to them not as an option but as our duty, that it was a necessity for us. They had their guards and kept trying to turn them off, but as we went by, we would always turn them on." Over time, the Russians became used to depressing news from the front and began to lose their self-confidence. Initially, when faced with questions about what they were doing in Chernobyl and against whom they were trying to defend the station, they had spoken about Ukrainian nationalists, but now they responded that they were simply following orders.[20]

Kostiantyn Karnoza, one of the stalkers, saw a Russian soldier, a Buriat by nationality, reading George Orwell's dystopian novel 1984. It described the dangers of totalitarianism and mass surveillance by "Big Brother," the leader of an authoritarian state. "We were surprised and complimented him, saying 'classy book' and the like," recalled Karnoza. "Then other soldiers were seen with that book, but no one read it seriously." The irony of the situation was obvious to Karnoza but apparently lost on the Russians in Chernobyl—soldiers of totalitarianism reading an anti-totalitarian book but not understanding its meaning. Or, if they did understand, they did not let on, probably realizing that Big Brother was watching.[21]

———

In the city of Chornobyl, which had fallen into Russian hands during the first hours of the invasion, the Ukrainian personnel of the Chernobyl nuclear station and the local inhabitants faced the same problems in dealing with the Russian occupiers: attempts to convert them to the "true faith," intimidation, and looting. But the latter two features of the occupation were much more pronounced in the city of Chornobyl than at the station.

Oleksandr Skyrda, who worked in the city of Chornobyl—his outfit ran the local hotel and oversaw other properties—learned of the out-break of war at 4:30 a.m., when the order came to start the evacuation of the facility. By 10:30 a.m. he saw Russian military vehicles entering the city and was shocked by the length of the columns. "My first thoughts were how all of them would find enough space in Kyiv," he recalled. Russian patrols appeared on the streets of Chornobyl on the third day of the occupation, stopping people and checking their identity. The Rus-sians did not expect to encounter anyone in the officially abandoned city. They asked the few remaining employees of the station and settlers in town, "Where did you all come from?"[22]

The Russian soldiers' behavior in the town of Chornobyl was noth-ing like that of their counterparts at the station. In the city they had no fear that their actions might cause a nuclear accident or radioactive retaliation. "They saw me: halt, lie down on the ground, hands along your trouser seams, and that's it," said Skyrda, recalling the moment of his detention by a patrol. "They put a machine gun to my spine; say who you are; they checked my documents and phone to see what was not right." "No one knew what was in their heads," recalled Skyrda, who presented the soldiers with a pass allowing him to be in the exclusion zone. "They guffawed and had a look," he added. "The most frighten-ing thing was walking away; lying on the ground was nothing, but as you walked away, you didn't know [whether they would shoot at you or not]." During the occupation, Skyrda was stopped and checked that way three times.

What was happening reminded Skyrda of World War II. He recalled the stories of his grandparents, who had survived the Nazi occupation of Ukraine. "I had found it interesting [to listen to them] in childhood but did not understand what occupation meant," he said later. Now he knew what it was. "It is weightlessness of life," Skyrda explained to a journalist after the liberation. "Everything is broken: everyday life, routine . . . many things became unimportant—time, day, and month were simply unnecessary; clocks and telephones, because they didn't work; in general, everything seemed to fall away. Sounds, hearing, and health were important, because you understood that if you fell ill, you would perish on the spot. If you can't detect a sound, it means that you won't hear something rustling somewhere, or you won't get away in time. That was important."[23]

The Russians moved along the streets in large groups of fifteen to twenty men, seemingly afraid of Ukrainian partisans, who they believed might emerge from the forests around Chernihiv—traditional partisan refuges. Their main task was to identify those who stayed in Chornobyl. The Russians encouraged them to leave the town and move to Belarus, but all those who stayed had to wear white armbands. Some were reminded of the armbands with the Star of David that the Nazis had forced Jews to wear in the ghettos—images familiar to all Ukrainians who had watched films about World War II. Now white armbands had returned to Chornobyl, a former Jewish shtetl and a Holocaust site. Skyrda recalled that the remaining citizens of Chornobyl used COVID masks in their possession to make the white armbands that the Russians demanded they wear.[24]

The occupiers were especially concerned about large gatherings of people. They rushed to the local Orthodox church, ready to fire, when elderly citizens lined up to receive humanitarian assistance. "They drove up and surrounded us; many, many of them, too many to count," recalled Skyrda. "Two 'Tiger' infantry vehicles, one 'Ural' truck; they leaped out and pointed their machine guns: 'Who are you? Stand still and don't move.'" Skyrda explained to the soldiers that the people had gathered at the church to receive some food. He pleaded that the elderly people be allowed to move around: "The little old ladies have their hands full; their bags are heavy and their legs sickly." The Russians wanted to know who had sanctioned the gathering. Skyrda responded with a question of his own: "Who should sanction it for us; whom should we ask?" There was no answer. The Russians eventually left.[25]

Aside from patrols and detentions, the greatest issue for the citizens of Chornobyl during the occupation was looting. If Heiko and Semenov at the power plant kept complaining about looting to the Russian generals, who moderated the looting spree of the rank-and-file soldiers, there was no one to stop the looting in Chornobyl, which took on truly industrial proportions. "They drove around here in Kamaz trucks and loaded them up," recalled Skyrda. "Groups of 17 to 20 [men] went around from morning to late evening. They did the rounds of all apartments and private homes. Everything. They broke into everything. They robbed. They carried everything out," said Liudmyla Besedina, echoing Skyrda. She was one of the old Chornobyl ladies who gave a name to a documentary, *The Babushkas of Chernobyl*, about squatters in the Chernobyl exclusion zone. Unlike Skyrda, an employee of the station, Besedina lived in Chornobyl illegally with her husband. The city was part of the 30-kilometer exclusion zone and considered too dangerous for continuous habitation.[26]

Before the Russian invasion, Besedina and her fellow squatters— she believed there were more than 200 such individuals in town—had been in a state of undeclared war with the local police, whose officers tried to force her and other "illegals" out of the city. Besedina was upset that with the start of the all-out war neither she nor the other squatters had been informed about the invasion. She learned about it from her sister, who worked at the Chernobyl plant and was therefore informed. Besedina was also aggrieved that the police officers had been among the first to be evacuated: allegedly they had dropped everything and left town ahead of the buses carrying civilians. But neither she nor the other grandmas and grandpas of Chornobyl were prepared to accept the Russian occupation.

"They came and greeted us," recalled Besedina. "They asked our opinion of the 'Russian World.' We said that we had no opinion about it." She put her own question to the occupiers: "And how would you react, guys, if we came to you with guns?" The Russians did not reply. But they had an explanation that they used on the citizens of Chornobyl: "You should have chosen a president [meaning Volodymyr Zelensky] correctly." Some Russians accused Zelensky of being a Nazi.

Besedina responded: "Well, we choose a president for ourselves, not for you. Why did you have to intrude here?" The only answer forthcoming was: "We have to. Because of your president." Arguments that because of Zelensky's Jewish ancestry he could hardly be a Nazi had no effect. The occupiers praised Putin and assured the citizens of Chornobyl that their life would not be disturbed under Russia.[27]

Besedina was terrified but ultimately glad that she and her husband had never left their house. Otherwise, it would have been robbed as well. It came as a shock to Besedina that what she considered anything but a comfortable life in abandoned Chornobyl was perceived as almost luxurious by the Russian soldiers, recruited from economically depressed areas of Russia. "They were amazed. They were amazed at everything," recalled Besedina. She overheard Russian soldiers conversing among themselves: "Oh, they even have asphalt. Oh, they even have water." They told her: "We don't even have homes like the brick shed where you keep your cow." Summarizing her impressions, Besedina said: "They came here and thought they'd found themselves in paradise. They don't have anything like it. . . . They were in shock and could not understand that people could live like this."

Besedina herself recalled her life before the occupation as paradise lost. "Even before the accident, as they say, we had a normal life," Besedina told a reporter and right away corrected herself: "before the war." Once again, her life was divided into "before" and "after." If earlier it had been before and after 1986, now it was before and after 2022. Born in Chornobyl, she had grown up, worked there, and was now retired in her hometown. In spite of the dangers of the occupation, her fellow citizens had always behaved humanely. As an example, she praised Viktor Yatsuk, the director of the Chernobyl power plant's food facility, who distributed food to the locals free of charge. Others were very grateful to the local doctor, Volodymyr Udovychenko, who kept visiting bedridden patients, as did his colleagues. The occupation had failed to kill such manifestations of human solidarity: on the contrary, people cooperated to help one another survive the ordeal.[28]

Among those who distributed clean water to the elderly citizens of

Chornobyl was the sixty-three-year-old former employee of the Chernobyl plant Leonid Struk. He was stopped more than once by Russian patrols who wanted to rob him of his vehicle. "Let us use it for a couple of days," one of the soldiers asked him. He refused, citing the need to deliver water. They backed down. There were two such attempts, but Struk kept his vehicle. He hid all the food he had been keeping at home and removed all valuable items to protect them from "confiscation" by marauding squads. As Struk described one of the numerous Russian looting parties he saw in the city: "The first of them carried a sledgehammer with the word 'crumb' on the handle. Beside him was a man with a crowbar for breaking down doors. Bringing up the rear were four men with sacks stretching from their chins to their knees." He commented later: "Could you say that I considered the military men an army? No. I saw criminals, marauders, alcoholics, paupers. I saw indigent people."[29]

Struk was known in town as a Ukrainian patriot and a brave soul. A former commander of a Ukrainian National Guard unit, Oleksandr Strenatkin, knew that he could count on Struk when he called him from Ukrainian-held territory and asked him to break into his office in Chornobyl to get the notebook and classified documents remaining there. Struk carried out the request and took the notebook and papers for safekeeping. He also regularly called a friend in Slavutych to inform him about Russian troop movements in Chornobyl. Despite the objections of some neighbors, Struk hid two Ukrainian prisoners of war who had been captured by the Russians near Kyiv and then released in the wilderness of the exclusion zone. The neighbors argued that the Russians would punish everyone if they found the men, one of whom was a member of the local council in the Ivankiv region, north of Kyiv, but Struk would not budge.[30]

One of the greatest problems for Struk and other Ukrainian patriots in Chornobyl was the lack of information from the "big land," the unoccupied part of Ukraine. Cell phones had to be hidden, and people no longer had radio sets. Moreover, the Belarusians jammed signals from Kyiv, letting only those from Moscow go through. Struk found a radio set in a neighbor's house and listened to the news from Kyiv with the former captives whom he had saved from hunger and possible death in the wilderness. "We were in seventh heaven, boys. For joy. That we had information. This hunger for information is probably worse than the hunger of someone who wants to eat, you understand."

The radio brought good news: the Ukrainian armed forces were fighting back, inflicting major casualties on Russian forces near the Kyiv suburbs of Irpin and Bucha. Struk had already heard news of Russian casualties at Bucha but was not sure whether to believe it. "You hear rumors; well, rumors are not what you need. You want to know all the true information," recalled Struk. Now he had confirmation: Kyiv was standing firm. "When you hear such information, you want to dance for joy," Struk told a reporter after the liberation.[31]

Among Struk's concerns was the situation at the Chernobyl power plant. One day he got into his car and, taking back roads, reached the plant to the shock and surprise of the Russians who believed that they controlled all the approaches to it. He asked the Russian commander whether he could take anyone from the station back to Chornobyl. "No problem. You can even take them all," came the answer. The commander stuck to the line that the occupiers were not holding anyone at the station against their will.

Struk was delighted. His only concern was that no more than six people would fit into his car. But the officer soon returned, saying that no one was willing to leave: the foreman had allegedly made an announcement, but there were no takers. Struk had worked at the station long enough to know that the announcement could have been made only through the public address system, and he had heard nothing. The Russians were simply lying. The men and women whom Struk had met at the station were hostages. So was he. Struk returned to Chornobyl empty-handed.[32]

9

SHADOW OF FUKUSHIMA

Oleksii Shelestii, the head of the electrical division shift, who had grown a substantial beard by that time, was sitting in his windowless concrete office late in the afternoon of March 9, monitoring the functioning of his electrical systems at the site and waiting for lunchtime. According to his instructions, Shelestii could not leave his post unless someone else took his place. A constant supply of electricity was a safety issue for the plant, which had ceased to produce electricity itself in 2000 and depended on outside power lines for its operation and the safety of its facilities. The engineer with whom Shelestii shared his office was away, and Shelestii was waiting for a colleague to replace him temporarily so that he could have lunch, when suddenly the electricity went off. "Darkness just like that—well, not complete darkness, of course; our emergency lights are always on," he recalled later.[1]

Shelestii would remember the time and date of the power loss for days and weeks to come: 11:22 a.m. on March 9, 2022. The darkness came as a shock, but the loss of electricity was not unexpected. Unlike the electricity going off in the control room of reactor no. 4 on the night of April 24, 1986, when the operators could not understand what had happened, Shelestii knew exactly what had gone wrong: this time it was military activity that had severed the supply line linking the station with the Ukrainian grid. Electrical lines had started to go out of service since the first day of the invasion. By March 6, the Chernobyl station had lost the electricity supplied by the second-last of its lines, called the Lisna (Forest) Line. The only one functioning was the Kyiv Line. If anything happened to it, Shelestii warned his colleagues, the station would lose all its electricity.

"There was a connection with Kyiv, and dispatchers told me that brigades would be dispatched . . . and would try to repair the lines," Shelestii recalled later. He knew how problematic the task was. He could not use his cell phone in the office because of its thick concrete walls, but during lunch breaks he checked the internet and knew that north of Kyiv, the source of electricity to the plant, open warfare was going on. "I could just imagine what they would be repairing if Hostomel, Vyshhorod, Bucha—that very direction—what could be repaired if there was blasting and shooting; there was full-scale warfare going on there. So of course we realized that this was highly, highly unlikely."[2]

After losing the Forest Line, Shelestii got in touch with Heiko: "The last line remains; if anything suddenly happens, then we 'drop to the floor,' that is, a complete loss of power takes place." Heiko ordered the entire management to get ready for a complete loss of electricity: that "all [components] be charged and that flashlights, diagrams, instructions, and plans for switching [to alternate sources of energy] in case of accident be prepared. So that everything will be ready to hand," recalled Shelestii. "Then the NSS [Heiko] ordered everyone not to go anywhere without a flashlight." Most of the rooms in the concrete industrial buildings had no windows, and that pertained especially to the hallways, so losing electricity even during the day meant that people might get lost and disoriented, not just unable to perform their functions.[3]

On March 9, all the plant facilities had lost electricity in a split second. The arch, the 1.5-billion-euro structure completed in 2019 by an international consortium led by the French company Novarka, was one of those facilities. Its equipment monitored processes taking place within the reactor's basement structures, which still contained elements of nuclear fuel and irradiated debris that required a constant supply of electricity.

So did the two spent nuclear fuel facilities, the "wet" Spent Nuclear Fuel Storage Facility 1 (ISF-1) and the "dry" Spent Nuclear Fuel Storage Facility 2 (ISF-2). ISF-1 had been built to store spent fuel from the Chernobyl reactors back in 1986, and ISF-2 had been completed and fully licensed in May 2021, a few months before the start of the war. Then there was the Centralized Spent Fuel Storage Facility (CSFSF), built to store spent fuel from the rest of the Ukrainian nuclear power stations. It had been completed only recently and had gone into cold testing a few weeks before the start of the war. The CSFSF had no radioactive materials in it when the Russians occupied the site.[4]

With electricity cut off, each of the plant's key facilities presented its own set of radiation safety issues. After the Russian takeover of the station, Heiko had ordered a stop to operations at ISF-2, but the complex still needed electricity to keep its equipment functioning. The situation was much worse with ISF-1. "We needed to support ISF-1, the security system of the Arch. According to all our instructions, in the event of complete power loss, voltage should be supplied on one of the lines within 30 minutes," recalled Shelestii a few weeks later. Ongoing operations at the arch could not be halted without risking radioactive contamination of the building and its environment. Nor could the circulation of water in the cooling pools be stopped without risking overheating of the assemblies and, potentially, another accident.[5]

Every Chernobyl-type RBMK reactor used more than 1,600 fuel assemblies consisting of fuel elements that contained uranium pellets to produce electricity. In the course of their lifetime, the three undamaged reactors produced more than 21,000 "spent" fuel assemblies. The uranium pellets in the assemblies had burned up by the time they were removed from the reactors, but the assemblies themselves remained highly radioactive and overheated. To render them harmless, they were first placed in the spent-fuel pools and then moved to ISF-1 for a longer period of cooling and storage.

ISF-1 had three main pools and one reserve pool for that purpose. The water in those pools had to be circulated, which required electrically powered pumps. If the pumps did not work, the water in the pools might evaporate, the fuel assemblies could become overheated and rupture, and that might cause a new nuclear accident at the Chernobyl plant. "ISF-1 cannot stop working," Shelestii explained later, "because it functions to sustain particular parameters in the spent-fuel pools, and that means water circulation, a mass of sensors, all kinds of systems . . . in our ISF 90 percent of the equipment is considered important for maintaining the security system."

Under optimal circumstances, the ISF-1 security system was considered a midterm solution of the spent-fuel problem. A Florida-based American company, Holtec International, offered a solution that was supposed to last up to 100 years—the world's newest and largest dry facility, ISF-2. Once the new facility was completed, the process of moving spent fuel from ISF-1 to ISF-2 could begin. The fuel had to be repackaged, and stored there for the next ten years. ISF-2 consisted of two units. In the first unit, the spent-fuel assemblies would be divided into two parts, placed in fuel tubes, and stored in double-wall-shielded steel canisters, with 196 fuel assembly halves fitting into one canister. The canisters would then be moved to the second unit of ISF-2 and placed into concrete modules for storage, where they could stay for up to a century. Should the supply of electricity be interrupted, the process of cutting and repackaging the spent-fuel assemblies might be stopped before completion, causing all sorts of radiation safety issues.[6]

It was the diesel generators, designed to replace lost electricity supply within minutes after an accident, that saved the situation. ISF-2 had two brand-new diesel generators of its own, but the rest of the complex had to rely on two "Made in Yugoslavia" electrical generators dating from the 1970s. No one knew how long they would last. At 11:35 a.m., thirteen minutes after the loss of electricity, Shelestii received an electrician's report that one of the generators had been turned on successfully and was beginning to produce electricity. "I restored lighting and signaling here at the central control panel, we partly restored the third block and then began supplying power to the production site," recalled Shelestii in one of his interviews.[7]

Oleksandr Babii, an engineer in the division for the treatment of radioactive waste, recalled that once power came back on, he and his colleagues rushed to turn off a monitor worth half a million euros and switch it to secure mode. But restoring the supply of electricity was a gradual process. "There were sites," recalled Shelestii, "that had been without lighting for eight to ten hours. First and foremost, we tried to restore service to places where people were working, as it was not May weather outside, and people were using fan heaters and electric boilers." According to Semenov, the transition of the whole station to generator-supplied electricity took fourteen hours.[8]

However useful they turned out to be, the generators were anything but a permanent solution to the Chernobyl station's problems. "Diesel generators are intended for short-term supply of electricity until normal supply is restored to the station," commented Heiko later. But no one knew when that would take place. In Slavutych, the acting director of the station, Valerii Seida, sounded the alarm, telling the BBC that "unless the supply of electricity is restored within 48 hours, we will completely lose all systems and equipment in our station." His main concern was ISF-1, the wet spent-fuel storage facility, because of possible radioactive contamination. "Perhaps not to the same extent as the first time," said Seida, referring to the 1986 catastrophe, "but all the same, [it threatens] the escape of radioactivity beyond the barriers established by the project."[9]

———

The worrisome developments at Chernobyl reminded many people not only about the events of 1986 but also of 2011. That was the year of the

Fukushima accident, in which a loss of electricity at a nuclear plant in Japan, resulting from a tsunami, caused multiple meltdowns of reactors and a catastrophe of global proportions.

Could something similar happen now at Chernobyl? Most of the world's leading experts were worried but believed that the situation at Chernobyl was different. Tony Roulstone of the Department of Engineering at Cambridge University thought that the loss of power might indeed lead to "overheating" of the spent-fuel assemblies, but the situation was "probably not as worrying as Fukushima because the Chernobyl reactors have already been shut down for a long time."[10]

In Vienna, Rafael Grossi tried to sound a positive note. In the press release update on the situation at Chernobyl, issued on the day the station lost its power supply, he stated that "the IAEA agreed with the Ukrainian regulator that its disconnection from the grid would not have a critical impact on essential safety functions at the site, where various radioactive waste management facilities are located. Specifically, regarding the site's spent fuel storage facility, the volume of cooling water in the pool is sufficient to maintain effective heat removal from the spent fuel without a supply of electricity. The site also has reserve emergency power supplies with diesel generators and batteries."[11]

Grossi's statement represented pretty much the consensus in the expert community with regard to the crisis at Chernobyl: a reason for concern—yes; possibility of damage to the equipment—yes; radiation leaks—unlikely but possible; but ultimately, should an accident happen, it would be local, not regional or global. That logic was completely unacceptable to Balthasar Lindauer, the director of the Nuclear Safety Department of the European Bank for Reconstruction and Development (EBRD), who tweeted a response on March 9 to the reassuring statements of the IAEA: "I am extremely astonished by self-declared experts to declare the #Chernobyl site safe from a comfortable distance. It is true that spent fuel stored in wet storage at the site is old and has decayed significantly. [But] loss of power to any nuclear facility is a serious risk."[12]

That was also the attitude of people at the Chernobyl site. "If we were to lose electricity, there might be a catastrophe," Chernobyl opera-tor Oleksandr Loboda later told the BBC. "A release of radioactive mate-rials might take place, and you can imagine its scale. I was not even so concerned for my life; I was afraid of what could happen if I were unable to manage the equipment. I feared that it might become a tragedy for mankind as a whole." The Ukrainians were growing desperate. What sounded to outsiders like a remote possibility of a local accident struck them as a clear and present danger to themselves and their loved ones.[13]

Grossi's expressions of concern and the reassurances offered by experts made little impression in Ukraine. When the Ukrainian nuclear inspectorate noted on its official Facebook page on March 11 that the IAEA was inspecting the Khmelnytskyi nuclear power plant in western Ukraine for the possible presence of undeclared nuclear materials—a routine inspection under the terms of the agreement on nonproliferation of nuclear weapons—some of the readers did not conceal their disappointment and irritation with the conduct of the Vienna-based agency.

"They found time for an inspection. Let them start by helping the Chernobyl nuclear power plant and the Zaporizhia nuclear power plant, and if they cannot manage that, then get rid of them," commented the nuclear engineer Varvara Tkachuk. "And couldn't the IAEA start by inspecting Chernobyl? One more unnecessary organization making inspections that nobody needs," commented another reader, Sviato-slav Plakhotiuk. "So? They're checking whether we might have nuclear weapons? Seriously?" wrote another engineer, Andrii Protokovylo. "What's next, biolaboratories with pathogens and migratory birds?" The latter reference was to Russian false claims about the existence of NATO laboratories in Ukraine and the use of birds to spread disease in the Russian Federation.[14]

On March 10, Rafael Grossi stated in his daily update on the sit-uation that "to ensure continued power, these lines [Kyiv and Lisna] would either need to be repaired or the generators holding fuel for two days would require additional diesel deliveries." The reference to diesel deliveries pertained to a Ukrainian request that had finally made its way into an IAEA press release. But how were the lines to be repaired and new supplies of diesel fuel to be arranged without cooperation with the occupiers? Grossi, now desperate, flew to Antalya, Turkey, where negotiations were being held between the Russian and Ukrainian governments. There he appealed for the safety of nuclear sites, with no apparent result.[15]

———

The first Russian reaction to the crisis was to accuse the Ukrainians of destroying the power lines in order to provoke a nuclear accident. The Russians claimed to have been trying to prevent such an accident by capturing the Chernobyl site on the first day of the war. A few hours after the attack on the Kyiv Line, Aleksandr Bastrykin, the head of the Russian Investigative Committee, a former KGB officer and a classmate of Putin's at Leningrad University Law School, ordered an investigation of the "criminal activity of Ukrainian military servicemen" that had allegedly led to the Chernobyl plant's loss of power.

On the same day, General Nikolai Pankov, Russia's deputy minister of defense, a former KGB officer whose responsibilities in the Russian army were human resources, sports, and youth, claimed that the power line had been deliberately destroyed by the Ukrainians. Pankov stated that "Russian specialists have taken operational measures to go over to reserve diesel-generator sources of supply." He deliberately confused the Ukrainian personnel with the Russian personnel. There simply were no "Russian specialists" at the plant. Also untrue was Pankov's statement that "in every way, the Ukrainian side is avoiding the organization of any efforts at repair and restoration."[16]

In fact, the Ukrainian foreign minister, Dmytro Kuleba, had called on the international community to demand that Russia halt military operations in the area and allow Ukrainian crews to repair the lines. The director of the plant, Valerii Seida, was seeking a way to restore the supply of electricity to the station. Ukrenerho, the Ukrainian state-owned grid operator, asserted that "combat operations in the region make it impossible to carry out repairs in order to restore the power supply." Time was running short. Kotin, the director of Enerhoatom, said that the situation might become critical if the station remained without electricity from the grid for the next seven days.[17]

Despite the false statements from Moscow, the Russian commanders on the ground seemed to be cooperative. General Mikhail Mizintsev, who would soon become known as the "butcher of Mariupol" for his savagery in that Ukrainian city, made a statement suggesting that the Russian army would help the Ukrainians restore the power lines. "Fully understanding the scope of the humanitarian catastrophe in blockaded population centers, we agreed even to the auxiliary routes proposed by the Ukrainian side," stated Mizintsev. He specifically mentioned a "corridor . . . from the city of Korosten in Zhytomyr oblast to the vicinity of the Chernobyl atomic electricity station for the passage of a repair brigade to the electricity supply line damaged by the nationalists."[18]

Mizintsev delivered on his promise. On the next day, the Ukrainian authorities stated that "attempts to restore the external power supply to the site are in progress." The Ukrainian electrical engineers were taking an enormous risk by crossing the Russian lines and working behind them. On one occasion a crew was detained by the Russian military, who roughed them up. Those who returned from that mission refused to go back, but volunteers were eventually found. Soon after 7:00 p.m. on March 13, the power line to the Chernobyl station was restored. The Ukrainian energy minister, Herman Halushchenko, was jubilant. He issued a statement calling the crew members heroes: "Today, thanks to the incredible efforts of the professionals of the Ukrenerho National Electricity Company, our nuclear scientists and electricians, we succeeded in restoring power to the Chernobyl atomic energy station, which was seized by Russian occupiers. Our Ukrainian energy specialists, risking their health and lives, managed to avert the risk of a possible nuclear catastrophe that threatened Europe as a whole."[19]

But Halushchenko's rejoicing was premature. As soon as electricity began to flow along the restored power line, it was damaged once again. "Marathon [a Ukrainian television news program] had just said at 8:30 a.m. that the Chernobyl atomic energy station had been linked to the Ukrainian energy system," recalled Valerii Semenov. "Fifteen minutes later, bang, the link was gone." The officials of the Ukrainian electricity company blamed the Russian occupiers. "Once again, the repair brigade of the Ukrenerho National Electricity Company is compelled to venture into occupied territory near the Chernobyl atomic energy station to search for new damage and liquidate it," read the company's statement. The fact that the line had been damaged both times near Chernobyl, deep in Russian-held territory, suggested Russian foul play.[20]

The Russians had a different plan from the outset: to connect the Chernobyl NPP to the Belarusian grid. Cutting off the power supply to the station on March 13 was probably the final move. On March 9, the day the Chernobyl plant lost its electricity, the Russian deputy minister of energy, Pavel Sorokin, hastened to declare that "Belarus efficiently handled the problem of restoring the energy supply by means of a permanent link with the Belarusian energy system." On the following day, another deputy minister of energy, Yevgenii Grabchak, announced that "The Mazyr-Chernobyl Atomic Energy Station electrical supply line has begun transmission. Thanks to the activity of the personnel operating the Chernobyl atomic energy station, it has become possible to transmit current to the station's electrical equipment."[21]

On March 10, the same day Grabchak made his announcement, the Belarusian strongman Aliaksandr Lukashenka stated publicly that he had discussed the situation at the Chernobyl power station with Putin. On the following day, March 11, during a visit to Moscow, Lukashenka declared: "Now we see what is going on in Chernobyl. You asked me to extend the electrical line there. But that's not what they [the Ukrainians] want, you see. But whatever may have been going on there, as they kept resisting, we extended the supply of electricity by force, as I promised, to the Chernobyl station." Putin thanked Lukashenka.[22]

On March 13, when all preparations for the switch to the Belarusian grid had been made, the recently restored Ukrainian line was conveniently damaged once again. The Russian government was either trying to exploit the existing crisis or, more probably, create one by destroying the Ukrainian power line to facilitate its next step in taking over the Chernobyl plant: cutting it off from the Ukrainian grid and connecting it to the one controlled by Moscow.

———

At Chernobyl, Heiko and his shift knew nothing about the high-level power games involving the station and were doing their best to prevent another accident.

When the crisis began, Heiko called on Semenov and asked him to bring General Aleksei Rtishchev and the Russian military commanders to his office. They showed up as requested. According to Semenov, Heiko addressed the Russians more or less as follows: "Here you are, looking so bright and handsome. You say that you can ensure the safety of the site. You say that everything is under your control. So come up with fuel. Or help us repair the power line. We have enough fuel for 14 hours." The response was not only prompt but also surprisingly positive. It pertained to the supply of diesel fuel. "No problem," said Rtishchev. "Thank God, we have diesel. We'll provide it. We'll fill you up," responded the general. This was followed by regular daily deliveries of up to 27 tons or four tank trucks of diesel fuel.[23]

Fuel was delivered for the next few days, and the staff felt good about making the Russian army spend fuel badly needed for tanks on the battlefield near Kyiv in Chernobyl instead. But on March 13, the fourth day of the crisis, the Russians cut off deliveries. "The general came to the office of the shift supervisor and stated that the diesel generators were guzzling as much diesel as half the front near Kyiv," said Semenov later, recalling what he had heard from Heiko. Rtishchev "presented an ultimatum giving us exactly twenty-four hours for consideration: the fuel already in the tanks would suffice for that period of consideration, and then there would be no more fuel. There was only one solution for us—to connect with the Belarusian power line."[24]

Heiko hesitated. He did not know what to do: accepting the Russian condition meant helping the enemy "steal" the station; rejecting it meant contributing to a new nuclear accident at Chernobyl. Semenov called the situation a "stalemate." What he actually had in mind was a "no-win" situation. He described Heiko's choices as "either to put the reactors in danger of a radiation accident when the fuel ran out or to connect after all." Semenov suggested to Heiko that they should accept the ultimatum, but on one condition: the Russians would have to connect not only the Chernobyl site to the Belarusian grid but also the city of Slavutych, which received its electricity from Chernobyl but had been cut off since the damage done to the Kyiv line on March 9.[25]

Semenov later recalled that the decision was a difficult one. The Ukrainian electrical crews were still not giving up hope of restoring the power lines, and switching to the Belarusian grid meant undermining the efforts of their own colleagues and letting their country down. "Ukrenerho tried every possible and impossible means," recalled Shelestii. "Green corridors for the repairmen were arrived at literally on the go." But he also did not think that the Ukrainian efforts would succeed. "The situation with the Ukrainian lines was quite clear," he recalled. "Warfare was going on: did it make sense to repair the lines?" There was also great concern that the generators, especially the Yugoslav ones, would not last much longer. "Station management called me every morning: What's going on? How are the generators?" recalled Shelestii.[26]

Finally, there was ongoing worry about the city of Slavutych, which had now been cut off from electricity for five cold March days. "We had been fueled by the diesels and seemed to be 'just fine' at the plant, in the main buildings," explained Shelestii to a reporter. "Then came awareness that Slavutych had been left without light." Telephone lines between the power plant and the city were working. So the operators at Chernobyl knew very well what was going on at home. Things were not good.[27]

Viacheslav Yakushev, the lead radiological safety engineer and a member of Heiko's crew, commented subsequently: "Because of the power outage, people began to grill food on campfires. My child is at least older, but what about little children? And in the twenty-first century it's simply abnormal to grill food on campfires." A city that relied on electricity, much of it produced by nuclear power in Ukraine, now reverted technologically not just to coal but to wood. There was only one saving grace: in a section of the city built by construction crews from Armenia after the Chernobyl disaster, every apartment block had its own public grill. Those grills helped to keep the Ukrainian city fed, if not warm: the temperature inside apartments fell to 5 degrees Celsius (41 degrees Fahrenheit.)[28]

Slavutych was wholly dependent on the Chernobyl plant for its power supply. With the Russians preventing the Ukrainians from supplying electricity to Chernobyl, the only hope for Slavutych became connecting the plant and through it the city to the Belarusian grid— Semenov decided that there was no choice but to accept the Russian ultimatum. "I came to Heiko in the morning," recalled Semenov, "and said: Valentyn Oleksandrovych, we have a stalemate; there's nothing we can do, so we'll have to connect. I suggest that we present them with a counter-ultimatum: we'll connect on one condition, that we add the town of Slavutych, knowing what is going on with our families." Heiko agreed. They called the Chernobyl plant headquarters in Slavutych, and the bosses there agreed.

The next step was to sell their response to the Russians. "We summoned the general," recalled Semenov, "and said that the plant administration had been informed, there was a stalemate, and now we had no choice." But the price of their agreement was the connection of Slavutych to the Belarusian grid. To their surprise, the Russians agreed on the spot. "Slavutych, no problem," responded Rtishchev. They were exhilarated. "Just like that," remembered Semenov. He and Heiko were convinced that the Russian "ultimatum" was the result of their spending too much Russian diesel at the plant. What they did not know was that Rtishchev's task was to make the connection as soon as the Belarusians were ready. He could not have cared less about including Slavutych in a package deal.[29]

Soon afterward, Belarusian officials started to bombard Shelestii with telephone calls, asking him to coordinate the connection process with officials at the Chernobyl nuclear plant and the Ukrainian grid. Since Shelestii was in Russian-occupied territory, he could hardly help them with that task. "I said that I could not reach the dispatchers of the Chernobyl plant because they were not in Chornobyl," said Shelestii, recalling one of his conversations with the Belarusian officials. "Why?" came the question. "Because, you motherfuckers, there are Russian troops in Chornobyl!" exploded Shelestii. He recommended that they get in touch with the Ukrainian grid dispatchers in Kyiv. His interlocutor was not pleased. "He stumbled and stumbled somehow and then sighed, 'Well, we can't,'" said Shelestii, recalling the reaction at the other end of the line.[30]

The switch to the Belarusian line took place on March 14. "At about 2:00 p.m., we connected the plant," recalled Shelestii. Slavutych was supposed to be next. "I asked the boss, who responded: wait, there are no negotiations yet, maybe we won't connect even today. We were upset. In the city, they were saying: little depends on us; we have to obtain permission from the energy system." It was a difficult decision not only for Heiko at the station but also for those in Kyiv. It was one thing to agree, after numerous attempts, to provide electricity to the nuclear plant by way of the Belarusian grid: at stake was the safety of the entire country and region. Agreeing to have the occupiers connect a Ukrainian city to a grid controlled by their forces was quite another.[31]

Shelestii was growing impatient. "That's not what we agreed," he told his boss at the station headquarters in Slavutych. "I said at the outset that we were connecting Mazyr for you for the sole purpose of providing electrical energy not only for ourselves but also for Slavutych." He reverted to the threat of turning off the entire line. "With a simple movement of my hand—I have two control keys—I will immediately either give the command to the engineer to turn off the Mazyr connection or do it myself, that's all." The officials in Slavutych tried to calm him down: "Oleksii, don't get mad. We'll work everything out right away; let's not be hasty." Shelestii agreed to wait.[32]

At about 5:30 p.m. he was alone in his office answering a telephone call when he received another on a different line. He lifted the receiver and placed it on the desk while he finished his current conversation. When he finally lifted the second receiver, he heard someone shouting: "Who's there, who's there? Is someone being butchered there?" Shelestii recalled his reaction to the strange sounds coming from the receiver. Finally he put it to his ear and heard a male voice saying, "Lekha, Lekha [Shelestii's nickname], they've given permission for Slavutych." There was jubilation at both ends of the line. "It was the brightest moment," said Shelestii later. "We successfully received current on the line, and I personally transmitted it to Slavutych," he recalled, not without a note of pride. "By eight or nine, there was light throughout the city."[33]

Kyiv went along with the decision made by Heiko and his staff—to connect to the Belarusian grid in order to save the plant from an accident and the city from freezing. Given the difficulty of acceding to the Russian ultimatum, neither the Ukrainian authorities nor the Ukrainian media reported that Ukraine would now be receiving electricity from Belarus, an enemy country. The Ukrainian nuclear inspectorate announced on its Facebook page: "According to information received from the Chernobyl NPP management, the power supply of all facilities located on the Chernobyl NPP site was restored on 14 March 2022, and at 17:45 the operation of all diesel generators providing emergency power to those facilities was stopped. At 18:14 the ChNPP-Slavutych high-voltage line was connected." The IAEA statement issued by Grossi repeated that information without mentioning Russia or Belarus.[34]

10

VOLUNTEERS

On March 15, 2022, the day after the electricity supply crisis at Chernobyl was finally resolved, the *Wall Street Journal* published a long article, "Inside Chernobyl, 200 Exhausted Staff Toil Round the Clock at Russian Gunpoint." The subtitle gave more details on the conditions with which the Ukrainian personnel had to cope. It read: "Trapped since their shift 3 weeks ago, the Ukrainians keeping the abandoned nuclear plant safe are ill-fed, stressed and desperate for relief." Reporters Joe Parkinson and Drew Hinshaw spoke with the plant administrators and relatives of the entrapped shift workers, who made it clear that the plant personnel were growing ever more desperate.[1]

According to the article, "Every morning at 9, the national anthem, 'Ukraine Has Not Yet Perished,' blares through the loudspeaker. The Ukrainian workers stand, palms pressed to chests, then return to work." But the personnel were emotionally exhausted. "That exhaustion is mutating into rebellion, with staff members arguing with their captors over the nature of Russia's war and staging acts of defiance," wrote the reporters. Indeed, on the night of March 11, the start of the sixteenth day of a shift scheduled for twelve hours, two staff members got involved in a standoff with the Russian military. According to the article, Valentyn Heiko, who spoke daily with his superiors at the Slavutych headquarters, told them that "the psychological situation is deteriorating."[2]

Heiko knew what he was talking about. He had convinced the Russians to give every staff member a daily medical check in which blood pressure was measured and psychological condition evaluated. "And we saw the statistics," recalled Valerii Semenov, "which showed that their emotional and physical condition was deteriorating with every passing day." Oleksandr Kalishuk, an engineer with the plant's physical safety service, recalled the case of a young colleague, about twenty-five years old, who lost control after weeks of occupation and shouted obscenities at the Russian guards. They were under orders not to react, but Kalishuk heard one of them saying: "Why think? Pull the trigger and fire." Kalishuk tried to talk sense to the young man: "Just imagine the reaction of an armed man. You're insulting him. He can use force. And heroism consists precisely in controlling yourself." The young man was responsive but told Kalishuk: "I hate them." Kalishuk kept working on him, asking the young man to think about his duty to his parents. It helped.[3]

"We worked almost round the clock. We rested a few hours according to schedule. We became exhausted," remembered Liudmyla Kozak. "We asked to be relieved, because we were already walking around like ghosts." Oleksii Shelestii recalled that he was close to having a nervous breakdown by the end of the second week of the shift. "What's up?" Shelestii asked his superiors in a phone call to the plant's headquarters in Slavutych. "Can't you come to an agreement there? Why? How can that be? We need to be relieved; we're tired. We weren't prepared for this morally or physically." He suspected that the managers were doing all they could, but that the authorities in Kyiv were not responsive.[4]

The Russian commanders at the station realized that they and their soldiers were sitting on an explosive nuclear barrel. The exhaustion and resentment of the Chernobyl personnel might very well lead to an accident that would claim the lives of the occupiers. The Russians were prepared to listen to Heiko and allow a shift change, but how were they to evacuate those on duty and bring in replacements from Slavutych? "And how did you get here before?" one of the Russian commanders asked Heiko. "Take a look," responded Heiko, "and count on your fingers: the highway bridge has been destroyed; nobody will take the route through Belarus because more people like you are stationed there, and no one will send people that way. The railway bridge that people used to take has also been destroyed, and we won't take that route either. So other routes of some kind have to be found." The Russian responded: "Fine, make your proposals."

Heiko and the plant managers in Slavutych ultimately decided that new personnel could be brought in only by the Belarusian route, crossing the Dnieper by boat. The alternative route, leading through Kyiv, was more dangerous than the one leading through Belarus. So Belarus it was. The Russians gave their approval. They would take the old shift as far as the Dnieper and pick up the new one, but the plant management would have to take care of travel arrangements to and from Slavutych. "At that moment, the director was faced with the following conditions: decide on your own, search on your own, act on your own," recalled Heiko.[5]

———

Valerii Seida, the director of the Chernobyl plant, first and foremost had to select members of the new shift—people ready to risk their freedom and perhaps their lives by going into Russian captivity. Slavutych was behind the Russian lines but still free, under the Ukrainian flag and control, while the Chernobyl plant was under occupation. A trip there might become a one-way ticket. Surprisingly, there was no lack of volunteers.

On the first day of the war, when Ihor Aleksandrov, the chief foreman of the plant, asked a roomful of operators for volunteers, everyone present responded positively. Many volunteers knew exactly whom they would replace. Serhii Niushev, for example, was ready to replace his next-door neighbor Viacheslav Yakushev. A woman from Slavutych volunteered to join the kitchen staff at the plant, as her husband and son were there—members of the National Guard unit captured by the Russians. She wanted to be with them.[6]

Two men, Volodymyr Falshovnyk and Serhii Makliuk, were selected to lead the new shift. This made sense: Heiko's experience had shown that with shifts lasting days and weeks rather than hours, there was more than enough work for two foremen. Falshovnyk and Makliuk, both in their fifties, were among the most experienced people at the station, but the key factors determining their selection was their family situation. Falshovnyk, a calm, soft-spoken family man, recalled that "in my case, thank God, my children provide for themselves, and that may be the reason why I was chosen, since the children of all the other shift foremen at the plant are of school age."[7]

Such considerations indicated how risky the mission was: if either foreman were killed or taken prisoner, his children, unlike those of other candidates, would not be left without support. "Hardest of all was convincing my wife that I had to go there," recalled Falshovnyk. For Makliuk, who came across as more emotionally involved than Falshovnyk, the most difficult decision was to leave his family behind in a city that might fall into enemy hands any day. "Of course, there was worry. There was the unknown; there was anxiety," he recalled later. "But, you know, it was probably less about how we would work there or what would happen than about our family in town."[8]

While everyone agreed that the shift at the Chernobyl plant had to be replaced, and volunteers were prepared to step in, there was no agreement with the Russian occupying force on how and when that could be achieved. "It was not clear how to do that," recalled Falshovnyk. "It was clear that in the next days and weeks we could only prepare; nothing would happen earlier, especially as active fighting was going on there, as well as near the station and closer to Kyiv." Falshovnyk, Makliuk, and the members of their shift, a total of forty-six men and women, could only wait.[9]

––––––––

According to Zoia Yerashova, plant employees knew that there were volunteers back in Slavutych ready to replace them. "Everyone said that there were people in the city prepared to go; that there were such heroes, heroes indeed, who knew where they were going; that our people were no longer [in charge] there; that there were foreigners who had seized the station, but there was a substitute for every worker; that everyone was prepared to go there for the rotation," recalled Yerashova.

But there was no telling whether a shift from Slavutych would safely reach the power plant, or what would happen to Heiko's shift— would they be allowed to go home or arrested on departure? Nadia Sira, another member of Heiko's shift, decided to go, but only with a group led by Heiko. "I said right away," recalled Sira, "that I would go only if the shift foreman and all the men went. If they brought only the women, who knew where they would take us. . . . Everyone wanted to go home, but only as long as everyone was on board."[10]

Shelestii recalled that preparations for the rotation began in mid-March with Heiko calling and asking him to prepare lists of his staff to be rotated in the first and second stages. No one trusted the Russians, and there was concern that they might bring in the new shift while keeping the old shift at the station or moving it somewhere else, still holding everyone hostage. Another problem was how to keep the station working during the shift itself. It was decided to rotate staff in two stages: the women and nonessential personnel would go first. Operators essential for the functioning of the station's equipment would leave after the first group of the new shift arrived. Everything was ready by the appointed time, but the dates kept changing, as the change of shifts required high-level coordination in both Russia and Ukraine. There was one false alarm after another. Groups of people gathered and then went back, either home or to their workplaces, both at the Chernobyl plant and in Slavutych.[11]

For Shelestii and others, their last day at the station arrived on March 20, the twenty-sixth day of the shift. Heiko ordered his staff to be ready for departure by 8:00 a.m. "They told us: be quick, girls; we're leaving; they're waiting for us, and we're leaving," remembered Zoia Yerashova. At the entrance to the administration building they were checked by Russian soldiers, whose numbers had dramatically increased, before they got on the buses. "The buses drove up; they tied white flags onto the buses," recalled Yerashova. "We boarded one by one, and they seated us. The Russian general Aleksei Rtishchev then made his appearance. He called out the names of those already on the bus and gave them permission to leave."[12]

Oleksandr Kalishuk, who was in the same bus, remembered that as they were all anxiously waiting to depart, they heard Heiko's voice on the public address system: the departure had been postponed once again. Heiko asked everyone to return to their workplaces, but the passengers, who had waited so long to go home, refused to leave the bus. Rtishchev went into the building to see what was going on and came back with even more disturbing news: the Ukrainians regarded the employees of the Chernobyl plant as collaborators and were refusing to accept them. It was a lie, but it did not matter: the buses were not moving.

Thoroughly disappointed, the employees left the bus and returned to their overcrowded living/working quarters. But Heiko's voice was soon heard again on the public address system: the rotation would go ahead; he was working on the organizational details and would keep everyone posted. Finally, at 10:00 a.m., came the long-awaited announcement. Heiko ordered the staff back into the buses. Rtishchev delivered his farewell speech, claiming credit for having solved the electricity supply crisis by connecting the station to the Belarusian grid and now for organizing the rotation. "But we sat and thought to ourselves," recalled Kalishuk, "if you hadn't come, you bastard, we wouldn't be having such problems at all."[13]

Fifty employees left the plant, including sixteen women, eight

Ukrainian national guardsmen, and one member of the fire brigade; the remainder were from the operational and kitchen staff. The Russians also released the four stalkers and one guardsman suffering from cancer. The rest of the group were male engineers and technicians. The buses, escorted by Russian armored personnel carriers, proceeded toward the town of Chornobyl, then to checkpoint Leliv on the border of the inner 10-kilometer exclusion zone, crossed the Prypiat River, and left the 30-kilometer (19-mile) exclusion zone at checkpoint Paryshiv. From there the column headed for the Belarusian border, crossing it near the village of Hdzen (Russian Gden) on the Brahinka River.[14]

"We proceeded under escort of the armored personnel carriers," recalled the nurse Liudmyla Mykhailenko. Along the road she saw dozens of Russian military vehicles. "It was frightening, so there was silence and fear," remembered Mykhailenko. "We were very frightened, because we had already heard that green corridors had been granted at some places in Ukraine; that they [the Russians] did not observe them; that some [evacuees] had been executed. We dismissed such thoughts, convincing ourselves that all would be well," recalled Yerashova. "I kept reassuring myself that we were going home," remembered Nadia Sira, with tears in her eyes. She was traveling with her son, also a shift worker, and was concerned for him more than for herself. "I wept very softly," remembered Sira. "My son said, 'Mama, they'll bring us home.' But I said, they're probably taking us as hostages or to Belarus or Russia."[15]

At the Belarusian border everyone was ordered to disembark and go through the Belarusian checkpoint one by one. The shift worker Viacheslav Yakushev noticed that the checkpoint was powered by diesel generators, suggesting that it was a mobile installation. Indeed, the Belarusian authorities did not place a border guard detachment at Hdzen until December 2021, two months before the start of the war. The Belarusian border guards checked the documents and personal belongings of the Chernobyl personnel. Nadia Sira could not hide her emotions. She was married to a Belarusian, and they had visited his family in Belarus only a few weeks earlier. "Don't cry, everything will be all right," said a Belarusian female officer, trying to calm her down.

Sira was inconsolable. "What do you mean, it will be all right? We were in your country a month ago, and everything was all right. . . . We will never see them again, that's it." Sira knew that the war had changed relations between the two neighboring countries and peoples for years, if not generations, to come.[16]

The Ukrainians got back onto the buses, and the column moved farther east on the road from Chornobyl to Slavutych: Ukrainian highway P56, Belarusian P35. They crossed an approximately 20-kilometer (12-mile)-wide "peninsula" of Belarusian territory protruding into Ukraine between the Brahinka and Dnieper Rivers. The bridge across the Dnieper connecting Belarus with Ukraine had been blown up, and the border checkpoint in the village of Komaryn had ceased to function. There were still border guards on the Belarusian side of the border, but none on the Ukrainian side. But awaiting the Ukrainian passengers was a welcoming party, led by the director of the Chernobyl plant, Valerii Seida, and the members of the new shift, headed by Falshovnyk and Makliuk.

It was Seida's task to get the two shifts across the river. Yevhen Kosakovsky, a volunteer from Falshovnyk's shift, recalled that there was a big, comfortable motorboat next to the crossing, but the Russians insisted on an open boat so that they could see everything and everyone. Kosakovsky remembered that it was not easy to find a fisherman willing to perform the task. "The negotiations were difficult and broke off several times," he said. "Some of the fishermen did not want to risk their lives and boats, while others said that taking our personnel across to an occupied station would make them collaborators."[17]

Eventually, Seida and his people turned to Natalia Muzyka, the mayor of the small village of Mnev, on the Ukrainian side of the river. Muzyka agreed to help. In ten minutes, two local fishermen, one named Serhii, the other Anatolii Chobotar, got into a small wooden boat of their own construction and headed twelve kilometers downriver to the place where Seida and the new shift workers awaited them. The Russians ordered Anatolii to put a white flag on the boat and did not allow him to take anyone to the Ukrainian side of the river until all the members of the new shift had been transported to the Belarusian bank.[18]

"It was agreed," recalled Oleksandr Loboda, a member of the new shift, "that the boat would take people to the right bank and come back with people whom we were replacing. That would mean that the agreement was being fulfilled." But to the surprise of Loboda and other members of the new shift, the boat that took their colleagues to the Belarusian side returned to the Ukrainian side empty. "And just imagine, the boat returned empty four times," recalled Loboda, "We were seriously apprehensive, thinking that it was a trap of some kind. But then, finally, the boat returned with the women. Then we breathed a sigh of relief."[19]

Russians armed with machine guns escorted people in groups of eight down the hill to the riverbank. Zoia Yerashova remembered that there was a soldier at the front of every group and another at the back. On reaching the bank, they would get into a small boat one by one. "There were people who had never seen a boat in their lives," recalled Chobotar. Among those getting into a small boat for the first time was Nadia Sira. She recalled: "It was frightening, since it was my first time riding in a boat. It was very frightening. Some people put on life jackets; others held them in their hands, hoping not to go under, sitting like little mice." Even the men, many of whom had some experience of fishing, were nervous. "It was quite unpleasant," recalled Viacheslav Yakushev, "since the boat was a kind of dugout with a motor, and the water came up quite high."[20]

A single crossing took between fifteen and twenty minutes. Altogether, the two fishermen made twenty-five trips across the river. The members of the two shifts first met on the Belarusian side of the river. "There came the highly emotional moment of our meeting with our replacements. We had literally seconds, at most a minute to embrace and shed tears," recalled Liudmyla Mykhailenko, from Heiko's shift. "We had spent 25 days in particular [limited] company, and here were our people from Slavutych." While the members of Heiko's shift were happy to meet their fellow citizens, the members of the new shift were taken aback to see how their friends had changed. "I crossed paths with the bus that brought the personnel from the station," recalled Kosakovsky, of the new shift. Taking a glimpse at his colleagues, he was shocked by the "gaze of people who perhaps were not afraid—hardly, it was probably exhaustion—but a gaze of such exhaustion that it will always be before my eyes. It was, of course, so terrible."[21]

Valentyn Heiko left the station with the second group late in the afternoon of March 20. To those who came to replace him he seemed completely unaffected by the stress of the previous weeks. "It was pleasant to see Valentyn Heiko, who was safe, sound, and active," recalled Falshovnyk. The other foreman, Serhii Makliuk, had the same impression: "I thought that he would be all exhausted and depressed, but no, he was in fine form. So energetic, ready to work; he told us everything." Although Makliuk considered Heiko typical of those who had stayed at the plant, he was quite unique in his demeanor. After bringing Falshovnyk and Makliuk up to speed, Heiko left the station and headed toward the river crossing. He still had a mission to perform as foreman: to report to the station director.[22]

When the last members of Valentyn Heiko's shift crossed the river, it was already dark. Director Valerii Seida welcomed his people on their return to the Ukrainian side of the border. He offered tea, coffee, and cigarettes. "We will do all we can for you," he told the returnees. Yakushev recalled that everyone thanked him. Then, as they boarded buses to go to Slavutych, Heiko, who had been among the last to cross the river, approached Seida. "I have a present for you," he told the director. Reaching into his small bag, he produced a blue-and-yellow Ukrainian flag, the one that he had convinced Colonel Frolenkov to give to him after the Russian takeover of the station. Seida accepted the flag. It was Heiko's last action as foreman of the shift that had lasted twenty-five days and nights. Keeping the flag had been an ultimate act of defiance.[23]

———

By the time Seida accepted the Ukrainian flag and welcomed his operators back home, the forty-six men and women of the new shift were
already on the Russian-controlled Belarusian side of the river, having
taken the same boat as Heiko and his colleagues. The Russians had
them board the buses, and the column, consisting of two armored personnel carriers in the lead, three buses with the new arrivals in the
middle, and a microbus full of Russian soldiers and another armored
personnel carrier at the back, moved slowly toward the station.[24]

Heiko considered the volunteers true heroes. "They were going into
the unknown," he said later. "No one knew how it would end or how
long they would be there. We had come out all right. I always said that
the stars had been in such a constellation that we were on duty that day
and had nowhere else to go, but those on their way there—it was all
much more complicated for them." Valerii Semenov fully agreed with
his boss. "It was no easy thing to enter occupied territory as hostages of
the occupier," he said on camera. "It's not simple. Thanks very much
to all 46 of them." Heiko and his crew had spent 600 hours on duty
at the occupied nuclear power plant. It was anyone's guess how long
Falshovnyk, Makliuk, and their shift would be there.[25]

Falshovnyk and Makliuk reached the station around 3:00 p.m.
on March 20. At 4:30, having received instructions and updates from
Heiko, Falshovnyk took over control of plant operations. Soon after,
the Russians paid a visit to the new foremen. "Their leaders came, the
colonels and generals, and said right away: guys, nothing here is your
Ukrainian property," recalled Falshovnyk. "We'll take what we need;
at best we'll let you know. Your response will be of no interest to us.
We'll take what we need." Falshovnyk already knew from Heiko that
"they dictate the rules of conduct and interaction." It was a shock nevertheless. "It was rude," he recalled. "It's galling that you're not master
in your own place, because we understood perfectly well that troops
were there."

"The first days were actually occupied with getting used to being
at war, "recalled Falshovnyk, "although there was no shooting here."
Heiko had left Falshovnyk a memo describing the structure of the Rus-

sian forces that occupied the station, which Falshovnyk greatly appreci-ated. "There were quite a few military organizations of all kinds on site: National Guard, special forces, normal armed forces, so to speak, and representatives of Rosatom," he recalled. He spent long hours trying to understand who he was dealing with.[26]

What helped the transition was that not all members of Heiko's shift had left the plant. Sixteen engineers and mechanics stayed behind for various reasons. Not everyone lived in Slavutych and could go home. Those who lived in Kyiv or in Chernihiv, east of Slavutych, had no chance of getting back home, as warfare was raging around both cities. The residents of Ivankiv, a settlement north of Kyiv, could not go back because their town was under Russian occupation. Others decided to stay so as not to expose themselves and those who would replace them to the risk of being detained by the Russians en route—no one knew what could happen to people on the road. Yet others, having learned that the supply of food in Slavutych was dwindling, decided not to make the situation more difficult for their families who had stayed in the city and were doing relatively well on their own.[27]

There was one more reason to stay at the plant. The new shift needed help: forty-six people simply could not manage the work nor-mally assigned to a hundred. Valerii Semenov, the man responsible for the physical safety of the plant and the chief liaison with the Russian military command, decided to stay. He later explained to a reporter that only seven people at the plant could do his job. He was the seventh. The other six were gone or incapacitated: three engineers had joined a Ukrainian territorial defense unit, two were stranded in Chernihiv, and one had two small children to take care of. Semenov also had a relative and a number of friends among the soldiers of the Ukrainian National Guard unit imprisoned at the station. Whatever was the rea-son, Semenov stayed, ensuring continuity in contacts between the Ukrainian personnel and the Russian commanders.[28]

A day after the arrival of the new shift, the Russians had a rota-tion of their own. General Aleksei Rtishchev, the commander of the Radiological, Chemical, and Biological Defense Troops, who had overseen the transfer of shifts, left the station. In a few months he would be promoted to acting commander of the Khabarovsk military district. The new Russian senior officer in charge of the station was General Oleg Yakushev, a deputy commander of the Siberian district of Russian Guard troops. His responsibility in Siberia was the protection of industrial sites. The Russian troops were also rotated: Falshovnyk noted that some vehicles left the station and new ones arrived. "The Chernobyl station was a 'rest base,' you might say, because when they came back from the front they were so gloomy and angry," recalled Falshovnyk. "Then they would somehow become more relaxed, but the rotation went on constantly."[29]

The Russians were under orders not to touch the personnel of the station, but discipline was hardly their strong point. Falshovnyk's colleague Serhii Makliuk recalled that at the station itself the Russian officers and soldiers did not threaten or intimidate the personnel, but outside the premises things could get rough. "When staff members drove or walked beyond the bounds of their immediate workplaces, there were incidents," recalled Makliuk. "They aimed grenade launchers at people. Such things happened. And when a vehicle was taking garbage to Leliv, they aimed machine guns at the driver on his way there and back. And there were similar incidents on the production site."[30]

––––––––

The greatest problem that Falshovnyk and Makliuk faced in dealing with the Russian occupiers was constant looting of anything and everything they could get their hands on. "Before we arrived, half the [administration] building was already smashed up, doors broken, and looted," remembered Falshovnyk. Russian looting of valuable equipment at the station made international headlines a few days after Falshovnyk and his shift arrived.[31]

On March 23, soon after the return of Heiko's shift to Slavutych, CNN reported that the Russian occupiers had destroyed the EU-funded radiation monitoring lab and removed samples of radionuclides. To deal with the international scandal, the Russian military television channel Zvezda (Star) sent its reporters to the Chernobyl site. The footage aired on Russian television left no doubt that the laboratory had indeed been ransacked. The camera showed destroyed computers with their hard drives ripped out, pieces of equipment scattered around the room, toilet paper, and an abundance of empty liquor bottles. The reporters claimed that the Ukrainians themselves had ransacked the lab. Allegedly, they had done a poor job of staging Russian "vandalism": the liquor bottles and the soldiers' belongings were improbably distant from each other, while the toilet paper and soap had been left intact.[32]

According to Russian television, all that had been done in order to "create a negative impression of the Russian military, of their activity on Ukrainian territory, and specifically on the territory of Chernobyl and the Chernobyl station." As if that were not enough, Russian television proposed another version of events leading to the destruction of the lab. The Ukrainians had allegedly staged it to cover up their nuclear research (apparently on a "dirty bomb") at Chernobyl. "The very first steps are accompanied by a threat," reported the Russian journalists. "The accompanying specialists warn of the danger of an explosion." The camera showed a dog named Samur, sent in to make sure that the building and its equipment were not booby-trapped. "The indicators on the control panel go wild," stated a Russian military reporter. "Radiation norms exceeded several hundred times. Now specialists will get to work here."[33]

Other Russian outlets assured their viewers that the Chernobyl plant was under the secure control of the Russian Guard, which was protecting the plant from possible attack by Ukrainian nationalist battalions. Despite the Russian media frenzy over the ransacked laboratory, neither Falshovnyk nor Semenov or their staff were ever questioned by the Russians or accused of destroying laboratory equipment. The Russian commanders knew only too well that it was the work of their own soldiers. Parts of computers had been stolen for sale outside the zone. Other parts would be found later in Russian trenches within the zone.[34]

The Russian commanders tried to stay on relatively good terms with the new shift, both because their own radiological safety depended on staff compliance and because they needed staff assistance with such mundane matters as garbage disposal. They also wanted the Ukrainians to help them clean the Russian officers' quarters, but the cleaning never took place. Relations between the occupiers and the staff deteriorated dramatically on March 24, the fifth day of the new shift.[35]

On that day Falshovnyk received a disturbing call from his wife in Slavutych: Russian troops had begun an attack on the city. The management at station headquarters in Slavutych confirmed the news. Slavutych, which had been behind the Russian lines, was about to become a battleground between the Russians and the city's territorial defense unit. Distressed, Falshovnyk turned to General Yakushev and the Russian military commanders. They had promised the personnel not to touch Slavutych, out of sheer self-interest, according to Falshovnyk, knowing that "the next personnel rotation was necessary: if active measures were to begin here, the personnel would simply scatter, and there would be no one to take our places."[36]

The Russians themselves appeared surprised. They assured Falshovnyk that they had nothing to do with what was happening in the city. They dialed superiors all the way up to the Russian Ministry of Defense. But the answer they passed on to Falshovnyk was as disappointing as it was cynical: "There are no regular troops of the Russian Federation at Slavutych." Falshovnyk and the others were shocked. As far as they were concerned, their informal arrangement with the Russians was now off. "We declared that we were terminating any cooperation with the occupiers until order was restored in Slavutych and until it was left in peace," recalled Falshovnyk.[37]

Vitalii Popov, a member of the new shift, recalled reaction to the news: "We all went nuts." Falshovnyk and Makliuk threatened the Russians that the shift would stop working if the attacks did not end: "That would simply threaten an ecological catastrophe. Look: you will be responsible for the consequences because, as a matter of fact, the personnel are working under your gun barrel." Popov and his colleagues pushed an even more radical line. "We didn't just sit idly by: we threatened the Armed Forces of the RF in every possible way, beginning with direct contacts: you will perish here, because we'll make you such a dirty nuclear bomb that you will never get out of here." Now, all that was left was to wait and see whether it would work.[38]

11

THE BATTLE FOR SLAVUTYCH

O n the evening of March 20, when Valentyn Heiko and the members of his shift finally got home to Slavutych, they entered a very different place from the one they had left twenty-five days earlier. The first sign of change was the checkpoint at the entrance to the city manned by their fellow citizens, members of a territorial defense unit. Slavutych remained under the Ukrainian flag but was visibly under siege.[1]

That day the city television station showed a report from a local school that was being used as a logistics center to distribute humanitarian aid, consisting mostly of food for city residents and refugees from neighboring villages and towns now under Russian occupation. The narrator pointed out that citizens could obtain humanitarian aid for themselves and, if need be, for their neighbors as well. The next distribution of aid was supposed to take place in a week. Meanwhile, everyone could receive coupons for bread, which would be available from the end of March. The camera showed a young man receiving a coupon.[2]

Liudmyla Mykhailenko, the nurse who had just arrived from the

Chernobyl plant, recalled the dinner that her sister prepared for her. "The festive table was probably laden by my sister with her very last supplies of food," remembered Liudmyla. She was very touched by that show of welcome, adding that "in many families there was a complete lack of foodstuffs." Oleksii Shelestii confronted the same shortage: "For the first time, on the following morning I saw a line on the square before the film-concert complex. They brought milk or whatever else, and that was across the whole square. I was smoking on the balcony. My wife came out and said: they brought milk. I said: that's a milk line? She said: yes, ha-ha, get used to it."[3]

Mykhailenko remembered the "endless sirens" in the city. "You come to understand the meaning of air-raid emergency and the threat of artillery barrage," she recalled. "It's all real, all frightening, it really is. I literally reacted to every sound, every rustle." Zoia Yerashova was equally shocked. "Everyone lived in fear, in basements and shelters of some kind," she recalled. "In some buildings they spread rugs in corridors [to avoid being near windows in case of attack]. People did not live their own lives. They lived and adjusted to nothing but war." Many returnees began to realize that they had had easier conditions at the power plant than their families at home in Slavutych. Still, they were all glad to get home at last and embrace their loved ones.[4]

———

The mayor of Slavutych, Yurii Fomichev, was faced with the difficult task of making sure that his citizens had enough food to survive another day. "The stores were empty. No foodstuffs, no medicine, no fuel. The town was isolated. Roads cut off, bridges blown up," he recalled.[5]

The fact that many inhabitants had left the city after the start of all-out war made Fomichev's task somewhat easier. The city officials gathered information about the number of individuals and families remaining in Slavutych. Of approximately 25,000 residents before the war, slightly more than 13,000 had stayed. That was still a large number, and there was not enough food for them. "We worked with the surrounding villages: farmers provided us with potatoes, vegetables, and milk." With the trade infrastructure broken, farmers did not know what to do with the milk they had. At first it was distributed in the city free of charge, then for a nominal price. "And they baked bread," recalled Fomichev. "With their own flour. And we got to a system whereby we could provide a loaf of bread for a small family every three days."[6]

Fomichev kept up his prewar routine of addressing his fellow citizens on television, explaining the current situation and offering instructions, advice, and reassurance. If his previous appearances had been occasional, he now spoke every day, sometimes twice daily. Like almost everyone else, he was shocked by the Russian invasion, as was apparent in his first address. But Fomichev regained his trademark calm on the following day. "We have survived the first day—the day of the invasion," Fomichev told his fellow citizens on the second day of the war. He called on them to stay united. "It is up to us to defend the city and to maintain it," he declared.[7]

The mayor's voice became more determined with each passing day, even though conditions in the city were growing desperate. "We spent the night in basements and shelters," a visibly weary Fomichev told his viewers on February 27, the fourth day of the war. "We are tired, it's hard for us, but we should endure." Fomichev explained what the sirens meant and how citizens should behave: "Three long hoots, each up to a minute long, followed by an announcement of danger or emergency. We go into safe places, we go into shelters and stay there until we hear three short siren calls and an announcement that the danger has passed."[8]

Fomichev called on the citizens of Slavutych, many of whom had come from Russia or had relatives and friends there, to open an information front in the war and try to tell their Russian counterparts what the Russian army was actually doing in Ukraine. "Stay in touch with your relatives in Russia. Explain the situation to them as it actually is. We should give them this message. We should give them the truth. They are being duped very intensively. The information there is absolutely different. This is the situation in which we're living. And when you're in touch with a relative, when you send a photograph or video of your hometown or of the city of Chernihiv, which they came to visit and now see what is going on, that changes the situation a little; that's also important for us."[9]

The Slavutych television channel showed a short video recorded by the city's most famous son, the singer and performer Ivan Dorn. The winner of a 2017 MTV European Music Award, Dorn was equally popular in Ukraine and Russia. Born in Cheliabinsk in 1988, he spent his childhood and youth in Slavutych, where his Russian parents moved two years after his birth. He married a high school sweetheart whose father worked at the Chernobyl nuclear power plant, and stayed in touch with relatives in the city. On the day of the invasion Dorn recorded a video calling on his Russian fans to "stop that catastrophe . . . take no part in that murderous war." He encouraged his Russian colleagues not to remain silent and to tell their audiences "that Ukraine is an independent sovereign state." Switching from Russian to Ukrainian, Dorn spoke emotionally to his homeland: "Ukraine, I am with you. Hold on, my dearest!"[10]

To the disappointment of many, the appeals of pop stars like Ivan Dorn and Oleksandr Usyk, a Ukrainian professional boxer with multiple heavyweight titles who was popular in Russia, had little impact on a Russian audience brainwashed by state media. Fomichev himself came to realize that as he communicated with his wife's relatives, who lived in Russia. "All my wife's family lives there," he said. "But in these . . . days everyone has understood who is who. We do not communicate even with our relatives—people who have lived here and know what Slavutych is say that they are freeing us from someone." If the citizens of Slavutych were to survive, they would have to fight back with more than words and appeals.[11]

———

As Fomichev was mobilizing citizens to deal with the challenges of living in the conditions of all-out war, his office was doing all it could to prepare the city to defend itself from invading Russian troops. The first priority was to create a territorial defense unit.

Serhii Shershen, a big silver-haired man in his late fifties who had retired from the army with the rank of captain and served before the war as head of the city's department of roads, took command of the newly formed detachment. Only a few days earlier he had appeared on local television to discuss his department's plans for the new year. At that time, his greatest ambition had been to repair the city's road edges. Now he was running a territorial defense company with the task of protecting the roads and pathways he had helped to build.[12]

Shershen and the deputy company commander, Major Valerii Khudolei, who had worked in the security department of the Chernobyl nuclear power plant, began to create a territorial defense company on the morning of February 24, the first day of the war. "Incredibly many people arrived," recalled Shershen. He was truly impressed by the desire of his fellow citizens to take part in the defense of the city. There were far more volunteers than could be accepted, and Shershen recalled that the rejects "were extremely offended that they could not be taken." "People came up to me personally and said that they had children dying in Chernihiv," recalled Oleksii Horny, a platoon commander of the Slavutych defense company. According to him, "everyone was ready to go to war. No one took thought for himself, for his own life, or anything else." They enlisted as many people as they had automatic rifles—168, courtesy of the Slavutych military commissar, Lieutenant Colonel Yurii Buialo, who obtained them from the army unit nearby.[13]

The rifles arrived on the evening of February 24. By the following morning, the new recruits were armed and ready to defend their city. The problem was that few, if any, had the slightest combat experience, although almost all had served in the Soviet or Ukrainian armed forces at some point. "We did what we knew, what we could, what our experience allowed us to do correctly," recalled Shershen. Platoon commander Horny knew from his military service that he had to keep his people busy in order to maintain their fighting spirit. Once platoons had been organized, they began fortifying entrances to the city. "And according to the principle that they taught me in the army, if you have nothing to fight with," recalled Horny, "then you have to do as much as possible to impede the enemy's advance."

The company needed help to establish positions around the city. Shershen recalled that businesses provided the defense unit with construction equipment and building blocks for fortifications. Ordinary citizens came not far behind, with everyone helping as best they could. "When we wrote on Facebook that we needed help, I was surprised," recalled Major Khudolei. "I see as if they were standing before me how many of our citizens responded. They brought useful things—some brought spare parts, others barbed wire, still others bottles filled with explosive mixtures."[14]

Shershen and his assistants studied the city map, identified weak points in their defenses, and began to build checkpoints—one at the entrance to the city; another on the southern road that Heiko's shift had followed on its return from the Chernobyl plant; and a third on the eastern approach from the Belarusian border and the town of Liubech. "We organized checkpoints that had not been there earlier. None of us had any experience of establishing and guarding them, but we did it," recalled Shershen. They put everyone to work. "Someone knew how to work with metal, someone else could work with wood, someone had power saws," recalled Horny. At the most dangerous approaches to the city "we blocked forests and trails, and additional engineering structures were built."[15]

All this helped to repel the first Russian attack on the city, which took place on the night of the second day of the war. On hearing gunfire, Shershen ordered his people to take positions at the entrance to the city. "They tried us from the cemetery side," recalled Shershen. "As I understand it, they encountered our return fire and understood that we were here. We were armed and would resist. Not knowing how many of us there were, what equipment and arms we had, they did not risk an advance." But the enemy did not retreat very far, and the company commanders kept watch. "The intelligence service was organized so that people called us from every surrounding village and told us what equipment they had seen," recalled Shershen.[16]

On March 21, the commanders received information that a Russian column was moving from the direction of Chernihiv toward the village of Pakul, located less than 20 kilometers (12 miles) south of Slavutych. The information was relayed to the Ukrainian armed forces, and Ukrainian artillery bombarded the column, causing numerous casualties. "In the vicinity of the village of Pakul, our forces destroyed a large group of occupiers, with many killed and wounded—clearly, their objective was Slavutych," reported Ukrainian media a few days later. Ukrainian evacuees leaving the Chernihiv area had to change their route to avoid Pakul. The highway was full of Russian troops evacuating their damaged equipment and wounded soldiers.[17]

Although the Russians managed to reach Pakul, they were in bad shape. "According to the operational information at my disposal," recalled Volodymyr Hrynenko, the commander of a Slavutych defense platoon, "when the forces of the Russian Federation took the village of Pakul, they had close to 300 men who were severely injured, and in the village of Pakul they found quarters in various residences, in the village club, in the cultural center, and they were very interested in medical assistance for their people." The Russians lacked medical facilities. Ironically, that was bad news for Slavutych. "It was imperative for the forces of the Russian Federation to obtain not only medical assistance for their personnel but also repair facilities," recalled Hrynenko. All that could be found only in Slavutych.[18]

In his late-night address to the citizens of Slavutych, Mayor Fomichev shared disturbing news: "There is enemy movement toward us. We are putting up a defense." Because the situation was becoming critical, Fomichev suggested that those who wanted to leave the city could do so. "Tomorrow, at their own risk, those who wish to drive away may do so after the departure of humanitarian assistance vehicles," declared the mayor. Everyone knew how risky escape from the city could be. During the first days of the war, a citizen of Slavutych had been killed in an attempt to get through a Russian checkpoint. "He got into his car with his wife and set off with a white rag of some kind by way of the checkpoint, heading for Chernihiv. But they were shot: the man was killed and his wife wounded," recalled Fomichev.[19]

The Russians were circling around the city, trying to get into Slavutych or find other way to Belarus. On March 22, a column of an estimated fifty vehicles moved toward the village of Dniprovske, next to a
bridge across the Dnieper River into Belarus. There they stopped six
trucks bringing humanitarian assistance for Slavutych. Their officers
established communications with the defenders of Slavutych. The Russians requested passage through the city in the direction of Liubech
and then toward the Belarusian border. They also indicated that they
wanted to take over the local hospital. The defenders would have none
of it. "Let them into the city for hospital accommodation?" recalled
Mykhailo Shynkarenko, the commander of the drone intelligence unit.
"But you understand that if they got into the hospital, a day later they
would have entered the warehouse of the Silpo food store, where there
was liquor. . . . And it does not bear imagining what might have happened in the city of Slavutych."[20]

On the next day, one of the commanders of the Slavutych company, Lieutenant Vladyslav Ihnatenko, asked a local volunteer who was
delivering insulin to patients in villages occupied by Russian forces to
tell the Russian commanders that if their troops laid down their weapons, the defenders of Slavutych would allow them to pass through the
city. The volunteer returned with a counteroffer—in fact, an ultimatum
from the Russians. The defenders of the city were given one hour to
lay down their weapons and allow the Russians to pass, otherwise they
would attack the city. Lieutenant Colonel Buialo, the region's military
commissioner and now the commander of the area self-defense units,
rejected the ultimatum.[21]

———

The all-out Russian attack on Slavutych began on March 23, about
3:30 p.m., with the bombardment of checkpoint no. 1 at the southern
entrance to the city. The mortar attack lasted an hour and a half, and
the volunteers counted thirty-five explosions in the city. Surprisingly,

there were no fatalities. "Nature itself protected us: on the battlefield and along the highway there were many trees that lost their crowns as they stood in the path of enemy shells," recalled one of the defenders, Volodymyr Hrynenko. "Thanks perhaps to God or to our boys' good luck, as well as their [the Russians'] lack of mastery, on the first day we managed to avoid serious losses among our personnel," said the platoon commander Vladyslav Ihnatenko, echoing Hrynenko.[22]

Addressing his citizens on the evening of March 23, Mayor Fomichev sounded both worried and relieved. "A difficult day," said the mayor as he described the Russian attack on the checkpoint. "There was no enemy advance toward us, but we understand that he is near, and everything is very complicated." His main concern was that mortar shelling might continue and wound or kill civilians standing in ever longer lines for such necessities as bread and milk. "To those who stood in line for milk—without you, your little children will not get milk," he said. He wanted people to head for shelters at the sound of the alarm. Fomichev ended by thanking the city's defenders: "We want to thank the armed forces, our defenders, who put up resistance. Ukraine is holding on. Ukraine will win."[23]

On the morning of March 24, after reconnoitering the Ukrainian positions with a drone, the Russians resumed their mortar attacks on the southern checkpoint. The attack was more massive than that of the previous day. "We were forced back to the second checkpoint," remembered Shershen. The Ukrainians suffered their first casualty—the soldier Andrii Novohonsky was wounded and evacuated to the city. But the Russians paid a high price for their success. "When our men withdrew from checkpoint no. 1, and the enemy, advancing toward us, had already passed it, the coordinates of his movement were relayed to our command," recalled Lieutenant Colonel Buialo. "And with the help of TOCHKA-U artillery we dealt a significant blow to enemy equipment." Buialo was referring to the Ukrainians' use of a Soviet-designed tactical ballistic missile.[24]

The battle for Slavutych continued. The Russians bombarded

the Ukrainian positions at checkpoint no. 2. Altogether, the defenders counted up to 200 explosions hitting the area. They began to lose comrades. In the evening someone called from the telephone of Serhii Sydorenko, a defender of checkpoint no. 1, who had gone missing. The caller asked Sydorenko's comrades about the disposition and number of troops defending the city. It became clear that Serhii had been either imprisoned or killed. There was a threat of Russian commando units breaking into the city. Buialo ordered that lights be switched on around the railway station, bridge, and highway to make it easier to spot the enemy. It helped. Throughout the night the city remained under Ukrainian control.[25]

Unable to capture Slavutych, the Russians retaliated against the citizens of Pakul. The village was under the control of the 7th combined armed company of the 74th Motorized Rifle Brigade from the city of Urga, not far from Russia's border with Mongolia. On the previous day the Russian soldiers had arrested two Ukrainian men, O. M. Parasiuk and S. M. Yakovenko. The first had photos on his mobile phone that the Russian soldiers considered a discredit to their armed forces. The second had a Ukrainian army badge belonging to his son, who was serving in the Ukrainian forces. Both men were tortured.

On the morning of March 25, they were visited by the Russian company commander, thirty-one-year-old Armen Abgarian, who demanded information about the Ukrainian armed forces and, upset that they provided none, opened fire at the captives. According to the Ukrainian prosecutor's office, Abgarian "fired twice at the right and left ulna bones and the right thigh of O. M. Parasiuk and three times at the right supraclavicular area, right cheek, and upper and lower lips of S. M. Yakovenko." Yakovenko lost five teeth. But both he and Parasiuk survived the ordeal. Ukrainian prosecutors would charge Abgarian with a war crime.[26]

On March 25, the day Abgarian opened fire on the civilian prisoners, his company made another attempt to capture Slavutych. The Ukrainians blocked the entrance to the city with old cars and returned to previously abandoned positions. "By morning we had returned to checkpoint no. 1 yet again," recalled Shershen. The Russians did not expect such audacity. "They could not comprehend how those people [the defenders of Slavutych] were fighting," recalled a local who over- heard conversations among the occupiers. "If a position is covered by mortar fire, they should abandon it and move to other positions. We approach and they are back in the trenches, and we don't understand what is going on."[27]

The Russians resumed their mortar attack on the city checkpoints. "On that day, in fact, there was a mine for every one of our fighters," remembered Hrynenko. "The grand total of mines fired at the check- points and directly at our people exceeded 150 units." "Then," recalled Shershen, "a tank approached, and they destroyed checkpoint no. 1 with a direct hit. By and large, we had nothing with which to defend ourselves and had to withdraw." Russian mobile groups began to pen- etrate the Ukrainian defensive lines. Two Ukrainian volunteers were shot in an encounter with one such unit. Serhii Barkhatov was killed on the spot. His body, along with that of another soldier killed in downtown Slavutych, had to be left unattended for almost twenty-four hours. "It was impossible to take them away," recalled Major Khudolei. "Emergency vehicles could not reach them, and no one could approach because of sniper fire." The paramedic Volodymyr Makarchuk tried to save another soldier wounded in battle but was wounded himself and died in the hospital. Altogether, four members of the company were killed, a number of volunteers were wounded, and four were taken prisoner.[28]

Late in the afternoon, news reached the defenders of Slavutych that the Russians were getting ready to open fire on the city with self- propelled 122 mm Grad multiple rocket launchers from the Pakul area. That might mean the destruction of a good part of the city. Hrynenko recalled that "the last time we launched the drone, we saw six armored vehicles. Six tanks alone! Plus armored personnel carriers, plus infan- try combat vehicles." The lightly armed defenders of the city had no chance of holding their ground. "We called one another and [decided] to withdraw," recalled Hrynenko. The commanding officers allowed the defenders to leave Slavutych if necessary, without weapons. On the evening of March 25, they began their retreat through the neighboring forests in small groups, but without abandoning their weapons. The city of Slavutych fell into Russian hands.[29]

On March 24, Mayor Fomichev broke tradition and did not appear on the evening television broadcast to reassure his fellow citizens that things were under control. They were not. Fomichev was busy smuggling his wife and their daughter, whose second birthday fell on that day, out of the city.

Fomichev's wife had earlier refused to leave him in the besieged city, but now they had no choice—the Russians were already breaking in, and everyone knew what awaited mayors and their families at the hands of the occupiers: the chances of their being kidnapped and even killed were extremely high. Fomichev managed to take his wife and daughter along forest roads across the front lines to Kyiv. From there they would go west toward the Polish border. The mayor would return to Slavutych. He recalled that once his family was safe, the fear that had dogged him previously disappeared. He was now ready to face his destiny.[30]

Fomichev spent the night of March 25–26 at a friend's house near Slavutych. In the morning he headed back to the city to lead a public rally that he and his aides had planned for the morning of March 26 to show the Russians that they were not welcome. They would do so by carrying a 100-meter-long blue-and-yellow national flag of Ukraine through the streets. An example of civil disobedience had been shown by another atomic city, Enerhodar, the site of the Zaporizhia nuclear power plant. "Twice or perhaps even thrice they drove out the occupiers precisely by means of peaceful protest," recalled Fomichev. "And we broadcast information that tomorrow at nine in the morning we would gather at the central square for a peaceful protest action against the occupiers."[31]

Fomichev's trip was cut short when a Russian patrol stopped him on the approach to the city. Russian soldiers showed up out of nowhere and ordered him out of the car. "Place your hands on the hood, take everything out of your pockets, and hand over your phone," Fomichev recalled his captors saying. "They took the phone and searched me. They tied my hands behind my back. They drove the car to the side of the road themselves. And they took me away to the forest." There were already several people with their hands tied behind their backs. Fomichev's fellow detainees were all citizens of Slavutych and knew him well. He signaled with his eyes that they should not identify him. No one betrayed him, but Fomichev would soon reconsider his original decision and identify himself. "Guys, you've hit the jackpot: I'm the mayor," he told his captors.[32]

What made Fomichev change his mind were the words of one of the Russians addressed to the group: "We told your mayor not to fight. We would have come in and not shot anyone. And now we'll do a cleanup operation here, pick out the military men, it will all be over in a few hours, and we'll let you go." Fomichev was shocked by what he heard. "I understood that we were gathering civilians [for the manifestation], but they [the Russians] were conducting a filtration, which was absolutely dangerous," he recalled. Fomichev knew that the "filtration," a compulsory security screening, could result not just in violence but in casualties. He felt that he had to do something to stop the Russian plans, so he identified himself. The Russians were taken aback: "Really the mayor?" He responded in the affirmative: "I am the mayor; there are no military people there. Bring your commander, stop the filtration: there is nothing to filter."

They decided to bring him to their commander a few kilometers away. Suddenly one of the soldiers turned to Fomichev: "May I take a picture with you?" Fomichev would recall that episode with laughter. He was in their custody, and they could do whatever they wanted with him, but they were clearly impressed by his status, if not his behavior. He saw an opening in the question. "To keep the situation under control, I had to make it clear who was in charge. And they respected superiors—that's their mentality," said Fomichev, recalling his thoughts at the time. He answered like a true Russian boss: "Don't you dare take a picture of me." It worked, and the soldier backed off, saying, "That's all, I've got it."[33]

As they began their walk of some three kilometers through the forest to the Russian headquarters, one thought preoccupied Fomichev: how to let his wife and the rest of the world know that he had been captured. He expected a call from his wife at any moment, but his phone was in the hands of his captors. Fomichev asked the soldier who had seized his phone to answer if a call came from his wife and say two words: "Everything's fine." The soldier did as he was told. Of course, Fomichev's wife understood immediately that nothing was "fine." She called Fomichev's deputy, Viktor Shevchenko, but there was no answer; Shevchenko was organizing the protest rally in downtown Slavutych and did not respond. She then called a friend who was on the square next to Shevchenko and told her what had happened. "The mayor has been taken prisoner," said Shevchenko into a loudspeaker a few minutes later. The news was out even before the Russian soldiers delivered Fomichev to their commanders.[34]

At the command post Fomichev noticed that the commanding officer was watching a video stream from a drone above the main square of Slavutych. By that time the Russians had entered the city and taken control of the local hospital. Their armored personnel vehicles were on the square, but citizens had shown up en masse, not intimidated by the Russian presence. Fomichev heard the sounds of firing from the officer's electronic device. "Why are you firing?" he asked. "Don't get excited, not at people," came the answer. When Fomichev asked how many people were on the square, the officer responded that there were about 500. He believed that there were armed defenders of the city in the crowd and was preparing to use force against them.[35]

Fomichev tried to convince the officer not to do so: all those with arms had already left the city, he told the Russian. The officer refused to believe him. Once again, Fomichev grasped the initiative. "We agreed as follows," he recalled. "I go there with him and walk in front of him. If there is any fire, it will hit me first." They got into an armored personnel carrier and drove downtown. It was flooded with people. "When we got out of the armored vehicle," recalled Fomichev, "I saw the people. There were no '500 souls' but thousands as far as the eye could see. . . . There were fewer than 15,000 people in Slavutych at the time, and most of them had come to the square." Fomichev was moved by the bravery and solidarity of his fellow citizens: "When they saw me, there was a hum: mayor, mayor, mayor . . . Incredible feeling. Inexpressible."[36]

————

Those who came to the square were mobilized through social networks. The Viber group alone, which was used to share information from the mayor's office, had more than 10,000 subscribers. Among those taking part in the rally were members of Valentyn Heiko's shift who had returned to the city a few days earlier. One of them, Mykola Pobiedin, recalled: "My wife sewed a flag, I got a fishing rod, we attached the flag and went to the square." Another member of the shift, Mykhailo Makhyna, was as moved as Fomichev by what he saw on the square. "Honestly, I never expected that so many people would gather. I did not even think that we had so many patriotic people."

There was good reason to be surprised and pleased. In the fall of 2020, a year and a half before the all-out invasion, candidates from "The Oppositional Platform—For Life," a Russian-supported political force, won seven of the twenty-six seats on the Slavutych city council— more than any other party or political group in the city. But the Russian invasion changed the mood of the town. The citizens were now united in the desire to defend their way of life and their hometown against the invaders. "We will defend our right to live freely in this city, in this state," declared a speaker from the podium. To his chant "Glory to Ukraine!" the entire square responded: "Glory to the Heroes!" Most popular was the chant "Slavutych is Ukraine!" Another was "Glory to the nation—death to enemies!" Until recently, such slogans had been considered nationalist. No longer. The occupiers had spilled the blood of their fellow citizens. That changed the thinking and the rhetoric.[37]

But the citizens of Slavutych were not the only ones changing. So were the Russian invaders. Valentyn Heiko, who joined the protesters on the square, noticed a difference in the behavior of the Russian troops. "I simply compared those [at the Chernobyl plant] with these [in Slavutych]. They were different. . . . The former, let's say, came in at that moment as cultured people thinking that they were bringing us some kind of civilization and freeing us from someone. And that is why they behaved more or less humanely and in cultured fashion. In my presence, at least! But here it was apparent that they were different. . . ." Indeed they were. When the protesters with the giant Ukrainian flag began their march across the city, shouting *"Doloi!"* (Down [with the Russians]) and "One and whole united Ukraine," the Russian soldiers opened fire, shooting above the heads of the people and throwing stun grenades into the crowd.

Viacheslav Yakushev, another member of Heiko's crew who came to the square, looked around as the Russians started to fire and saw a bleeding man next to him. "I thought to myself that the worst scenario was probably beginning across town," he recalled. People were shocked but did not retreat or run away: instead, they charged toward the Russian troops. "Here all these people, the whole stream, appeared to stop and fall into a stupor, but then adrenaline. . . . They went, went, went. . . . Start crushing them!" recalled Makhyna.[38]

Among the charging protesters was a priest in full Orthodox regalia. Father Ioann Shepynda belonged to the jurisdiction of the Moscow Patriarchate, which many considered a pro-Russian branch of the Ukrainian Orthodox Church, but his jurisdiction did not matter under the circumstances. He was with his people. He had been conducting a service in his church when he heard the gunfire. "At about nine I glanced out the window," he recalled. "I saw a crowd. I saw a boy fall . . . I thought that mass execution had begun. Then I did not fear death. Dressed just as I was, I went." Others recalled him saying words of prayer before addressing the Russians: "Infidels! Those wearing crosses, take them off, for Christians do not aim machine guns at ordinary people."[39]

The troops were taken aback. One of them said to Father Ioann:

"What is this? You, a priest, are shouting such things at us? But we are also Christians; we are also Orthodox." The priest responded that no one was welcoming them with bread and salt—a traditional greeting. When one of the Russian soldiers decided to try his knowledge of Orthodox theology on the rebellious priest and told him that he and his fellow citizens were being punished for their sins, Father Ioann replied that the Russian soldiers were worse than Satanists and that he was not afraid to die. He had made his confession, God was with him, and no one could defeat God and the truth. He was dressed in white and ready for his funeral; neither he nor the people were afraid of the soldiers.[40]

It was at that moment of stalemate that the Russians brought Yurii Fomichev to the square. The camera of the Slavutych television operator who filmed the whole rally showed Fomichev heading toward the crowd with two Russian officers. "As I got out of that armored car of theirs, I saw people with flags extending to the horizon," recalled Fomichev. "A few moments later an Orthodox priest carrying a huge wooden cross ran through the crowd, shouting, 'Antichrists, take off your crosses.' That was probably the climax. The Russians were also surprised and stood silent." According to Fomichev, the Russian commander asked the protesters whether they and the soldiers were going to shout at one another or try to reach an agreement. Father Ioann could not understand what the Russians wanted him to do. Any compromise with the occupiers seemed unimaginable to him.[41]

Fomichev, joined by members of the city council who attended the rally, opened negotiations with the Russian commander. It took some time, and the results were anything but clear. But then people saw the Russian vehicles retreating. Fomichev, loudspeaker in hand, asked the protesters to leave the area where the confrontation had taken place and return to the main square. There, at 11:00 a.m., they continued the rally. Fomichev addressed the people once again, beginning with the words "Glory to Ukraine!" The rally responded: "Glory to the Heroes!" Fomichev continued: "Slavutych is a Ukrainian city. With a Ukrainian flag, a Ukrainian constitution, and our code of ethics." Father Ioann, holding the big cross, stood next to the mayor. Fomichev explained what he had agreed on with the Russians: they would check the city for arms, and leave if there were none. He asked the citizens to comply.[42]

On the next day, March 27, the Russians checked the local police building and a number of other locations for weapons, finding nothing. They left the city limits before the end of the day. On the following day, one of Russia's chief propagandists, Olga Skabeeva, announced in the *60 Minutes* talk show on the Russia One channel that Slavutych was under complete Russian control. In fact, the Russians limited their presence in the city to the checkpoint at its entrance. Nor did they interfere on March 30, when Father Ioann performed a church service for the three fallen defenders of the city: Volodymyr Makarchuk, Aleksandr Zatsepin, and Sergei Barkhatov. On the wooden crosses Makarchuk's name was written in Ukrainian and those of Zatsepin and Barkhatov in Russian, reflecting the ethnic origins of the fighters. In church they lay in similar coffins next to one another, covered with the Ukrainian national banner.[43]

Slavutych managed to avoid the fate of Pakul and other villages in the area, where Armen Abgarian and his soldiers from the 74th Motorized Rifle Brigade engaged in acts of terror and looted everything they could lay their hands on. The heroism with which the fighters of the territorial defense company and, finally, the citizens resisted became an important factor in saving Slavutych from Russian occupation. But probably even more important was the position taken by the personnel of the Chernobyl nuclear power plant, who threatened to end all cooperation with the invaders.[44]

Fomichev had heard that the plant personnel told the commanding officers: "If anything happens to our families, we will blow up the station." He knew that they were bluffing. "Understandably, there was nothing with which to blow it up, but still, Chernobyl carries an emotional charge that could be used for blackmail," he recalled. The mayor believed that one of the reasons the Russians took over Chernobyl was to be able to blackmail Ukrainians and the world community. Now it appeared that the personnel had used the same weapon against the occupiers and helped to save the city.[45]

12

LIBERATION

At the Chernobyl nuclear power plant, March 30, the day on which the citizens of Slavutych bade farewell to their defenders at the funeral service led by Father Ioann Shepynda, became a day of promise. Late in the evening, the Russians took down a 35-meter-tall antenna that they had installed near the plant's administration building. On learning the news, the shift foreman, Volodymyr Falshovnyk, told his colleagues: "Oh, they're probably leaving us." He would later recall having said that more in jest than in genuine expectation. Yet his words turned out to be prophetic.[1]

Next morning, Falshovnyk looked out his window and saw armed Russian soldiers in the gallery that led toward the large meeting hall where the occupiers interned members of the Ukrainian National Guard during daylight hours. The internees, who slept in two different locations, usually walked to the meeting hall and back on their own. Now they were guarded by the Russian soldiers. Falshovnyk tried to ask the Ukrainian internees and then their Russian guards what was going on, but all he learned was that the Russians had ordered the Ukrainians into the meeting hall.[2]

Falshovnyk returned to his office just in time to get a call from Valerii Semenov, who on his surveillance cameras spotted fourteen paddy wagons approaching one of the station's checkpoints. He grasped what was going on: the Russians were about to take the Ukrainian guardsmen away. At 9:00 a.m., they ordered the guardsmen out of the building, searched and handcuffed them, and started to put them into the wagons one by one. Falshovnyk was shocked. In recent days, when he had spoken with the Russian commanders about the future of the station, they had suggested that as many as forty Ukrainian guardsmen would continue their duties at the station, while the rest would be allowed to go home. But now it looked as if the Russians had lied once again. They had promised not to touch Slavutych and broken their promise; now they were doing the same with regard to the guardsmen, many of them relatives and friends of station personnel.[3]

Upset by this development, Falshovnyk locked himself in his office, then asked his colleague, Serhii Makliuk, to guard the door and allow no one to enter. He made an announcement on the station's public address system. He informed his staff that the Russians were taking the handcuffed Ukrainian guardsmen to an undisclosed location. Falshovnyk soon heard loud sounds outside his office: someone was trying to break in. He unlocked the door and saw General Oleg Yakushev, the commander of the Russian forces at the station. "Why are you creating provocations?" barked the angry general. Falshovnyk responded that he was just telling his staff what he had seen. Yakushev ordered Falshovnyk and Makliuk into Falshovnyk's office and placed an armed guard at the entrance. They were forbidden to use telephone lines or any other means of communication, or to leave the premises.[4]

The Russians returned after noon, demanding that Falshovnyk and Makliuk sign a one-page document. Titled "Act of Acceptance and Transfer of Protection of the Chernobyl Atomic Station," it was dated March 31, 2022. Surprisingly, the location was given not as the Chernobyl plant itself or the nearby city of Prypiat but as the city of Chornobyl, ten miles distant from the station. The document stated that between February 24 and March 31, the troops of the Russian Guard had provided "reliable protection and defense" of the Chernobyl nuclear station. They were now transferring those functions to the Ukrainian personnel. Falshovnyk and Makliuk were supposed to attest with their signatures that the administration of the "site under protection" had no complaints about the Russian Guard. On behalf of the Russians, the document was signed by General Yakushev as commander of the Russian Guard troops at the station and Nikolai Nikolaevich Muliukin, identified as a representative of the Russian nuclear monopoly Rosatom.[5]

Makliuk later recalled that the men, carrying automatic rifles, demanded that he and Falshovnyk sign the document or they would be arrested and sent away with the Ukrainian guardsmen. The two men found themselves in an impossible situation. De facto captives of General Yakushev, they knew that the Russians had looted the station before and most likely would do so again. "At the moment of our arrival, the third-floor premises of Administration/Service Building 1 had all been broken into," recalled Falshovnyk. The Russians continued looting on Falshovnyk's watch as well. "They broke into the storerooms. Every morning we received regular reports from our non-departmental security," Falshovnyk said. "Makliuk and I would drive to the location with representatives of Rosatom to verify the fact of break-in." Now they were supposed to sign a document saying that they approved such conduct.[6]

Makliuk believed that the Russians forced him and Falshovnyk to sign the document in order to blame the Ukrainians for the looting that they knew was going to happen afterward. Faced with the threat of arrest, the two foremen decided to sign. The only change they managed to introduce was to add the time of signing—12:13 p.m., March 31— next to their signatures. They added the time to avoid taking responsibility for whatever the occupiers might do afterward.[7]

The Ukrainian personnel's worst apprehensions were soon confirmed. Mass looting of the station's premises began at about 3:00 p.m., soon after the Ukrainian guardsmen had been taken away in the paddy wagons, and continued into the evening. The most senior officers left the station about the same time. "Well, I think that was done deliberately," Valentyn Heiko observed later. "You know, they gave them those 3 hours as a payoff. Here you are, 3 hours: go and grab." And they did. "When they finally allowed us to leave the office, the loading of heaters and fans continued near Administration/Service Building 1 on the production site, where their vehicles were parked—trucks and armored personnel carriers," recalled Falshovnyk. "We saw and observed all that." One episode made an especially strong impression on him. The occupiers tried to squeeze a heater stolen from one of the offices into their car, but it did not fit. "It was a horrible sight," commented Falshovnyk later. To make space for looted objects, the Russians removed four brand-new spare tires from an armored personnel carrier and left them behind.[8]

Semenov recalled that some officers were ashamed of what was going on and told him that not all Russians were the same. According to Semenov, the looting was done mostly by the officers and soldiers whom he called "obsessed." "Those who had come with an exalted mission to free us," continued Semenov, "they freed us only of things. Moreover, they ["freed"] the station premises of office equipment, as well as of personal items—military ones. Those were such things as tablets and notebooks that were among personal possessions." Falshovnyk tried to intervene, to no avail. "And when one told them that you are 'freeing' us of material valuables, then he (a Russian officer), instead of replying, would simply remain silent and take offense, not understanding," recalled Falshovnyk.

Before long, one of the station's security cameras captured an image of a Russian soldier leaving the square with a Russian flag trailing behind him like the low-hanging tail of a defeated dog leaving the battlefield. "The last truck left Administration/Service Building 1 rather late; it was growing dark," recalled Falshovnyk.[9]

———

The Russian withdrawal from the Chernobyl zone came as a pleasant surprise to Volodymyr Falshovnyk and his shift at the station. What had happened? Why did the Russians leave? Was it indeed due to their exposure to radiation and the resulting panic?

The real reason for the Russian withdrawal was the success of the Ukrainian counteroffensive north of Kyiv. The inability of Russian paratroopers to capture and hold the Hostomel airport in the first few days of the war led eventually to the abandonment of their whole operation in northern Ukraine. Kyiv repelled the Russian attack, and by mid-March Ukrainian troops were on the offensive. By March 21, they had reclaimed the important village of Moshchun on the Irpin River, stopped the Russian movement toward Kyiv, and threatened to encircle Russian units advancing on the capital. On March 28, they liberated the city of Irpin, and the next day the Russians officially announced their withdrawal from the Kyiv region.[10]

The Russians declared that the cutback in operations around Kyiv and Chernihiv would be undertaken to increase the level of trust between the Russian and Ukrainian diplomatic delegations, which had resumed talks that day in Istanbul. But the previous weeks had destroyed any remnants of trust between the two sides. President Volodymyr Zelensky suggested that the Russian withdrawal was meant to facilitate the resumption of attacks on the city of Irpin. On March 30, the Russians continued to bombard the outskirts of Kyiv. Yet, they were already on the run, and on March 31, left the Chernobyl nuclear power plant.[11]

By retreating from the Chernobyl exclusion zone, the Russians freed the Ukrainian personnel of their oppressive presence. Concerns about the imprisoned guardsmen and looted equipment aside, the overwhelming feeling among the Ukrainians was satisfaction. "We've breathed a sigh of relief, thank God; finally it's become more peaceful," recalled Yevhen Kosakovsky, of Falshovnyk's shift. "At least there's no ponderous weight hanging over you!" But the personnel had neither the resources nor the capabilities to defend the plant if another Russian military unit or group of marauders were to show up at their gates.[12]

On their first night free of the Russian presence, Falshovnyk and his staff used everything at their disposal, from metal chains to brooms, to secure the doors of the buildings and checkpoints. Semenov, responsible for the physical security of the plant, was particularly worried. "Because I was concerned that they might 'roll back' from there, beaten and hungry, and feared what they might do on our premises," he recalled, with reference to the departing Russian troops. Early in the morning of April 1, a Russian tank was indeed spotted near the plant, but it was heading for Prypiat and the Belarusian border, apparently trying to catch up with the rest of the retreating army.[13]

On April 2, the second day after the Russian departure, Falshovnyk felt more confident but realized that something was missing at the plant besides the property looted by the Russian marauders. The Ukrainian banner, which had waved on the flagpole near the administration building, had been removed by Heiko in the first days of the occupation. Falshovnyk called Heiko in Slavutych and learned that he had managed to smuggle the banner out of the station during the shift change. But Falshovnyk needed a flag. He made an announcement on the public address system and soon had more flags than he could use. It turned out that five banners stashed away in people's lockers and desks had survived the occupation.[14]

Falshovnyk announced a ceremonial flag raising to be held during the lunch break so that more people could attend. He asked the shift foreman of the electrical division, Yevhen Sosnovy, to arrange a transmission of the national anthem over the public address system. Sosnovy promised to do his best. But when everyone had gathered, Sosnovy surprised his colleagues by performing the anthem a cappella himself. Everyone was emotionally overwhelmed. Falshovnyk would retell that episode, trying to hide his feelings, but his voice would betray them anyway.

The members of staff were free and independent once again.[15]

———

The excitement of the raised Ukrainian flag aside, for the Ukrainian operators of the plant the most emotionally charged day was still ahead. It came the next morning, April 3. Although it was a Sunday, for those on duty like Semenov, who was beginning his fortieth day at the station, it was as much a working day as any since the start of the war.

Semenov and two colleagues were having coffee while following their monitors when, about 10:15 a.m., they heard a voice from the station's public address system. "Good morning. We are the Armed Forces of Ukraine. Please let us in," said a male voice in Ukrainian. Semenov recalled that he and the others were shocked. "Our jaws dropped, and we were unable to speak. You won't believe that we delayed all of 30 seconds!" he recalled. The operators tried to gather their thoughts and figure out what was going on. Their cameras were of little help—they were pointed at the perimeter of the station, but the voice came from one of the observation points outside the perimeter. Finally, Semenov mastered all his faculties and said what was on everyone's mind: "So where are you?" The speaker identified his location, and Semenov explained how he could proceed to administration building no. 1. He then rushed to the checkpoint.[16]

Semenov reached the checkpoint first, just in time to see a Ukrainian Kozak (Cossack) armored personnel carrier and two trucks pulling up to the entrance. An officer in Ukrainian uniform came out—Semenov estimated him to be about twenty-five years old. His soldiers followed, some of them as old as sixty. They all looked tired. "It took us two weeks to make our way to you. With battles and everything," the young officer told Semenov. He then ordered a tablet to identify his position on the map. Once Semenov had done that, the officer told him: "Fine, our mission here is accomplished." The station personnel who had gathered offered the soldiers freshly brewed coffee. The soldiers drank it and bade them farewell. Volodymyr Falshovnyk remembered their parting words: they told the staff that they had returned to the zone "For a long stay; forever."[17]

Later that day, Ukrainian media broadcast a statement: "Today, April 3, units of the Air Assault Corps of the Ukrainian Armed Forces took control of the environs of the city of Prypiat and a sector of the State Border of Ukraine with the Republic of Belarus. We continue to carry out our combat tasks!" Next to the news item was a photo of a young Ukrainian officer posing with the national flag against the background of the new confinement arch over the damaged reactor no. 4. The soldiers whom Semenov met that morning belonged to air force units—the 95th and 80th separate air assault brigades.[18]

The same units also liberated the city of Chornobyl. As at the station, the Russian units departed before the Ukrainian troops showed up. The locals rejoiced in their victory. "When we found out that they had already left, there was such an inner feeling as if of a real victory; it was such ultimate freedom; everyone really felt such euphoria that it was inexpressible, not even like a first sexual experience," recalled Oleksandr Skyrda. He was under the impression that nature itself was celebrating the liberation of his city. "The Orcs [Russians] departed, and in two or three days so many storks flew by; there were a million of them, on the roofs, on houses, on the ground, on the main street; they went around grazing—it was simply too much, there were so many of them here," recalled Skyrda. He added: "Old women say that if the storks have arrived, it means that Chornobyl will live." Back in 1986, the cleanup workers had had the same feeling when they saw the storks returning to the exclusion zone. It was returning to life.[19]

Ukrainian media outlets and social media accounts were flooded not only with images of Ukrainian soldiers retaking the Chernobyl station but also with gruesome photos of the massacre committed by Russian troops in the city of Bucha, north of Kyiv. Ukrainian forces reclaimed Bucha on March 31. What they found there shocked not only them but the world at large. One of the streets of Bucha, Yablunska (Apple Village Street), was lined with corpses, some of them with their hands tied behind their backs. Satellite images suggested that eleven of those corpses had been lying there since March 11, twenty days before they were located and filmed on April 1 by a member of the city council.[20]

According to the UN High Commissioner for Human Rights, seventy-three civilians had been killed by Russian forces during their occupation of the city. The total of victims in Bucha was close to 500 individuals, including nine children, killed by a combination of bombardment and war crimes committed by Russian troops. In many ways,

Bucha was just the tip of the iceberg. According to the Ukrainian general prosecutor's office, in the Bucha district alone Russian soldiers had committed more than 9,000 war crimes and killed more than 1,400 civilians, including thirty-seven children. In Kyiv province as a whole, military action had damaged 26,000 houses, 5,000 of them totally destroyed. If one did not count fallen members of the territorial defense unit, no civilians were killed in Slavutych, a testament to the heroism of its defenders and the determination of the Chernobyl station staff, who made the safety of their city a condition of continuing work at the plant.[21]

On April 5, the third day after the return of the Chernobyl station under Ukrainian control, reporters from the "Ukrainian Witness" project visited to collect video evidence of the war. Their camera recorded images of a weary but cheerful man with long sideburns and a beard showing them the premises. It was Semenov, working the forty-third day of his shift; with the situation still very uncertain in the region, neither he nor his colleagues could go back to Slavutych. The camera showed Semenov guiding the reporters through the looted premises of the station. He and Makliuk led them to the basement, where the Russians had held the imprisoned Ukrainian guardsmen. The place had been turned upside down by Russian marauders after the guardsmen were taken away from the station, explained Semenov.[22]

As more Ukrainian reporters began to arrive in the Chernobyl zone, the extent of looting conducted by the retreating Russian troops became more evident. Among the places ransacked was the museum of the 1986 accident, known as "The Star Called Wormwood." The occupiers had stolen television sets from the museum and, as Ukrainian journalists joked, "enriched" its collection with the garbage they left there. They left behind strips used for detecting traces of drugs in urine, empty cans of meat produced in Buriatia, and empty cigarette packages from Belarus.[23]

The Russians' living quarters were full of garbage as well. Among the items left by the occupiers was a homemade poster with the image of a Russian armored personnel carrier emblazoned with the letter "V," used to identify Russian troops in northern Ukraine, and with a catchphrase popular among the Russian military from the 2000 Russian blockbuster *Brother 2*, which read, "Strength lies in Truth." Also written on the poster were the place names "Krasnoiarsk," "Irkutsk," and "Altai," supplemented by the unit numbers "24 Rus" and "38 Rus," suggesting that the poster had been produced by soldiers of Russian Guard units from Siberia. Soldiers had also inscribed their first names on the walls and left inscriptions such as OMON, the special-purpose police detachment of the Russian Guard.[24]

The extent of the damage and looting done by the Russian occupiers at the plant was astounding. During the first weeks after the Russian retreat, the Ukrainians could not locate 133 sources of ionizing radiation originally held at the looted laboratory. Their total radiation activity was estimated at 7 million becquerels, roughly equal to 1,534 pounds of radioactive waste. It is not clear whether and when the Ukrainians were able to locate the sources, but according to their inventory as of early June 2022, they lacked 1,500 radiation dosimeters, 698 computers, and 344 vehicles, amounting to a total value of $135 million. Some of the stolen equipment was furnished with GPS tracking, which showed that some vehicles had been driven to Belarus and were transmitting signals as late as early June. The signals were coming not only from Homel, close to the Ukrainian border, but also from the Belarusian capital of Minsk.[25]

The Chernobyl station, which had been constantly in the news during the occupation, and where the top Russian commanders had lived, turned out to have been looted considerably less than neighboring areas within and outside the exclusion zone. The town of Chornobyl, through which Russian units moved toward Kyiv and then retreated to Belarus, suffered numerous waves of marauding soldiers. The first news of looting in the town reached Ukrainian media in mid-March, but its scope became fully clear only after the Russian retreat. "All of Chernobyl has

been looted," Anatolii Solivon, a firefighter from the town, told reporters. "Automobiles, tractors—they took them all to Belarus. They drove
all that could be driven and pulled the rest. Computers, household
appliances, apparatus—they took even black-and-white television sets,
which have long been useless to anyone here. They simply went from
house to house and looted: one went with a sack, another with a sledgehammer, smashing in doors and emptying the contents."[26]

In the village of Sydorovychi, a few dozen kilometers south of the
Chernobyl exclusion zone, the Russian marauders hit almost every
household. "If the door was not opened to them, they broke in the doors
and windows, stealing all they could—household appliances and food.
People lived in fear," recalled local resident Tetiana Mukhoid. Before
leaving the city, the Russians took an Israeli flag from the local library.
The village was the birthplace of Nehemiah Rabin, the father of the
Israeli prime minister Yitzhak Rabin. The villagers, all of them Ukrainian, had been preparing to mark the centennial of Yitzhak Rabin's
birth on March 1, 2022. Five days earlier, the village was occupied by
Russian troops. The celebration never took place, and now the flag was
gone, too.[27]

———————

Aside from spare tires and equipment removed from their vehicles
to make space for looted goods, and the destruction of looted houses,
the retreating Russian soldiers left behind an increased level of radiation. Oleksandr Loboda, the head of the radiation safety division on
Falshovnyk's shift, recalled that on March 30, when the Russians were
getting ready to withdraw from the station, he registered a significant
spike in the radioactivity level in the exclusion zone. It had increased by
more than forty times.[28]

There was widespread suspicion outside the exclusion zone that
this time high radiation levels had been caused by more than moving
vehicles. On March 31, the day the Russians left the station, officials of
Enerhoatom, the Ukrainian company that runs the country's nuclear

power plants, including the one in Chernobyl, confirmed something that the Ukrainian and world media had been discussing throughout the previous week. The Russians, said the officials, had dug trenches in one of the exclusion zone's most contaminated areas, a space of four square miles close to the power plant known as the Red Forest. The Red Forest made it into almost every book on Chernobyl and was depicted in the 2019 HBO blockbuster *Chernobyl*. Now it was in the news once again.

The first report about Russian fortifications in the Red Forest surfaced soon after Heiko's shift returned to Slavutych. On March 24, Oleksandr Syrota, head of the Civic Council of the Directorate for the Management of the Chernobyl Zone, published a Facebook post that read: "Good people are saying that the motherfuckers have dug trenches not just anywhere but in the most strategic forest of the Chernobyl zone—the 'Red Forest.' Our sincerest wishes to them—DIG DEEPER, STAY LONGER! Amen." A Kyiv television channel reported the story the following day. By March 29, news of the Russian exploits in the Red Forest had been picked up by Reuters, whose reporters interviewed two members of Heiko's shift, now back in Slavutych. They said that they had seen Russian vehicles and heavy equipment moving through the vicinity of the Red Forest at the time of the invasion.[29]

On April 1, 2022, April Fool's Day, Ukrainian media broadcast information from the "Military Medical Service of the Russian Federation" that one person had died, twenty-six had been admitted to the hospital, and seventy-three sent for rehabilitation after exposure to radiation in the Chernobyl zone. Iryna Vereshchuk, the vice prime minister of Ukraine in charge of the occupied territories, had posted on her Facebook account one day earlier: "I consider that the Russian servicemen who dug trenches in the forest in the exclusion zone of the Chernobyl atomic energy station fully deserve to be nominated for the Darwin Prize this year. For they voluntarily received doses of radiation so high that the consequences will be explained to them by doctors in special protective suits. This is a case in which the enemy horrifies one with the sawdust in his head." The Darwin Award was a tongue-in-cheek "honor" of the Usenet discussion system recognizing those who became sterile, thereby contributing to human evolution. Vereshchuk posted her comment on the eve of April Fool's Day.[30]

All jokes aside, the Enerhoatom officials who examined the station confirmed information about the fortifications. They also suggested that the Russians had been affected by radiation, which was one of their reasons for leaving the zone. "We shall note," read the Enerhoatom statement, "that information about fortifications—trenches that the rashists [contraction of "Russians" and "fascists"] dug in the Red Forest itself, the most polluted forest in the whole exclusion zone—has also been confirmed. No wonder, then, that the occupiers received significant doses of radiation and panicked at the first signs of illness. And they appeared very quickly. Accordingly, something close to mutiny began to develop among the soldiers, and they made preparations to leave."[31]

Belarusian doctors confirmed that cases of Russian soldiers from Chernobyl had been treated in the country's Republican Research Center for Radiation Medicine and Human Ecology, but no independent data surfaced to suggest any immediate consequences of their presence in the area. Olena Pareniuk, a bioscientist at the Kyiv-based Institute for the Safety of Nuclear Power Plants, considered that information about radiation poisoning was wishful thinking on the part of her fellow Ukrainians. "It would be fine if only that were true," she told a journalist. Her calculations and those of her colleagues suggested that Russians in the Red Forest could have received a dose of radiation no greater than 0.2 sieverts. The development of acute radiation syndrome in the average person requires a minimum dose of 1 sievert.[32]

The Ukrainian journalists who came to the zone soon after its liberation produced plenty of video evidence substantiating the original report that Russian soldiers had dug trenches in the Red Forest area. Although there have been no confirmed cases of acute radiation syndrome among the Russians stationed in the Chernobyl zone, one discovery resulting from exposure to low doses of radiation after the 1986 Chernobyl disaster was that their impact could manifest itself years if not decades after exposure. The mayor of Slavutych, Yurii Fomichev, coined a phrase that summarized not just the hopes of Ukrainians but also their experience of dealing with the consequences of the nuclear accident: "The Russian troops have left Chernobyl, but Chernobyl will never leave them."[33]

———

By May 2022, the Ukrainian Security Service had collected enough information about Russian presence in and around the Chernobyl zone to charge three Russian commanders at Chernobyl for violating "the laws and customs of war." They were generals Sergei Burakov and Oleg Yakushev and Colonel Andrei Frolenkov.[34] General Yakushev was charged, inter alia, with ordering or allowing the looting of 2,000 items on the territory of the Chernobyl zone amounting to an estimated value of 26 million Ukrainian hryvnias.[35]

But Russians were not the only ones charged by the Ukrainian authorities in connection with the occupation. Criminal cases were also opened against Ukrainians accused of collaboration. At the top of the list of Russian agents was Andrii Derkach, the former head of Ener-hoatom, the company managing Ukraine's nuclear facilities. Derkach was a Ukrainian politician whose father, Leonid, had served as head of the Ukrainian Security Service (USS) in the late 1990s and early 2000s under President Leonid Kuchma. Entering Russia's Federal Security Service Academy during the last years of the USSR's existence, Andrii Derkach graduated in 1993 and became head of Enerhoatom in 2006. In that position he signed a number of agreements that deepened the dependence of the Ukrainian nuclear energy sector on Russia. In June 2022, Derkach was charged with having received more than half a million dollars from the Russian security services to fund private security firms that were to be used as a fifth column during the Russian invasion. By that time Derkach had left Ukraine, not having been seen since the start of the all-out war.[36]

In March 2022, the Ukrainian Security Service arrested Oleg

Boiarintsev, a former parliamentary assistant to Derkach and, at the time of his arrest, vice president of Enerhoatom in charge of personnel.[37] In July 2022, the USS arrested one of its own, Oleh Kulynych, the head of the Crimea directorate. Kulynych who had served as a vice president of Enerhoatom under Derkach in 2006–7, was accused not only of providing Russia with information on the USS Crimean network and its plans to defend southern Ukraine but also of orchestrating the appointment of Russian intelligence agents to the service's top positions.[38]

Another USS officer accused of spying for Russia was Andrii Naumov. Before becoming head of internal security of the USS, Naumov had spent time at the agency controlling access to the Chernobyl zone, where he became known for extorting bribes from tour operators.[39] The Chernobyl zone allegedly served as a meeting place between Russian intelligence officers and their Ukrainian agents. The Ukrainians failed to capture Naumov as he fled the country just before the invasion. He was later detained for currency smuggling by Serbia, which refused to return him to Kyiv.[40]

Ukrainian counterintelligence made most of its arrests of nuclear energy employees on charges unrelated to the fall of the exclusion zone into Russian hands on February 24, 2022. There was one exception— the arrest of the deputy director of the Chernobyl nuclear station in charge of security, the USS colonel Valentyn Viter. It was Viter who, on the morning of February 24, suggested to the commander of the Ukrainian guardsmen at the plant, Yurii Pindak, that he "spare his people." Viter took sick leave before the invasion and then left Kyiv for Transcarpathia, Ukraine's westernmost region. He was arrested there in March 2022, charged with abandoning his post in time of war, and held on suspicion of treason.[41]

Russian intelligence services and spies in the Chernobyl zone aside, the question of whether the Ukrainian guardsmen did the right thing by not resisting the Russian military takeover of the Chernobyl plant is anything but a clear-cut matter in both Ukrainian and international law. At the station itself, no one considered them traitors. The plant personnel would have looked with suspicion on anyone who tried to leave the plant under occupation. In their eyes, loyalty required staying on duty in order to prevent another nuclear accident from happening, no matter what the conditions.

At the end that became the position of the Ukrainian government as well. The members of both shifts received high government awards from President Zelensky, and the national guardsmen serving at the Chernobyl plant returned from Russia one by one as heroes as a result of prisoner-of-war exchanges. But the operators were also questioned by the Ukrainian Security Service and kept emphasizing in numerous interviews that what they had done was fully in keeping with Ukrainian and international law. Valerii Semenov, the go-between at Chernobyl, joined the Ukrainian territorial defense unit after the liberation of the site, some believe in an attempt to shield him from accusations of treason and disloyalty. The question of what constitutes loyalty in such circumstances has not been clarified in either international or domestic branch of jurisprudence.[42]

———

Yaroslav Yemelianenko of Chornobyl Tour was among the first non-military individuals to visit the Chernobyl zone after its liberation by the Ukrainian army. One of his tasks was to locate those of his employees who had found themselves under Russian occupation and provide humanitarian assistance to them and their neighbors. In the town of Ivankiv, located between Kyiv and Chernobyl, he let an old man use his Starlink to call his son. The old man was shaken and hesitated at first: what if his son had not survived? He eventually called; the son answered and told the old man that he was now a grandfather—his grandson had been born in Kyiv while Ivankiv was under occupation.[43]

Yemelianenko was also in the zone to lay the groundwork for the establishment of a museum of the Russian occupation of Chernobyl. He was on the lookout for artifacts to represent that frightening period in the history of the nuclear exclusion zone. Yemelianenko was disgusted by the sight of burned-out Russian military vehicles along the road and did not think that they should be represented in the future museum. But he selected items found in those vehicles that had been looted by Russian soldiers in neighboring villages. Among them was an old video player. Yemelianenko told a journalist that such equipment "is now of no use to anyone and can be found in garbage dumps. But this person [a Russian soldier] stole the video player from a Ukrainian and even signed it with his name and the name of his unit to keep his own Russians from stealing this stolen article. All these facts make it possible to understand what kind of people came to us."[44]

Before the all-out war, Yemelianenko and his staff at Chornobyl Tour had been determined to transform the image of the Chernobyl zone from a place of disaster to one of rebirth. He remained loyal to that idea throughout the weeks of occupation and believed that the new museum should serve the same purpose. "The basic idea of associating the war with Chernobyl is to show that the Soviet Union was the cause of the Chernobyl disaster," Yemelianenko told a reporter in December 2022. "With our culture and labor we transformed this problematic place in the Soviet Union into a zone of Rebirth. And this zone of Rebirth has already been Ukrainized; it has now helped us once again in our struggle against Muscovy, which has come to us for the nth time in an attempt to kill us."[45]

The Chernobyl disaster of 1986 had returned in a new guise. Yemelianenko now had to account for both. He was thinking about the new meaning of the Chernobyl zone as he would present it to new generations of tourists. The tourist season for which he had been preparing in January 2022 did not materialize, but he knew that future seasons were coming. People would need to see a place of two tragedies, one caused by the Soviet-made disaster of 1986, the other by the Russian-made war of 2022. The world would need to learn from both in order to avoid destruction by a new nuclear cataclysm.

EPILOGUE

On April 26, 2022, the thirty-sixth anniversary of the 1986 disaster, the president of Ukraine, Volodymyr Zelensky, presented state awards to those now considered the new heroes of Chernobyl, members of the two wartime shifts at the nuclear power plant. He thanked those who "remained at the station and ensured continuous operation of the Chernobyl atomic energy station in truly inhuman conditions—under occupation, with direct threat to their lives." Among the thirty-one individuals awarded the Order of Courage were Valentyn Heiko, Volodymyr Falshovnyk, Serhii Makliuk, Valerii Semenov, Nadia Sira, Oleksii Shelestii, Liudmyla Kozak, and Zoia Yerashova, whose testimonies appear in this book and helped me piece together the story of the Russian occupation of the Chernobyl plant.[1]

On the same day, Rafael Mariano Grossi, the director general of the International Atomic Energy Agency in Vienna, made a long-awaited visit to the Chernobyl plant. It was the third visit of a director general since the accident of 1986. The first occurred in May 1986, a few days after the explosion, when Hans Blix, who headed the IAEA at the time, circled the troubled reactor in a helicopter. Yukiya Amano, who held that position between 2009 and 2019, visited the plant in April 2011 to mark the twenty-fifth anniversary of the disaster. The purpose of Grossi's visit was less to commemorate the disaster than to prevent another one.[2]

Grossi came to the Chernobyl NPP to assure the world that everything was under control and that, despite spikes in radiation levels during the Russian occupation of the site, radiation levels had been checked with appropriate equipment to conduct "radiological and other assessment at the facility" and had returned to the norm. The IAEA team that followed him came to help the Ukrainians repair remote data-control systems incapacitated by the Russian forces, which had made it impossible to monitor radiation levels in the exclusion zone from the agency's headquarters in Vienna. That was pretty much all the agency could do under the circumstances. Like a police sheriff in Hollywood movies who always arrives after the main character has already defeated the villain on his own, Grossi came to Chernobyl as a symbol of law and authority that he and the IAEA had been unable to enforce.[3]

When a few months later the Board of Governors of the IAEA adopted a resolution calling on Russia "immediately to cease all actions at and against nuclear facilities in Ukraine," the resolution was ignored, and there was little that the IAEA could do about that either. The Chernobyl station was safe, having been liberated by the Ukrainian army. But the Zaporizhia nuclear power plant, the largest in Europe, remained under Russian control. It was becoming more dangerous with every passing day of Russian occupation. Four thousand of the 10,000 workers originally employed at the Zaporizhia nuclear power plant in Enerhodar had left the station and the town, sharing with the world their stories of intimidation, arrest, and torture at the hands of the Russian occupiers. The nuclear power plant was in danger not only because of continuing shelling in the area but also because of the lack of experienced and qualified personnel.[4]

The situation became even worse in June 2023, when the Russians blew up their section of the Kakhovka dam, emptying the Kakhovka reservoir and raising concerns about the water supply for the station's cooling pond. Grossi led one more IAEA mission to the plant, but little was achieved by that act of personal courage, as the station remained under Russian control. If the worst were to happen in Ukraine—another Chernobyl or multiple meltdowns of the Fukushima type at the country's four nuclear power plants—the impact would be felt not only in Ukraine but in the rest of Europe as well.[5]

————

Russia's aggression against Ukraine brought the Chernobyl plant to world attention for the second time in slightly more than thirty-five years. The causes of both Chernobyl crises, Chernobyl I and Chernobyl II, lay not only in human actions but also in decisions made in Moscow. In the first case, it was a decision to repurpose reactors originally designed to produce nuclear weapons in order to generate electricity while keeping the characteristics and shortcomings of those reactors secret from those who would operate them. In the second case, it was a decision to seize a nuclear energy station by armed intervention, with all the risks of open warfare involved in such a venture, in order to achieve the Kremlin's geostrategic goals.

The Chernobyl crisis of 1986 showcased the humanitarian and ecological consequences of the world's greatest nuclear accident to date. It symbolized the arrogance of humankind in handling nuclear power, the inherent defects of Soviet technology, and the world's lack of preparation for dealing with global disasters in the context of the Cold War. The Chernobyl crisis of 2022 demonstrated the threat posed to the world by revisionist authoritarian regimes, the ease with which atoms for peace could be turned into atoms for war, and the vulnerability of nuclear sites to military takeover.

The story of the Russian occupation of the Chornobyl nuclear power plant tells a lot about today's Russia and Ukraine. It explains the reasons why Russia failed to conquer a newly independent country, which did not collapse in the first weeks of warfare, as many had expected. It explains the "Ukrainian miracle" as a phenomenon produced by citizens united across ethnic and religious lines and determined to defend their dignity and way of life. With no clear laws and very few instructions or regulations to guide them, the operators, engineers, military personnel, and kitchen staff at the Chernobyl station had to make decisions on the fly. This meant rethinking and testing their identities and loyalties while protecting themselves, their country, and the world from the occurrence of another nuclear accident at Chernobyl. They managed to outsmart their captors and turn the tables on them in a dangerous game of nuclear blackmail.

Why did the Russians bring the war to the nuclear sites? They did that to achieve their geostrategic goals while showing complete disregard for the health and lives of their soldiers, to say nothing of legal norms and their country's international obligations. Their main target in the war was Kyiv, so to get there they not only did what the Germans undertook back in 1914 by attacking France from the territory of Belgium—in the Russian case it was the territory of Belarus—but they also used the Chernobyl Exclusion Zone, unprotected by the Ukrainian army, to make their way to the Ukrainian capital. In preparing the attack, the Russian top commanders made plans for the takeover of the Chernobyl nuclear power plant either by threatening the use of force or using it if the defenders refused to surrender.

The official explanation for the takeover of the Chernobyl station given by the occupiers was the need to control the site to avoid provocations from Ukrainian nationalists. That explanation fit the general narrative of the Russian war on Ukraine: the liberation of the Ukrainians from nationalists and Nazis. After being silent on the day of the takeover of Chernobyl, the Russian media subsequently admitted the capture of the station, assuming in that way the responsibility of the Russian government for what had happened and would be happening at the station. Not having any expertise to run the plant, and dependent on the cooperation of the Ukrainian personnel to avoid a nuclear accident that first and foremost would affect the Russian military operations in the area, the Russian commanders made almost every effort possible not to alienate further the kidnapped personnel of the station. It worked only to a degree, as the rejection of the Russian occupation and hatred toward the occupiers on the part of the Ukrainian personnel grew in intensity and became more and more visible with every passing day of the occupation.

As the "special military operation" turned into all-out war, the occupiers started to use the Chernobyl station as a nuclear shelter—a place immune to the Ukrainian attacks because of the danger of a nuclear accident, and for that reason suited as a base for the Russian operations in the area. The Russians also started to turn the station into a fortress, establishing firing positions and digging fortifications in some of the most contaminated areas of the zone. At the Zaporizhia nuclear power plant they mined some of the facilities and used the station and its environs to launch artillery and missile attacks on Ukrainian targets, including on urban areas. They tried, with different degrees of success, to switch both nuclear sites from the Ukrainian electric grid to the grid controlled by Russia, and in the case of Zaporizhia not only to steal electricity produced by the nuclear power plant but also to claim ownership of the plant itself.

What started as a disregard for the values of human life and nuclear safety rules ended with attacks on the nuclear sites, hijacking of the personnel, use of the nuclear power plants as bases for military operations and even firing positions, and theft of the electricity and nuclear facilities. The Ukrainian government deemed these actions acts of nuclear terrorism and repeatedly warned the world about the Russian plans to cause a nuclear accident at the Zaporizhia nuclear power plant to achieve military advantage on the front line. Such warnings became especially credible after the Russian troops blew up the Kakhovka dam, causing ecological catastrophe and endangering the supply of water to the Zaporizhia nuclear power plant. With the destruction of the Kakhovka dam, the purposeful act of nuclear terrorism causing another nuclear accident became more likely than ever.

The Russian occupation of the Chernobyl and Zaporizhia nuclear power plants should serve as a wake-up call to the world, showing how unprepared we all are to deal with acts of nuclear terrorism perpetrated by a major nuclear power. The main characters in this book, the staff of the Chernobyl nuclear power plant, found themselves pioneers in managing unexpected dangers of the nuclear age. They had to deal with an attack that was not only illegal under international and domestic law but also difficult if not impossible to imagine, either by them or by leaders of governments and international organizations. In dealing with the crisis they had to manage with little guidance or help from their own government or the international community, whose efforts did not produce the results they wanted and expected.

Why the leadership of the International Atomic Energy Agency refused to name the Russian Federation as an aggressor and demand the withdrawal of Russian troops from a nuclear site was a question on the mind of many Ukrainians during the first weeks of the war. There were several reasons why the IAEA took the position it did. The agency's public stance of neutrality was not only in line with the long-established policy of international institutions toward their members and sponsors but also kept the door open for negotiations. Rafael Grossi's travels to both Kyiv and Moscow may have had a positive influence on developments at Chernobyl and, later, at Zaporizhia. But there are also good reasons to argue that by not calling a spade a spade and refusing to demand action from Russia, the IAEA failed not just Ukraine but the international community as well.

One of the central problems revealed by the Chernobyl crisis was the inability of the IAEA to influence the behavior of one of its key members. The core of the problem was not the position taken by Rafael Grossi as director general of the IAEA or the actions of the agency's bureaucracy. Aside from Grossi's public statements, he had shown that he was personally courageous, leading IAEA missions to the Zaporizhia nuclear plant in spite of direct threats to his life and the lives of his employees. The problem lay much deeper than the rhetoric employed or actions undertaken by leaders of international organizations. It consisted in the lack of mandate and resources of the IAEA or any other international institution in dealing with military aggression against nuclear sites.

The reasons for the IAEA's failure to prevent or terminate Russia's hostile takeover of Ukrainian nuclear sites boil down to the following. At present we lack effective legal instruments that could stop aggressors from targeting such sites. There are no international treaties dealing specifically with military attacks on nuclear power plants. Existing treaties prohibiting warfare on nuclear sites treat their power-generating facilities as if they were no more dangerous than dams and dikes. The most important such treaty, an additional protocol to the Geneva Conventions on the conduct of war, dates from the late 1970s and has huge loopholes, permitting an aggressor to get away with an attack on a nuclear site if it is perceived to be assisting the enemy.[6]

There is little doubt that the war in Ukraine exposed major problems with the international legal order and demonstrated the inability of international organizations to protect the nuclear sites. By doing that, it delivered one more blow to the prestige of nuclear energy, highlighting the vulnerability of reactors in conditions of conventional warfare and the inability of the international community to prevent another nuclear catastrophe, caused this time by deliberate military attack. Unless nuclear reactors are protected from attack in wartime, there can be no serious consideration of nuclear energy as a solution to the problem of climate change. Nuclear power would instead solidify its reputation as a terminator of human life and an agent of ecocide.

The Chernobyl crisis of 1986 produced an international reaction that contributed to the signing of a number of important agreements strengthening international cooperation and control over the nuclear industry. In the USSR, the disaster contributed to the rise of democratic movements that established public control of nuclear power in a number of post-Soviet republics. What will be the outcome of the Chernobyl crisis of 2022 and the continuing occupation of the Zaporizhia nuclear power plant? For now, the response is mixed. While some countries, such as Germany, have stayed the course and divested themselves fully of nuclear energy, others, such as France, have decided to increase their reliance on nuclear power. The Chernobyl and Zaporizhia crises notwithstanding, global interest in the nuclear industry has increased owing to Europe's renunciation of energy imports from Russia.

What has been absent so far in the variety of international responses to Chernobyl II is any concentrated effort to rethink the international legal order and reform the International Atomic Energy Agency to make it capable of reacting in a timely and effective manner to crises such as the one recounted here. We need reform of both legal and institutional frameworks to prevent acts of war against nuclear sites. Such actions must incur the severest possible punishment. If the world is to survive, it must make warfare against nuclear sites as much a taboo as the use of nuclear weapons became after Hiroshima and Nagasaki.

ACKNOWLEDGMENTS

Many people helped me to research and write this book, sometimes not fully understanding what they were doing. For a long time I myself did not realize that my interest in what was going on at Chernobyl during the Russian occupation of the site would lead to this book.

My meeting in Vienna in May 2022 with Sergii Mirnyi, a former Chernobyl cleanup worker and founder of "Chornobyl University," a Chornobyl Tour program designed to train tour guides, put me on the road leading to this book. Sergii was not only the first to tell me about the Chornobyl Tour camera working in the Chernobyl zone during the Russian invasion but also warned me to be cautious in assessing media reports about levels of irradiation of Russian soldiers in the zone. The founder of the Chornobyl Tour, Yaroslav Yemelianeko, shared with me his memories about his and his colleagues' attempts to attract public attention to the dangers caused by the Russian occupation of the zone.

Nataliya Gumenyuk, daughter of a Ukrainian nuclear engineer, a prominent Ukrainian journalist and a key figure behind "The Reckoning Project: Ukraine Testifies," organized by journalists to document war crimes, alerted me to the project's program of interviewing witnesses to the Russian occupation of the Chernobyl exclusion zone. I am extremely grateful to Nataliya and her colleagues Oleksiy Radynski and Lyuba Knorozok for allowing me to use interviews conducted by project participants for this book. I am also grateful to Oleksiy, who took most of those interviews, for sharing with me the first drafts of his articles on the subject and giving me an opportunity to view his film *Chornobyl 22*, which is referenced in this book. Oleksiy also was one of the readers of the book manuscript and made excellent suggestions on how to improve it.

As always, my wife, Olena, read numerous versions of the manuscript and helped to improve it with her comments and advice. Special thanks go to Myroslav Yurkevich, who once again did an excellent job of editing my writing. A fellowship offered by the Slavic and Eurasian Center at Hokkaido University in Sapporo, Japan, gave me time to complete and revise the manuscript. I am especially grateful to the center's director, Motoki Nomachi, and professors David Wolff and Yoko Aoshima, for making my stay at the center both pleasant and productive.

At the Wylie Literary Agency, Sarah Chalfant and Emma Smith supported the idea of the book from the very start and helped me convince my wonderful publishers, Casiana Ionita at Allen Lane/Penguin and John Glusman at W. W. Norton, to adjust their editing and publishing schedules to accommodate it. I am very grateful to them both for allowing it to appear shortly after the publication of my *Russo-Ukrainian War*.

Finally, my gratitude goes to the main characters of this book—the men and women of the Chernobyl Nuclear Power Plant, who did all they could to ensure that while Chernobyl returned to world headlines in 2022, it never came back in the same disastrous way as in 1986. They bought us time to learn, think, and react. The rest depends on us.

NOTES

1. Countdown

1. Yaroslav Yemelianenko, Facebook page, January 18, 2022, www.facebook.com/yaroslav.chernobyltour.
2. Amanda Macias, "Biden talks with European leaders as situation at Ukraine-Russia border deteriorates," CNBC, January 24, 2022; "Ukraine—Level 4: Do Not Travel," US Embassy in Ukraine, https://ua.usembassy.gov/ukraine-level-4-do-not-travel-2/.
3. Yaroslav Yemelianenko, Facebook page, January 24, 2022, www.facebook.com/yaroslav.chernobyltour.
4. Shane Harris, Karen DeYoung, Isabelle Khurshudyan, Ashley Parker, and Liz Sly, "Road to war: U.S. struggled to convince allies, and Zelensky, of risk of invasion," *Washington Post*, August 16, 2022.
5. Harris et al., "Road to war."
6. Kateryna Liubezna, "Zelensky in Glasgow told about two 'eco-bombs' and Ukraine's goals in combating climate change," *Suspil'ne Krym*, November 2, 2021, https://crimea.suspilne.media/en/news/6045; "Priroda v Chernobyle vosstanavlivaetsia namnogo bystree—Zelenskii," *Bagnet*, November 2, 2021, www.bagnet.org/news/society/1321888/priroda-v-chernobyle-vosstanavlivaetsya-namnogo-bystree-zelenskiy.
7. "Chornobyl' maie staty zonoiu vidrodzhennia–Zelens'kyi," *Ukrinform*, June 7, 2021, www.ukrinform.ua/rubric-tourism/3260200-cornobil-mae-stati-zonou-vidrodzenna-zelenskij.html.
8. "Ukraïna perekyne na kordon z Bilorussiu dodatkovi 8,5 tysiach sylovykiv," *Ievropeis'ka pravda*, November 11, 2021, www.eurointegration.com.ua/news/2021/11/11/7130165/.
9. Andrew Roth, "Belarus escorts hundreds of migrants towards Polish border," *The Guardian*, November 8, 2021; "Kolejna próba sforsowania granicy. Strzały pod Białowieżą," *Kraj*, November 11, 2021, www.rp.pl/kraj/art19095101-kolejna-proba-sforsowania-granicy-strzaly-pod-bialowieza.
10. Margaret Besheer, "Western Nations Condemn Belarus at UN Security Council," *Voice of America*, November 11, 2021.

11. Mariia Avdieieva and Yurii Panchenko, "Lukashenko pidnimaie stavky: Shcho dast' dyktatoru shantazh Briukselia khvyleiu mihrantiv," *Ievropeis'ka pravda*, November 10, 2021, www.eurointegration.com.ua/articles/2021/11/10/7130078/; "Ukraïna perekyne na kordon z Bilorussiu dodatkovi 8,5 tysiach sylovykiv."

12. Serhii Fomenko, "Aviatsiia ta 8500 viis'kovykh: U Kyïvs'kii oblasti ukripliuiut' kordon z Bilorussiu," *Depo Kyïv*, November 25, 2021, https://kyiv.depo.ua/ukr/kyiv/aviatsiya-ta-8500-viyskovikh-u-kiivskiy-oblasti-ukriplyuyut-kordon-z-bilorussyu-foto-video-202111251394776; Andrii Statsiuk, "Chornobyl's'ka zona ta AES. Chy hotovi vony do mozhlyvoho viis'kovoho vtorhnennia," *Suspil'ne Novyny*, February 14, 2022, https://suspilne.media/206675-cornobilska-zona-ta-aes-ci-gotovi-voni-do-mozlivogo-vijskovogo-vtorgnenna/.

13. David Batashvili, "Geostrategic Activities," *Rondeli Russian Military Digest*, no. 118 (January 24–30, 2022), https://web.archive.org/web/20220205173445/https://www.gfsis.org/russian-monitor/view/3121; "Russian Hybrid Threats Report: Troops arrive in Belarus as propaganda narratives heat up," Digital Forensic Research Lab, Atlantic Council, January 21, 2022.

14. "Russian forces arrive in Belarus for joint military drills," Reuters, January 17, 2022; "Allied Resolve 2022 Exercise: Russia Brings Troops from Far East to Belarus," SLDinfo.com, January 23, 2022, https://sldinfo.com/2022/01/allied-resolve-2022-exercise-russia-brings-troops-from-far-east-to-belarus/; Zachary Basu, "U.S. warns Russia may attack Ukraine from Belarus," *Axios*, January 18, 2022.

15. Harris et al., "Road to war."

16. "Defend Chernobyl During an Invasion? Why Bother, Some Ukrainians Ask," *New York Times*, January 22, 2022.

17. "Defend Chernobyl During an Invasion?"

18. Oleksandra Komisarova, "Rieznikov: My ne sposterihaiemo formuvannia udarnykh hrup u Bilorusiï ta Rosiï," *Suspil'ne Novyny*, February 3, 2022, https://suspilne.media/203539-reznikov-mi-ne-sposterigaemo-formuvanna-udarnih-grup-u-bilorusii-ta-rosii/.

19. Ian Berrell, Will Stewart, and Chris Pleasance, "Ukraine bares its teeth in CHERNOBYL: Troops practice fighting off invasion in training exercises in the abandoned city of Pripyat where radiation levels are still deadly 35 years after disaster," *Mail Online*, February 4, 2022.

20. Valera Mironenko, "Ukrainskie voennye nachali obstrelivat' Pripiat," YouTube, www.youtube.com/watch?v=oMYniqMwMhE.

21. Berrell et al., "Ukraine bares its teeth in CHERNOBYL."

22. Yaroslav Yemelianenko, Facebook page, February 4, 2022, www.facebook.com/yaroslav.chernobyltour; Lala Tarapakina, Facebook page, February 10, 2022, www.facebook.com/lalatarapakina.

23. Bill Chappell, "Russia holds a massive military exercise with Belarus, raising concerns in Ukraine," NPR, February 10, 2022.

24. Tara John, Adrienne Vogt, Melissa Macaya, and Maureen Chowdhury, "The latest on the Ukraine-Russia border crisis," CNN, February 18, 2022; "Za 4 kilometra vid kordonu Ukraïny cherez richku Pryp'iat' u Bilorusi rozhornuly pontonnyi mist," *Inform Napalm*, February 16, 2022, https://informnapalm.org/ua/v-4-km-vid-kordonu-ukrainy/?fbclid=IwAR3YDx6HmTyz4LPRiO-PP5Yve_

USkGMiawiWM4X_wE9rzQ4uo1mzI-7AiXM; Verkhovna rada Ukraïny, Zasidannia 5, February 18, 2022, www.rada.gov.ua/meeting/stenogr/show/7959 .html.

25. "U Zelenskogo znali, chto rossiiane zashli v Chernobyl'skuiu zonu esche do shturma," *Kommentarii.ua*, May 18, 2022, https://kyiv.comments.ua/news/ politics/domestic-policy/9922-u-zelenskogo-znali-chto-rossiyane-zashli-v -chernobylskuyu-zonu-esche-do-shturma.html; Verkhovna rada Ukraïny, Zasidannia 5, February 18, 2022.

26. Derzhavne ahenstvo Ukraïny z upravlinnia zonoiu vidchuzhennia, February 19, 2022, www.facebook.com/dazv.gov.ua; "Russia and Belarus extend military drills amid Ukraine tensions," Al Jazeera, February 20, 2022.

27. David Martin and Melissa Quinn, "U.S. has intel that Russian commanders have orders to proceed with Ukraine invasion," *CBS News*, February 20, 2022.

2. Exclusion Zone

1. Serhii Plokhy, *Chornobyl: History of a Tragedy* (London, 2018); Serhii Plokhy, *Atoms and Ashes: A Global History of Nuclear Disasters* (New York, 2022).

2. "Chornobyl Radiation and Ecological Biosphere Reserve," Chernobyl R&D Institute, https://dazv.gov.ua/en; http://chornobyl.institute/en/news/2020/08/04/65/ view; https://chernobyl-tour.com/english/.

3. Chornobyl'ska AES. Struktura pidpryiemstva, DSP CHAES [Specialised State Enterprise "Chornobyl nuclear power plant"] 2023, https://chnpp.gov.ua/ua/ about/struktura-pidpryiemstva.

4. Volodymyr Shovkoshytnyi, *Chornobyl': ia bachyv* (Kyiv, 2019), 304–5.

5. Plokhy, *Chernobyl*, 341–42; Paulina Deda, "Chernobyl's $1.7B nuclear confinement shelter revealed after taking 9 years to complete," *FOX News*, July 3, 2019.

6. Shovkoshytnyi, *Chornobyl'*, 307.

7. "Chornobyl'ska AES. Struktura pidpryiemstva"; Hanna Chornous, "Chornobyl' i ioho maibutnie. Rai dlia 'zelenoï' ekonomiky, zapovidnyk, chy turystychna meka," *BBC News Ukraine*, April 26, 2019.

8. Brandon Specktor, "Chernobyl's nuclear fuel is 'smoldering' again and could explode," *Live Science*, May 14, 2021; Chornous, "Chornobyl' i ioho maibutnie."

9. Trevor English, "First Spent Nuclear Fuel from Chernobyl Is Safely Stored After 34 Years," *Interesting Engineering*, December 24, 2020; "Nuclear Power in Ukraine (updated January 2023)," World Nuclear Association, https://world -nuclear.org/information-library/country-profiles/countries-t-z/ukraine.aspx; "Promyslovyi kompleks z povodzhennia z tverdymy radioaktyvnymy vidkhodamy," DSP CHAES. Chornobyl'ska AES. September 5, 2022, https://chnpp .gov.ua/ua/185-2011-11-16-11-58-26/zaversheni-proekty/29-2010-09-13-07-24 -4929.

10. Ukaz Prezydiï Verkhovnoï Rady Ukraïns'koï RSR pro prysvoiennia naimenuvannia mistu, shcho buduiet'sia v Chernihivs'kii oblasti," 1987, https://zakon.rada .gov.ua/laws/show/3617-11#Text; "Slavutych tvoryt' maibutnie," Slavutyts'ka mis'ka hromada, https://web.archive.org/web/20071213003823/http://www .e-slavutich.gov.ua/; Iryna Kremenovs'ka, "Podorozh do Nerafy. Slavutych," *Hovory!*, https://vilneslovo.com/%D0%BF%D0%BE%D0%B4%D0%BE%D1% 80%D0%BE%D0%B6-%D0%B4%D0%BE-%D0%BD%D0%B5%D1%80%D0

%B0%D1%84%D0%B8-%D1%81%D0%BB%D0%B0%D0%B2%D1%83%D1%82%D0%B8%D1%87/.

11. Vadym Aristov, "Dnipro-Slavutych," *Ruthenica* 14 (2017): 215–17, chrome-extension://efaidnbmnnnibpcajpcglclefindmkaj/https://ekmair.ukma.edu.ua/server/api/core/bitstreams/02995d68-6eda-44c3-9410-ed569ed8a1c5/content.

12. Vseukraïns'kyi perepys naselennia, 2001, http://2001.ukrcensus.gov.ua/results/general/nationality/kyiv/; Leonid Kapeliushnyi, "Desit' let s Chernobylem," *Izvestiia*, April 24, 1996; Anna Balakir, " 'V odin moment iz Slavuticha vyekhalo 6 tysiach chelovek,'—kak zhivet gorod rabotnikov ChAĖS," *Gazeta.ua*, April 19, 2017, https://gazeta.ua/ru/articles/reportage/_v-odin-moment-iz-slavuticha-vyehalo-6-tysyach-chelovek-kak-zhivet-gorod-rabotnikov-caes/767209; "Reportazh s Chernobyl'skoi AĖS: godovshchina avarii, voina, pomoshch MAGATE," *Novosti OON*, April 26, 2022, https://news.un.org/ru/story/2022/04/1422642.

13. "Slavutych tvoryt' maibutnie"; "Vsesoiuznaia perepis' naseleniia 1989 g.," *Demoskop*, www.demoscope.ru/weekly/ssp/sng89_reg2.php.

14. "U Slavutychi pereimenuvaly kvartaly, sproiektovani rosiianamy," *Khmarochos*, July 27, 2022, https://hmarochos.kiev.ua/2022/07/27/u-slavutychi-perejmenuvaly-kvartaly-sproyektovani-rosiyanamy/.

15. "Zasidannia vykonavchoho komitetu," *TV MediaDim Slavutych*, February 16, 2022, www.facebook.com/100063654212599/videos/498079725252986.

16. "President: Today, the people of Ukraine must show unity and confidence in their state," President of Ukraine, February 14, 2022, www.president.gov.ua/en/news/prezident-ukrayinskij-narod-sogodni-maye-pokazati-yednist-i-72897#:~:text=In%20order%20to%20strengthen%20the,2022%20the%20Day%20of%20Unity; Darya Korsunskaya and Natalia Zinets, "Ukraine president calls for 'day of unity' for Feb. 16, day some believe Russia could invade," Reuters, February 16, 2022.

17. "Zasidannia vykonavchoho komitetu."

18. "Zasidannia vykonavchoho komitetu."

3. Invasion

1. Roman Romaniuk, "From Zelenskyy's 'surrender' to Putin's surrender: How the negotiations with Russia are going," *Ukraïns'ka pravda*, May 5, 2022, www.pravda.com.ua/eng/articles/2022/05/5/7344096/.

2. "Zelensky's full speech at Munich Security Conference," *Kyiv Independent*, February 19, 2022.

3. "Putin: Ukraine's threat to develop nuclear weapons not an empty bravado," TASS, February 21, 2022; Georgiy Erman, "Mozhet li Ukraina vernut' sebe iadernoe oruzhie? I vo chto ėto oboidetsia?" *BBC News, Russian Service*, February 22, 2022.

4. "Address by the President of the Russian Federation," President of Russia, February 21, 2022, http://en.kremlin.ru/events/president/news/67828.

5. "Na Ukraine raskryli skhemu bystrogo sozdaniia atomnoi bomby Kievom," *RIA Novosti*, February 23, 2022, https://ria.ru/20220223/skhema-1774566379.html?in=t.

6. "Mizhnarodnyi den' ridnoï movy u Slavutychi," *TV MediaDim Slavutych*, February 23, 2022, www.facebook.com/100063654212599/videos/501975491137960606.

7. "Fomichev Iurii Kyrylovych. Mis'kyi holova Slavutycha," *LB.ua*, March 28, 2022, https://lb.ua/file/person/5208_fomichev_yuriy_kirilovich.html; "Dos'e: Udovichenko Vladimir Petrovich," *KyivVlada*, July 23, 2021, https://kievvlast.com.ua/base/dose-udovichenko-vladimir-petrovich.

8. Dmytro Fionik, "Apokalipsys ne s'ohodni," *Liga.net*, July 23, 2022, https://projects.liga.net/apocalypse-is-not-today/; "ChAES: Okupatsiia," *Novyny ChAES*, 3 (1531), April 26, 2022, chrome-extension://efaidnbmnnnibpcajpcglclefindmkaj/https://chnpp.gov.ua/images/pdf/2022-04-26_1.pdf.

9. "Pro uchast' mis'koho holovy u forumi Bezpechni ta spromozhni hromady maibutn'oho," *TV MediaDim Slavutych*, February 23, 2022, www.facebook.com/100063654212599/videos/701584461168014; "Bezpechni, spromozhni hromady maibutn'oho," Ivankivs'ka selyshchna rada Vyshhorods'koho raionu Kyïvs'koï oblasti, February 21, 2022, https://ivankiv-gromada.gov.ua/ua/news/667.

10. "Putin ob'iavil o nachale voennoi operatsii v Donbasse. Vot rasshifrovka ego rechi," *Bumaga*, February 24, 2022, https://paperpaper.ru/putin-obyavil-o-nachale-voennoj-operac/; "Putin postoianno ugrozhaet miru iadernym oruzhiem," *Meduza*, September 22, 2022, https://meduza.io/feature/2022/09/22/putin-postoyanno-ugrozhaet-miru-yadernym-oruzhiem-a-ved-kogda-to-on-podpisyval-dogovor-o-sokraschenii-chisla-boegolovok.

11. Michael Schwirtz, Anton Troianovski, Yousur Al-Hlou, Masha Froliak, Adam Entous, and Thomas Gibbons-Neff, "How Putin's War in Ukraine Became a Catastrophe for Russia," *New York Times*, December 16, 2022.

12. Schwirtz at al., "How Putin's War in Ukraine Became a Catastrophe for Russia"; Sergei Morfinov, "Kolonna, kotoraia ne proshla v Kiev," *BBC News*, February 24, 2023, www.bbc.com/russian/features-64761517.

13. Roman Kravets' and Roman Romaniuk, "Dva plany Kremlia, Khto mav keruvaty Ukraïnoiu iakby vpav Kyïv," *Ukraïns'ka pravda*, February 28, 2023, www.pravda.com.ua/articles/2023/02/28/7391273/.

14. "Rosiis'ka tekhnika pishla na proryv u Kyïvs'kii oblasti," Operatyvnyi ZSU, 6:23 a.m., February 24, 2022, https://twitter.com/operativno_ZSU/status/1496807919266013191; Oleksa Shkatov, "Radioaktyvnyi napriamok: pontonnyi mist cherez Pryp'iat' v Bilorusi prokladaie shliakh navkolo kordoniv Ukraïny," *DepoKyiv*, February 17, 2022, https://kyiv.depo.ua/ukr/kyiv/radioaktivniy-napryamok-pontonniy-mist-cherez-pripyat-v-bilorusi-prokladae-shlyakh-navkolo-kordoniv-ukraini-202202171425628; "RF sporudyla pontonnyi mist cherez Pryp'iat' na kordoni z Bilorussiu: Suputnykovi znimky," *Ievropeis'ka pravda*, February 25, 2022, www.eurointegration.com.ua/news/2022/02/25/7134641/.

15. Maksim Kamenev, "Kak rossiiskie okkupanty zakhvatili ChAĖS i zonu otchuzhdeniia, a zatem bezhali, razgrabiv stantsiiu," *Ukraina kriminal'naia*, June 10, 2022, https://cripo.com.ua/main/kak-rossijskie-okkupanty-zahvatyvali-chaes-i-zonu-otchuzhdeniya-a-zatem-bezhali-razgrabiv-stantsiyu/.

16. Yaroslav Yemelianenko, Facebook page, February 23, 2022, www.facebook.com/yaroslav.chernobyltour.

17. Petro Didula, "Okupovana rosiianamy Chornobyl's'ka zona ta okopy v Rudomu

lisi—pershyi u sviti pryklad mizhnarodnoho iadernoho teroryzmu," Ukraïns'kyi katolyts'kyi universytet, July 25, 2022, https://ucu.edu.ua/news/okupovana -rosiyanamy-chornobylska-zona-ta-okopy-v-rudomu-lisi-pershyj-u-sviti-pryklad -mizhnarodnogo-yadernogo-teroryzmu-yaroslav-yemelyanenko/; Miriam Berger, "A Chernobyl tour group secretly helped track Russia's invasion," *Washington Post*, August 21, 2022.

18. Berger, "A Chernobyl tour group secretly helped track Russia's invasion"; " 'Zona sprotyvu': Chornobyl's'kyi operator orhanizuvav pidpillia navkolo okupovanoï ChAES," Tsentr natsional'noho sprotyvu, *Novyny*, July 19, 2022, https://sprotyv .mod.gov.ua/2022/07/19/zona-sprotyvu-chornobylskyj-operator-organizuvav -pidpillya-navkolo-okupovanoyi-chaes/.

19. Yaroslav Yemelianenko, Facebook page, February 24, 2022, www.facebook.com/ yaroslav.chernobyltour.

20. Anton Herashchenko, Facebook page, February 24, 2022, www.facebook.com/ anton.gerashchenko.7/posts/4864179457002196; "Tochat'sia zapekli boï u Chor- nobyl's'kii zoni—Herashchenko," *Malakava*, February 24, 2022, www.malakava .if.ua/articles/34172.

21. "Rosiia namahaiet'sia zakhopyty ChAES, tse oholoshennia viiny Ievropi— Zelens'kyi," *Panoptikon*, *Novyny Zaporizhzhia ta Zaporiz'koï oblasti*, February 24, 2022, https://panoptikon.org/ukraine/139454-rosija-namagayetsja-zahopiti -chaes-ce-ogoloshennja-vijni-yevropi-zelenskij.html.

4. Holdup

1. Joe Parkinson and Drew Hinshaw, "Inside Chernobyl, 200 Exhausted Staff Toil Round the Clock at Russian Gunpoint," *Wall Street Journal*, March 15, 2022; Olga Osipova, "Ia ostalsia na rabochem meste. Ia ne imeyu prava ego pokidat'," *Meduza*, April 1, 2022, https://meduza.io/feature/2022/04/01/ya-ostalsya-na -rabochem-meste-ya-ne-imeyu-prava-ego-pokidat; Chornobyl NPP. Chronicle of Occupation. Part 1: Beginning, www.youtube.com/watch?v=mqE8cDib3n8.

2. Oleksiy Radynski, "What Were the Russians Doing in Chernobyl?" *The Atlan- tic*, September 6, 2023; Interview with Valentyn Heiko, The Reckoning Project, 2022; Parkinson and Hinshaw, "Inside Chernobyl"; Chornobyl NPP. Chronicle of Occupation. Part 1: Beginning.

3. Interview with Valentyn Heiko, The Reckoning Project, 2022.

4. Chornobyl NPP. Chronicle of Occupation. Part 1: Beginning; Nataliia Pavlenko, "Rosiis'ki irody vlashtuvaly isteryku: Chomu do vas rytual'na sluzhba pryïkhala? Koho vy vbyly?" *Gazeta.ua*, May 5, 2022, https://gazeta.ua/articles/people-and -things-journal/_rosijski-irodi-vlashtuvali-isteriku-comu-do-vas-ritualna-sluzhba -priyihala-kogo-vi-vbili/1084325; Osipova, "Ia ostalsia na rabochem meste."

5. Chornobyl NPP. Chronicle of Occupation. Part 1: Beginning.

6. Parkinson and Hinshaw, "Inside Chernobyl"; Maksim Kamenev, "Rebiata, vy ser'ezno? Vy ponimaete kuda vy edete? Istoriia rossiiskoi okkupatsii Chernobyl'skoi atomnoi stantsii i zony otchuzhdeniia," *Graty*, June 9, 2022, https://graty.me/ rebyata-vy-serezno-vy-ponimaete-kuda-vy-edete-istoriya-rossijskoj-okkupaczii -chernobylskoj-atomnoj-stanczii-i-zony-otchuzhdeniya/; Faustine Vincent, "Cher- nobyl: The story of 35 days of Russian occupation," *Le Monde*, June 16, 2022.

7. Nataliya Gumenyuk, " 'Atomnyky taki sami liudy iak i inshi. My tezh boïmosia

bezgluzdykh liudei'—mer Slavutycha," *Suspil'ne Novyny*, September 7, 2022, https://suspilne.media/279175-atomniki-taki-sami-ak-j-insi-mi-tez-boimosa -bezgluzdih-ludej-mer-slavutica/; "Informatsiia vid mis'koho holovy Slavutycha Iu. Fomicheva na 12:30," *TV MediaDim Slavutych*, February 24, 2022, www .facebook.com/100063654212599/videos/1068880923657665; Dmytro Fionik, "Apokalipsys ne s'ohodni," Liga.net, July 23, 2022, https://projects.liga.net/ apocalypse-is-not-today/.

8. Fionik, "Apokalipsys ne s'ohodni"; Kamenev, "Rebiata, vy ser'ezno?" "Oni iskali preslovutye amerikanskie laboratorii; rabotnik ChAËS ob okupatsii," *ICTV*, May 9, 2022, www.youtube.com/watch?v=D-THwUDkiUE.

9. Stanislav Paniuta and Konstantin Karnoza, UNIAN Fotobank, https://photo .unian.net/photo/833208-stanislav-panyuta-i-konstantin-karnoza; Sofiia Bogut- skaia, "Rasprashivali pro amerikanskie bazy i o banderovtsakh. Istoriia chetyrekh sportsmenov, vyzhivshikh v okkupatsii na ChAËS," *Vikna TV*, April 26, 2023, https://vikna.tv/ru/istorii/rassprashivali-ob-amerikanskih-bazah-i-banderovczah -istoriya-chetyreh-sportsmenov-vyzhivshih-v-okkupaczii-na-chaes/; Wendell Stea- venson with Marta Rodionova, "The inside story of Chernobyl during the Russian occupation," *The Economist*, May 10, 2022.

10. Chornobyl NPP. Chronicle of Occupation. Part 1: Beginning.

11. "Pod Gostomelem razgromili kolonnu rossiiskogo spetsnaza, sredi pogibshikh— chechenskii komandir Tushaev—SBU," *Gordon.ua*, February 27, 2022, https:// gordonua.com/news/war/pod-gostomelem-razgromili-kolonnu-rossiyskogo -specnaza-1597340.html; "'Rosgvardiia' po respublike Chechnia v okrestnos- tiakh Pripiati," February 27, 2022, www.youtube.com/watch?v=zk1POhPkq088.

12. "'Zadachei byla okhrana ulits i perekrestkov Kieva,' Sotrudniki Rosgvardii dali pokazaniia po odnomu iz ugolovnykh del," *Meduza*, May 23, 2022, https:// meduza.io/feature/2022/05/23/zadachey-byla-ohrana-ulits-i-perekrestkov -kieva; "Prisoner of war of the Russian Federation—Spiridonov Evgeny Viktoro- vich," *Russoldat.info*, https://russoldat.info/voenoplennyj-rf-spiridonov-evgenij-v/; "Magomed Tushaev: 'Ia tot, kogo 'truslivye zaitsy' v internete nazvali mertvym,'" *Chechnia segodnia*, March 13, 2022, https://chechnyatoday.com/news/353808; "Ogii stal geroem Kuzbassa," *Kuzpress*, January 25, 2023, https://kuzpress.ru/ society/25-01-2023/92808.html.

13. Interview with Valerii Semenov, The Reckoning Project, 2022; interview with Valentyn Heiko, The Reckoning Project, 2022; Radynski, "What Were the Rus- sian Doing in Chernobyl?"

14. "Komandir rosgvardeitsev rasskazal o vziatii pod kontrol' Chernobyl'skoi AËS bez edinogo vystrela," *NTV programma: segodnia*, Aleksandr Konevich, March 27, 2022, www.ntv.ru/video/2102851/; "Oni iskali preslovutye amerikanskie labora- torii;" Interview with Valerii Semenov, The Reckoning Project, 2022; interview with Oleksandr Kalishuk, The Reckoning Project, 2022.

15. "Komandir rosgvardeitsev rasskazal o vziatii pod kontrol' Chernobyl'skoi AËS bez edinogo vystrela"; "Stavshie geroiami Rossii rosgvardeitsy raskryli podrobnosti provedennoi spetsoperatsii," *Izvestiia*, May 20, 2022, https://iz.ru/1337526/2022 -05-20/stavshie-geroiami-rossii-rosgvardeitcy-raskryli-podrobnosti-provedennoi -spetcoperatcii; Steavenson with Rodionova, "The inside story of Chernobyl dur- ing the Russian occupation."

16. Katerina Abrashina, "Na ChAES ustanovili pamitnik likvidatoru Lelechenko," *Vesti.ua*, April 23, 2021, https://vesti.ua/strana/na-chernobylskoj-aes-ustanovili -pamyatnik-likvidatoru-lelechenko-foto.

17. Chornobyl NPP. Chronicle of Occupation. Part 1: Beginning; interview with Oleksandr Kalishuk, The Reckoning Project, 2022.

18. Steavenson with Rodionova, "The inside story of Chernobyl during the Russian occupation"; Parkinson and Hinshaw, "Inside Chernobyl"; "Chornobyl' pid chas viiny. Okupanty mohly sprovokuvaty novu trahediiu," *Ochi*, April 26, 2022, www .youtube.com/watch?v=B6HmtSBVq-U; Chornobyl NPP. Chronicle of Occupation. Part 1: Beginning; interview with Valerii Semenov, The Reckoning Project, 2022.

19. Interview with Oleksandr Kalishuk, The Reckoning Project, 2022; Mari Saito and Maria Tsvetkova, "The Enemy Within," Reuters, July 28, 2022; Fionik, "Apokalipsys ne s'ohodni."

20. Chornobyl NPP. Chronicle of Occupation. Part 1: Beginning; Saito and Tsvetkova, "The Enemy Within"; Pavlenko, " 'Rosiis'ki irody vlashtuvaly isteryku.' "

21. Chornobyl NPP. Chronicle of Occupation. Part 1: Beginning; "Komandir rosgvardeitsev rasskazal o vziatii pod kontrol Chernobyl'skoi AĖS bez edinogo vystrela"; Rossiiskoe obshchestvo Znanie, Prosvetitel'skii marafon "Znanie o geroiakh," 5:40; Pavlenko, " 'Rosiis'ki irody vlashtuvaly isteryku.' "

22. Chornobyl NPP. Chronicle of Occupation. Part 1: Beginning.

23. Interview with Valentyn Heiko, The Reckoning Project, 2022.

24. Radynski, "What Were the Russians Doing in Chernobyl?" Cf. Radynski, "Deja Vu in Chornobyl," The Reckoning Project, www.thereckoningproject.com/; Chornobyl NPP. Chronicle of Occupation. Part 1: Beginning; "Chornobyl' pid chas viiny. Okupanty mohly sprovokuvaty novu trahediiu"; Steavenson with Rodionova, "The inside story of Chernobyl during the Russian occupation."

25. Oleg Gorodkov, "Kak buriaty chitali Oruella i ukrali trusy u dneprovskikh stalkerov na ChAĖS," *Kust*, May 12, 2022, https://kustdnipro.com/ru/kak-buryaty -chytaly-oruella-y-ukraly-trusy-u-dneprovskyh-stalkerov-na-chaes/.

26. Rossiiskoe obshchestvo Znanie, Prosvetitel'skii marafon "Znanie o geroiakh," November 3, 2022, https://vk.com/video-135454514_456243012, 5:40; Steavenson with Rodionova, "The inside story of Chernobyl during the Russian occupation"; "Chornobyl' pid chas viiny. Okupanty mohly sprovokuvaty novu trahediiu."

27. Steavenson with Rodionova, "The inside story of Chernobyl during the Russian occupation"; "Chornobyl' pid chas viiny. Okupanty mohly sprovokuvaty novu trahediiu."

28. Interview with Valentyn Heiko, The Reckoning Project, 2022.

29. Iuliia Mamoilenko, "Sytuatsiia na kordoni z Bilorussiu znovu nebezpechna— interv'iu z nachal'nykom Chornobyl's'koï zony," *S'ohodni*, July 7, 2022, www .segodnya.ua/ua/strana/intervyu/maroderily-35-dney-ne-ostalos-ni-odnih -ucelevshih-dverey-v-kakom-sostoyanii-chernobyl-posle-deokkupacii-1629307 .html; Parkinson and Hinshaw, "Inside Chernoybl."

30. Bogutskaia, "Rasprashivali pro amerikanskie bazy i o banderovtsakh."

31. "Komandir rosgvardeitsev rasskazal o vziatii pod kontrol' Chernobyl'skoi AĖS bez edinogo vystrela."

32. Fionik, "Apokalipsys ne s'ohodni"; "Chornobyl' pid chas viiny. Okupanty mohly sprovokuvaty novu trahediiu"; "Frolenkov Andrei Anatol'evich," Geroi strany,

https://warheroes.ru/hero/hero.asp?Hero_id=32392; "Burakov Sergei Dmitrie-vich," Geroi strany, https://warheroes.ru/hero/hero.asp?Hero_id=32878.

33. Interview with Valentyn Heiko, The Reckoning Project, 2022; "Sergey Dmitrie-vich BURAKOV," *Open Sanctions*, https://www.opensanctions.org/entities/NK-87sQjqCeN4jXGshYRt5vPY/; "Andrey Anatolyevich FROLENKOV," *Open Sanctions*, https://www.opensanctions.org/entities/NK-JQNcwqthNfTMjeySkhqvCH/.

5. International Crisis

1. [Rafael Mariano Grossi], "Nuclear Safety, Security and Safeguards in Ukraine. Summary Report by the Director General, February 24–April 28, 2022" (Vienna, 2022), 5.

2. Derzhavna inspektsiia iadernoho rehuliuvannia Ukraïny, Facebook page, February 24, 2022, www.facebook.com/profile.php?id=100064837892613.

3. "Rafael Mariano Grossi, Director General," IAEA International Atomic Energy Agency; "La agenda nuclear internacional," Consejo Argentino para las Relaciones Internacionales, December 22, 2015, www.cari.org.ar/recursos/cronicas/nuclear22-12-15.html; Michael Hirsh, "Rafael Grossi Has a Plan to Stop Future Pandemics," *Foreign Policy*, March 24, 2021.

4. "IAEA Director General Statement on the Situation in Ukraine," IAEA Press Releases, February 24, 2022.

5. Derzhavna inspektsiia iadernoho rehuliuvannia Ukraïny, Facebook page, February 25, 2022, www.facebook.com/profile.php?id=100064837892613.

6. Derzhavna inspektsiia iadernoho rehuliuvannia Ukrainy. Facebook page, February 25, 2022.

7. "Update 1 - IAEA Director General Statement on Situation in Ukraine," IAEA Press Releases, February 25, 2022.

8. Initials of the Russian Federation deliberately lowercased to show contempt.

9. Oleksandr Lavrenchuk's comment at Derzhavna inspektsiia iadernoho rehuli-uvannia Ukraïny, Facebook page, February 24 and 25, 2022, www.facebook.com/profile.php?id=100064837892613.

10. Lara Marlowe, "What are Russia's designs on the two nuclear power plants it has seized?" *Irish Times*, March 21, 2022.

11. "Scale of Assessment of Member States' Contributions Towards the Regular Budget for 2023 (Revised)," IAEA, General Conference, chrome-extension://efaidnbmnnnibpcajpcglclefindmkaj/https://www.iaea.org/sites/default/files/gc/gc66-11_0.pdf; "Head of the Department of Nuclear Energy," IAEA, Organizational Structure.

12. "Greenpeace calls for IAEA to suspend deputy over ties to Russian state nuclear energy corporation," Greenpeace, Press Releases, Energy, March 15, 2022; "Switzerland demands Russian UN nuclear official be debarred," *Daily Sabah*, April 21, 2022, www.dailysabah.com/world/europe/switzerland-demands-russian-un-nuclear-official-be-debarred.

13. Derzhavna inspektsiia iadernoho rehuliuvannia Ukraïny, Facebook page, February 27, 2022, www.facebook.com/profile.php?id=100064837892613; David Dalton, "European Regulators Call for Russia to Hand Back Control of Nuclear Facilities," *NucNet, the Independent Nuclear News Agency*, March 4, 2022.

14. "Rossiiskie voennye v Chernobyle i vseobshchaia mobilizatsiia," TASS, February

25, 2022; Channel One Russia, "Novosti," February 26, 2022, www.1tv.ru/news/issue/2022-02-26/18:00#1.

15. Channel One Russia, "Novosti," February 26, 2022.

16. Rustam Abdullin, "V Gomele zhdut Zelenskogo na peregovory 'khotia by do kontsa dnia' i ne ponimaiut, pochemu on ne edet," *AfishaDaily*, February 27, 2022, https://daily.afisha.ru/news/60440-v-gomele-zhdut-zelenskogo-na-peregovory-hotya-by-do-konca-dnya-i-ne-ponimayut-pochemu-on-ne-edet/; "Peregovory Rossii i Ukrainy v Belarusi. Pripiat'. Podgotovka k peregovoram. Priamoi efir," Informatsionnoe agentstvo BelTA, February 28, 2022, www.youtube.com/watch?v=vBCSsZsvW_8.

17. "Press-sekretar Zelenskogo poiasnil prichinu otkaza Ukrainy ot peregovorov v Gomele," *Interfax*, February 27, 2022, www.interfax.ru/world/824915; "Podoliak pro perehovory z RF v Homeli: Ukraïna katehorychno vidmovylasia vid ul'tymatumiv," *Kurs Ukraïny*, February 27, 2022, https://kurs.com.ua/novost/793462-podoljak-o-peregovorah-s-rf-v-gomele-ukraina-kategoricheski-otkazalas-ot-ultimatumov.

18. "GosSMI skryvali, chto peregovory proidut v rezidentsii Lukashenko, no vse ravno proboltalis'," *The Village*, February 28, 2022, www.the-village.me/village/city/news-city/291649-ont-skryvalo; "Liaskovichi. Pripiatskii natspark," https://ekskursii.by/?Goroda_Belarusi=470_Lyaskovichi_Pripyatskiy_nacpark.

19. Joe Parkinson and Drew Hinshaw, "Inside Chernobyl, 200 Exhausted Staff Toil Round the Clock at Russian Gunpoint," *Wall Street Journal*, March 15, 2022; "Bez bud'-iakykh obov'iazkovykh ul'tymatumiv,"—Podoliak pro perehovory z Rosiieiu shchodo zakinchennia viiny proty Ukraïny," TSN, February 28, 2022, https://tsn.ua/politika/peregovori-vazhki-podolyak-pro-peregovori-z-rosiyeyu-schodo-zakinchennya-viyni-prot-ukrayini-1992274.html.

20. Parkinson and Hinshaw, "Inside Chernobyl"; Chornobyl NPP. Chronicle of Occupation. Part 1: Beginning, www.youtube.com/watch?v=mqE8cDib3n8; Halyna Vorona, "U Buchi znyshchyly kolonu vorozhoï tekhniky-video vid mera Fedoruka," Big Kyiv, February 28, 2022, https://bigkyiv.com.ua/u-buchi-znyshhyly-kolonu-vorozhoyi-tehniky-video-vid-mera-fedoruka/.

21. Marta Kushka, "V Buche ne tolko podniali flag, no i vosstanovili elektroenergiiu," 24 Kanal, March 3, 2022, https://24tv.ua/ru/buche-ne-tolko-podnjali-flag-vosstanovili-jelektrojenergiju_n1888765.

22. Chernobyl Nuclear Power Plant, Facebook page, March 1, 2022, www.facebook.com/ChornobylNPP/posts/256145750039647/; Tetiana Vorzhko, "Personal vysnazhenyi, sytuatsiia—nebezpechna. Shcho vidbuvaiet'sia na ChAES," Voice of America, March 1, 2022.

23. Chernobyl Nuclear Power Plant, Facebook page, March 1, 2022.

24. Maksim Kamenev, "Rebiata, vy ser'ezno? Vy ponimaete kuda vy edete? Istoriia rossiiskoi okkupatsii Chernobyl'skoi atomnoi stantsii i zony otchuzhdeniia," *Graty*, June 9, 2022, https://graty.me/rebyata-vy-serezno-vy-ponimaete-kuda-vy-edete-istoriya-rossijskoj-okkupaczii-chernobylskoj-atomnoj-stanczii-i-zony-otchuzhdeniya/.

25. Derzhavna inspektsiia iadernoho rehuliuvannia Ukraïny, Facebook page, March 1, 2022, www.facebook.com/profile.php?id=100064837892613.

26. Derzhavna inspektsiia iadernoho rehuliuvannia Ukraïny, March 1, 2022.

27. [Grossi], "Nuclear Safety, Security and Safeguards in Ukraine," 24; "Update 5 -

IAEA Director General Statement on Situation in Ukraine," IAEA Press Releases, March 1, 2022.

28. "The IAEA Board of Governors in Vienna adopted a Resolution on nuclear safety, security and safeguards in Ukraine," National Atomic Energy Agency (Poland), March 3, 2022, www.gov.pl/web/paa-en/the-iaea-board-of-governors-in-vienna -adopted-a-resolution-on-nuclear-safety-security-and-safeguards-in-ukraine.

29. "Update 6 - IAEA Director General Statement on Situation in Ukraine," IAEA Press Releases, March 2, 2022; "Update 7 - IAEA Director General Statement on Situation in Ukraine," IAEA Press Releases, March 2, 2022; "IAEA Director General's Introductory Statement to the Board of Governors," March 2, 2022.

30. [Grossi], "Nuclear Safety, Security and Safeguards in Ukraine," 5, 13; "Spil'ne zvern-ennia shchodo faktu zakhoplennia zbroinymy formuvanniamy RF Chornobyl's'koï AES," *Holos Ukraïny*, March 3, 2022, www.golos.com.ua/article/356717.

31. IAEA Board of Governors, "The Safety, Security and Safeguards Implications of the Situation in Ukraine," Resolution adopted on March 3, 2022, during the 1613th Session, chrome-extension://efaidnbmnnnibpcajpcglclefindmkaj/https:// www.iaea.org/sites/default/files/22/03/gov2022-17.pdf; "The IAEA Board of Governors in Vienna Adopted a Resolution"; Francois Murphy, "IAEA board 'deplores' Russian invasion of Ukraine, only two votes against," Reuters, March 3, 2022.

32. "Spil'ne zvernennia shchodo faktu zakhoplennia zbroinymy formuvanniamy RF Chornobyl's'koï AES."

6. God's Grace

1. "Ukraine asks IAEA for 30km safe zones around nuclear plants," *World Nuclear News*, March 1, 2022.

2. "Zaporizhzhia: boï za Melitopol', rosiiany pid Berdians'kom i oboronni sporudy pid oblasnym tsentrom," *Radio Svoboda*, February 25, 2022, https://web.archive .org/web/20220227141127/https://www.radiosvoboda.org/a/news-berdiansk -rosiyski-viyskovi/31723154.html; "Rossiiskie zakhvatchiki gotoviat shturm Kieva i nastuplenie na neskol'kikh napravleniiakh—Genshtab VSU," *Dzerkalo tyzhnia*, March 8, 2022, https://zn.ua/UKRAINE/rossijskie-zakhvatchiki-hotovjat -shturm-kieva-i-nastuplenie-po-neskolkim-napravlenijam-henshtab-vsu.html; "Komandyr 58-ï zahal'noviis'kovoï armiï pivdennoho viis'kovoho okruhu Mykhailo Zus'ko," *Bees*, December 24, 2022, https://informnapalm.org/ osintbees/2022/12/24/komandyr-58-yi-zahalnoviiskovoi-armii/.

3. "Naibil'sha v Ievropi Zaporiz'ka AES vpershe u svoii istoriï vyishla na povnu potuzh-nist'," *LB.ua*, January 15, 2021, https://web.archive.org/web/20211107190306/ https://lb.ua/economics/2021/01/15/475267_naybilsha_ievropi_zaporizka_aes .html; Vitalii Kniazhans'kyi, "Tsina vidkladenykh rishen'. Maibutnie iadernoï energetyky riasniie . . . 'bilymy pliamamy,' " *Den'*, September 7, 2017, https://web .archive.org/web/20220628055120/https://day.kyiv.ua/uk/article/ekonomika/cina -vidkladenyh-rishen; "Zaporiz'ka AES. Fil'm 'Iadernyi shantazh.' Do richnytsi okupatsiï Zaporiz'koï AES," www.youtube.com/watch?v=6_ORg-7nrbo.

4. Kamen Kraev, "Ukraine. Energoatom Shuts Down Zaporozhye-5 and -6 As Rest of Fleet Remains Safe and Operational," *NucNet, the Independent Nuclear News Agency*, February 25, 2022; "Zaporizhzhia NPP," Enerhoatom, https://web

.archive.org/web/20201027004706/; Serhii Plokhy, *Chernobyl: The History of a Nuclear Catastrophe* (New York, 2018), 301–30.

5. "Enerhodar," *Velyka ukrains'ka antsyklopediia*; 'Istoriia mista Enerhodar,' Enerhodar—misto na piskakh," https://sites.google.com/site/energodarmistonapiska/home/den-mista/malovnicij-energodar/karta-energodaru; Katia Stasenko and Anna Skorospielova, "Enerhodar vid A do Ia. Abetka nashoho mista—pro podiï, mistsia ta liudei," *EnerhodarCity*, https://energodar.city/articles/171794/energodar-vid-a-do-ya-abetka-nashogo-mista-pro-podii-miscya-ta-lyudej-; Ol'ha Zvonariova, "Dmytro Orlov, mis'kyi holova Enerhodara: V okupatsiï vidchuttia, shcho vas vidkynuly na 30 rokiv nazad," *Ukrinform*, May 24, 2022, www.ukrinform.ua/rubric-regions/3490854-dmitro-orlov-miskij-golova-energodara.html.

6. "Enerhodars'ka mis'ka rada. Rezul'taty vyboriv deputativ vid 25 zhovtnia 2015 r." Tsentral'na vyborcha komisiia, https://web.archive.org/web/20151118092533/http://www.cvk.gov.ua/wvm2015/pvm057pid112=30pid102=10960pf7691=1096optoo1fo1=100rej=optoo_too1fo1=100.html.

7. "Mis'kyi holova Pavlo Muzyka stav milionerom," *EnerhodarCity*, April 14, 2019, https://energodar.city/articles/29618/miskij-golova-pavlo-muzika-stav-miljonerom-yak-zminyuvalisya-jogo-statki-na-posadi-z-2015-po-2018-r-; Ol'ha Iakovleva, "Na vyborakh mis'koho holovy Enerhodara chynnyi holova prohrav mistsevomu aktyvistu," *Suspil'ne Novyny*, November 10, 2020, https://suspilne.media/78512-na-viborah-miskogo-golovi-energodara-cinnij-golova-prograv-miscevomu-aktivistu/.

8. Ievhen Kozlov, "Rosiis'ki viis'ka pidiishly do Enerhodaru," *Ukraïns'ka pravda*, February 27, 2022, www.pravda.com.ua/news/2022/02/27/7326530/; "Update 4 - IAEA Director General Statement on Situation in Ukraine," IAEA, February, 28, 2022; "Russian forces take control of Ukraine's Berdyansk, Enerhodar - Russian Defense Ministry," *Interfax*, February 28, 2022; "Segodnia, 28 fevralia, v Energodar popytalas' zaiti kolonna voennoi tekhniki Rossiiskoi Federatsii," *1 Pervyi zaporozhskii*, February 28, 2022, http://1news.zp.ua/ru/zhiteli-energodara-bez-oruzhiya-ostanovili-kolonnu-rossijskih-okkupantov-video/.

9. Violetta Orlova, "Ukraïns'ki viis'kovi vedut' bii z rosiis'kymy okupantamy v raioni Enerhodaru – MVS," *UNIAN*, March 1, 2022, www.unian.ua/war/ukrajinski-viyskovi-vedut-biy-z-rosiyskimi-okupantami-v-rayoni-energodaru-mvs-novini-donbasu-11724181.html.

10. "Sytuatsiia shchodo rosiis'koho vtorhnennia 2.03.2022 stanom na 18:00," Zaporoz'ka oblasna derzhavna administratsiia, Facebook page, March 3, 2022, www.facebook.com/zoda.gov.ua/posts/265209855788873; Denis Karlovskii, "Rossiiskie okkupanty ugovarivaiut pustit' ikh 'sfotografirovat'sia' na ZAES i oni uidut," *Ukraïns'ka pravda*, March 2, 2022, www.pravda.com.ua/rus/news/2022/03/2/7327550/; Zvonariova, "Dmytro Orlov, mis'kyi holova Enerhodara."

11. Ol'ha Zeniuk, "Rada oborony Enerhodara pereishla na tsilodobovyi rezhym roboty, misto v otochenni," *061 Sait mista Zaporizhzhia*, March 1, 2022, www.061.ua/news/3340996/rada-oboroni-energodara-perejsla-na-cilodobovij-rezim-roboti-misto-v-otocenni; " 'Taka hordist' bula za svoie misto.' Zhytel'ka Enerhodara rozpovila pro opir mistsevykh u pershi tyzhni okupatsiï," *Suspil'ne*, Novem-

ber 13, 2022, https://suspilne.media/315858-taka-gordist-bula-za-svoe-misto
-zitelka-energodara-rozpovila-pro-opir-miscevih-u-persi-tizni-okupacii/; Olena
Roshchina, "Zhyteli Enerhodara staly stinoiu na zakhyst mista," *Ukraïns'ka
pravda*, March 2, 2022, www.pravda.com.ua/news/2022/03/2/7327506/.

12. "'Taka hordist' bula za svoie misto.' Zhytel'ka Enerhodara rozpovila pro opir mistsevykh u pershi tyzhni okupatsiï"; Roshchina, "Zhyteli Enerhodara staly stinoiu."

13. "'Taka hordist' bula za svoie misto.' Zhytel'ka Enerhodara rozpovila pro opir
mistsevykh u pershi tyzhni okupatsiï"; Roshchina, "Zhyteli Enerhodara staly stinoiu"; "Sytuatsiia shchodo rosiis'koho vtorhnennia 2.03.2022 stanom na 18:00";
"Enerhodar: liudy ne puskaiut' kolonu RF v misto," *Militarnyi*, March 2, 2022,
https://web.archive.org/web/20220313043006/https://mil.in.ua/uk/news/
energodar-lyudy-ne-puskayut-tanky-v-misto/.

14. "'Taka hordist' bula za svoie misto.' Zhytel'ka Enerhodara rozpovila pro opir
mistsevykh u pershi tyzhni okupatsiï"; "Viis'ka Rosiï aktyvizuvaly sproby zakhopyty Zaporiz'ku AES," *Ukrinform*, March 3, 2022, www.ukrinform.ua/rubric
-ato/3419318-vijska-rosii-aktivizuvali-sprobi-zahopiti-zaporizku-aes.html.

15. "Viis'ka Rosiï aktyvizuvaly sproby zakhopyty Zaporiz'ku AES"; "'Taka hordist'
bula za svoie misto.' Zhytel'ka Enerhodara rozpovila pro opir mistsevykh u pershi
tyzhni okupatsiï"; "Na Enerhodar sune ponad 100 odynyts' vazhkoï tekhniky—
uzhe obstrilialy blokpost," *5 Kanal*, March 3, 2022, https://web.archive.org/
web/20220303152510/https://www.5.ua/regiony/na-enerhodar-sune-ponad-100
-odynyts-vazhkoi-tekhniky-uzhe-obstrilialy-blokpost-270059.html; "V Enerhodari rosiis'ki viis'ka obstrilialy blokpost ta robliat' sprobu proryvu do mista,"
Suspil'ne, March 3, 2022, https://suspilne.media/213449-v-energodari-rosijski
-vijska-obstrilali-blokpost-ta-roblat-sprobu-prorivu-do-mista/.

16. Viktoriia Roshchyna, "'My tut iak raby 21-ho stolittia': Shcho vidbuvaiet'sia na
Zaporiz'kii AES v okupovanomu Enerhodari," *Ukraïns'ka pravda*, March 10, 2023,
www.pravda.com.ua/articles/2023/03/10/7392758/; "Zaporiz'ka AES. Fil'm 'Iadernyi shantazh,'" www.youtube.com/@atomzaes, 4:30.

17. Geoff Brumfiel, Meredith Rizzo, Tien Le, and Alyson Hurt, "Video analysis reveals
Russian attack on Ukrainian nuclear plant veered near disaster," NPR, March 11,
2022; Derzhavna inspektsiia iadernoho rehuliuvannia Ukraïny, Facebook page,
March 3, 2022, www.facebook.com/profile.php?id=100064837892613; Roman
Petrenko and Ievhen Rudenko, "V Enerhodari zahynuly troie natshvardiitsiv.
Zaiavy mera pidozril—MVS," *Ukraïns'ka pravda*, March 4, 2022, www.pravda
.com.ua/news/2022/03/4/7328175/; Liubov Velichko, "Mir pod udarom. Kak ros-
siia grozit iadernoi katastrofoi na ukrainskikh AĖS i pochemu molchit MAGATE,"
The Page, June 8, 2022, https://thepage.ua/economy/rossiya-ugrozhaet-yadernoj
-katastrofoj-na-aes.

18. Zvonariova, "Dmytro Orlov, mis'kyi holova Enerhodara"; "Dombrovskii Aleksei Iur'evich. Podrobnoe opisanie prestuplenii," May 23, 2022, https://russian
-torturers.com/ru/profile/327.

19. Brumfiel et al., "Video analysis reveals Russian attack on Ukrainian nuclear
plant veered near disaster"; "Obstril Zaporiz'koï AES: U DSNS rozpovily, de
same vynykla pozhezha," *5 Kanal*, March 4, 2022, https://web.archive.org/
web/20220304075143/https://www.5.ua/regiony/obstril-zaporizkoi-aes-u-dsns

-rozpovily-de-same-vynykla-pozhezha-270109.html; Derzhavna inspektsiia iad-ernoho rehuliuvannia Ukraïny, Facebook page, March 3, 2022.

20. Brumfiel et al, "Video analysis reveals Russian attack on Ukrainian nuclear plant veered near disaster."

21. "Lidery ES prizvali obespechit' bezopasnost' iadernykh ob»ektov Ukrainy," *RIA Novosti*, March 25, 2022, https://ria.ru/20220311/bezopasnost-1777583139 .html.

22. Dmytro Kuleba @DmytroKuleba, March 3, 2022, https://twitter.com/Dmytro Kuleba/status/1499543775240196099; "Iakshcho bude vybukh – tse kinets' vsim. Kinets' Ievropi."—Zelens'kyi pro ZAES," *Ukraïns'ka pravda*, March 4, 2022, www.pravda.com.ua/news/2022/03/4/7328011/; "March 4, 2022, Russia-Ukraine news," CNN, www.cnn.com/europe/live-news/ukraine-russia-putin -news-03-04-22/h_1f73598a8edc48dcd10cea81c3c37be5.

23. Derzhavna inspektsiia iadernoho rehuliuvannia Ukraïny, Facebook page, March 3, 2022.

24. Derzhavna inspektsiia iadernoho rehuliuvannia Ukraïny, Facebook page, March 4, 2022, www.facebook.com/profile.php?id=100064837892613.

25. "Update 11 - IAEA Director General Statement on Situation in Ukraine," IAEA, March 4, 2022.

26. "Security Council debates Russian strike on Ukraine nuclear power plant," *UN News*, March 4, 2022.

27. "DiCarlo: Military operations around nuclear sites are unacceptable and highly irresponsible," United Nations, Political and Peacebuilding Affairs, March 4, 2022; "Security Council debates Russian strike on Ukraine nuclear power plant."

28. "Security Council debates Russian strike on Ukraine nuclear power plant"; "V OON potrebovali obespechit' MAGATE dostup k iadernym ob"ektam v sluchae neobkhodimosti," *United Nations News*, March 4, 2022, https://news.un.org/ru/ story/2022/03/1419242.

29. "Zaporiz'ka AES. Fil'm 'Iadernyi shantazh'"; "Rosgvardia spoke about a large number of weapons at the Zaporozhye nuclear power plant," *Pledge Times*, March 9, 2022; "Zolotov zaiavil ob okhrane Rosgvardiei Chernobyl'skoi i Zaporozhskoi AÈS," *Interfax*, March 11, 2022, www.interfax-russia.ru/main/zolotov-zayavil-ob -ohrane-rosgvardiey-chernobylskoy-i-zaporozhskoy-aes.

30. Viktoriia Roshchyna, "Zaporiz'ka AES pid kontrolem rosiis'kykh okupan-tiv," *Ukraïns'ka pravda*, March 4, 2022, www.pravda.com.ua/news/2022/03/ 4/7328064/; Rudenko, "V Enerhodari zahynuly troie natshvardiitsiv"; "'Taka hordist' bula za svoie misto.' Zhytel'ka Enerhodara rozpovila pro opir mistsevykh u pershi tyzhni okupatsiï."

31. "Ukraine: Russia-Ukraine War and Nuclear Energy," World Nuclear Association (updated June 2, 2023); Viktoriia Roshchyna, "V Enerhodari na proshchannia z heroiamy pryishly kil'ka soten' liudei," *Ukraïns'ka pravda*, March 7, 2022, www .pravda.com.ua/news/2022/03/7/7329077/.

32. Hanna Arhirova, "Ukraine nuclear workers recount abuse, threats from Rus-sians," Associated Press, October 5, 2022; "V Enerhodari mistiany vyishly na akt-siiu protestu proty okupatsiï ta vykradennia posadovtsia mis'koï rady," *Suspil'ne*, March 20, 2022, https://suspilne.media/219639-v-energodari-mistani-vijsli -akciu-na-protestu-proti-okupacii-ta-vikradenna-posadovca-miskoi-radi/.

33. "'Taka hordist' bula za svoie misto.' Zhytel'ka Enerhodara rozpovila pro opir mistsevykh u pershi tyzhni okupatsiï."

34. "'Taka hordist' bula za svoie misto.' Zhytel'ka Enerhodara rozpovila pro opir mistsevykh u pershi tyzhni okupatsiï."

35. "'Taka hordist' bula za svoie misto.' Zhytel'ka Enerhodara rozpovila pro opir mistsevykh u pershi tyzhni okupatsiï"; "Okkupantami v Énergodare rukovodit rossiiskii general-maior: on otdal prikaz zhestoko razognat' 'miting,'" *Inform ZP.UA*, April 7, 2022, www.inform.zp.ua/ru/2022/04/07/147242_okkupantami -v-energodare-rukovodit-rossijskij-general-major-on-otdaval-prikaz-zhestoko -razognat-miting/.

36. "Dombrovskii Aleksei Iur'evich. Podrobnoe opisanie prestuplenii"; Oleksandr Chornovalov and Kira Tolstiakova, "'Zaharbnyky atoma.' 'Skhemy' identyfikuvaly komandyriv Roshvardiï iaki zakhopyly Zaporiz'ku AES," *Radio Svoboda*, May 26, 2022, www.radiosvoboda.org/a/skhemy-komandyry-roshvardiya-zaes/31869790 .html.

7. Dirty Bomb

1. "Chornobyl 22," a film by Oleksiy Radynski, The Reckoning Project (2023), 14:00; interview with Valentyn Heiko, The Reckoning Project, 2022; Yuras Karmanau, Jim Heintz, Vladimir Isachenkov, and Dasha Litvinova, "Putin puts nuclear forces on high alert, escalating tensions," *AP News*, February 27, 2022.

2. Rossiiskoe obshchestvo "Znanie," Prosvetitel'skii marafon "Znanie o geroiakh," November 3, 2022, https://vk.com/video-135454514_456243012 5:40; "Kak polkovnik Rosgvardii ne dopustil vtorogo Chernobylia," *Mir tesen*, November 12, 2022, https://sovsojuz.mirtesen.ru/blog/43979398162/Kak-polkovnik-Rosgvardii -ne-dopustil-vtorogo-Chernobyilya.

3. Interview with Valentyn Heiko, The Reckoning Project, 2022; interview with Serhii Dediukhin, The Reckoning Project, 2022; Oleksiy Radynski, "What Were the Russians Doing in Chernobyl?" *The Atlantic*, September 6, 2023.

4. "Muliukin, Nikolai Nikolaevich," *Mirotvorets*, https://myrotvorets.center/ criminal/mulyukin-nikolaj-nikolaevich/; interview with Vitalii Popov, The Reckoning Project, 2022; Radynski, "What Were the Russians Doing in Chernobyl?"

5. "Oni iskali preslovutye amerikanskie laboratorii: rabotnik ChAÉS ob okkupatsii," *ICTV*, May 9, 2022, https://www.youtube.com/watch?v=D-THwUDkiUE&t=182s, 5:53; "Chornobyl' pid chas viiny. Okupanty mohly sprovokuvaty novu trahediiu," *Ochi*, April 26, 2022, www.youtube.com/watch?v=B6HmtSBVq-U&t=210s, 4:00; Nataliya Gumenyuk, "'Atomnyky taki sami liudy iak i inshi. My tezh boïmosia bezgluzdykh liudei'—mer Slavutycha," *Suspi'lne Novyny*, September 7, 2022, https://suspilne.media/279175-atomniki-taki-sami-ak-j-insi-mi-tez-boimosa -bezgluzdih-ludej-mer-slavutica/; "Chornobyl' 22," film (2023), 10:13.

6. Interview with Valerii Semenov, The Reckoning Project, 2022.

7. Interview with Valentyn Heiko, The Reckoning Project, 2022.

8. Interview with Valentyn Heiko, The Reckoning Project, 2022.

9. "Ukraina mogla sozdat' iadernoe oruzhie v blizhaishei perspektive— informatsionnyi istochnik v RF," *Interfax*, March 6, 2022, www.interfax.ru/ russia/826642.

10. Dmitrii Kochetkov, "Ukrainskie spetsialisty zanimalis' izgotovleniem 'griaznoi

bomby' na territorii Chernobyl'skoi AĖS," *1 Kanal, Novosti,* March 6, 2022, www.1tv
.ru/news/2022-03-06/422787-ukrainskie_spetsialisty_zanimalis_izgotovleniem_
gryaznoy_bomby_na_territorii_chernobylskoy_aes; "Igor' Korotchenko," *24 SMI,*
https://24smi.org/celebrity/130987-igor-korotchenko.html; "Sredi lits uzhe pod
sanktsiiami: Korotchenko Igor' Iur'evich," *Voina & sanktsii,* https://sanctions.nazk
.gov.ua/ru/sanction-person/2221/.

11. "Ukrainskie spetsialisty zanimalis' izgotovleniem 'griaznoi bomby' na territorii
Chernobyl'skoi AĖS"; "Andrei Koshkin," *Svobodnaia pressa,* https://svpressa.ru/
experts/andrey-koshkin/; "Rossiiskie voennye dostavili gumpomoshch personalu Chernobyl'skoi AĖS," *Izvestiia,* March 7, 2022, https://iz.ru/1301875/2022
-03-07/rossiiskie-voennye-dostavili-gumpomoshch-personalu-chernobylskoi
-aes; "Nikulin, Igor Viktorovich," *FederalPress,* https://fedpress.ru/person/
2952514.

12. "Oni iskali preslovutye amerikanskie laboratorii; rabotnik ChAĖS ob okkupatsii,"
15:49.

13. Interview with Valentyn Heiko, The Reckoning Project, 2022.

14. Viktoriia Bilous, "Vony pryishly: deputaty Slavutyts'koï mis'koï rady VIII sklykannia," *KyivVlada,* November 13, 2020, https://kievvlast.com.ua/text/voni-projshli
-deputati-slavutitskoi-miskoi-radi-viii-sklikannya; "Oni iskali preslovutye amerikanskie laboratorii; rabotnik ChAĖS ob okkupatsii"; Dmytro Fionik, "Apokalipsys ne s'ohodni," *Liga.net,* July 23, 2022, https://projects.liga.net/apocalypse-is
-not-today/.

15. Fionik, "Apokalipsys ne s'ohodni"; "Oni iskali preslovutye amerikanskie laboratorii; rabotnik ChAĖS ob okkupatsii," 6:30, 9:35.

16. "Chornobyl' pid chas viiny. Okupanty mohly sprovokuvaty novu trahediiu," 5:53.

17. Iuliia Titok, "'Tse ne trahediia—tse anekdot': iak rosiiany okopalysia v radio-
aktyvnomu 'Rusomu lisi' bilia Chornobylia," *Suspil'ne Novyny,* June 17, 2022,
https://suspilne.media/251124-ce-ne-tragedia-ce-anekdot-ak-rosiani-okopalisa
-v-radioaktivnomu-rudomu-lisi-bila-cornobila/; Maksim Kamenev, "Rebiata, vy
ser'ezno? Vy ponimaete kuda vy edete? Istoriia rossiiskoi okkupatsii Chernobyl'skoi
atomnoi stantsii i zony otchuzhdeniia," *Graty,* June 9, 2022, https://graty.me/
rebyata-vy-serezno-vy-ponimaete-kuda-vy-edete-istoriya-rossijskoj-okkupaczii
-chernobylskoj-atomnoj-stanczii-i-zony-otchuzhdeniya/; "Iakushev Oleg Vladi-
mirovich," *Russian Torturers,* https://russian-torturers.com/ru/profile/1143; Fionik,
"Apokalipsys ne s'ohodni."

18. Interview with Valerii Semenov, The Reckoning Project, 2022.

19. Interview with Valentyn Heiko, The Reckoning Project, 2022; interview with
Serhii Dediukhin, The Reckoning Project, 2022.

20. Nataliia Pavlenko, "Okupatsiia ChAES: rosiiany v Rudomu lisi ïly, spaly, a zi stantsiï vkraly navit' servizy," *Pereiaslav.City,* September 3, 2022, https://pereiaslav
.city/articles/234076/okupaciya-chaes-rosiyani-v-rudomu-lisi-ili-spali-a-zi
-stancii-vkrali-navit-servizi; Fionik, "Apokalipsys ne s'ohodni"; "Oni iskali preslovutye amerikanskie laboratorii; rabotnik ChAĖS ob okkupatsii," 9:35.

21. Interview with Liudmyla Kozak, The Reckoning Project, 2022.

22. "Oni iskali preslovutye amerikanskie laboratorii; rabotnik ChAĖS ob okkupatsii," 6:30, 9:35; "Chornobyl' pid chas viiny. Okupanty mohly sprovokuvaty novu
trahediiu," 19:46.

23. Interview with Valentyn Heiko, The Reckoning Project, 2022.

24. Pavlenko, "Okupatsiia ChAES."

25. Interview with Valerii Semenov, The Reckoning Project, 2022.

26. Interview with Valerii Semenov, The Reckoning Project, 2022.

27. Stephen Mulvey, "Chernobyl's continuing hazards," *BBC News*, April 25, 2006; Pavlenko, "Okupatsiia ChAES."

28. "Chornobyl' pid chas viiny. Okupanty mohly sprovokuvaty novu trahediiu;" Iogita Limaie, "Chernobyl' vo vremia russkogo vtorzheniia: 'My vorovali u rossiian toplivo, chtoby ne dopustit' katastrofu,'" *BBC News, Russian Service*, April 9, 2022, www.bbc.com/russian/news-61046931.

29. "Chornobyl' pid chas viiny. Okupanty mohly sprovokuvaty novu trahediiu," 5:53, 16:53; "Oni iskali preslovutye amerikanskie laboratorii; rabotnik ChAĖS ob okkupatsii," 12:11.

30. Interview with Valentyn Heiko, The Reckoning Project, 2022.

8. Hostages

1. "Rosgvardiia vziala pod okhranu Chernobyl'skuiu i Zaporozhskuiu AĖS," *Lenta.ru*, March 11, 2022, https://lenta.ru/news/2022/03/11/rosgva/.

2. "Voennye RF dostavili gumanitarnuiu pomoshch personalu Chernobyl'skoi AĖS," *RenTV*, March 6, 2022, https://ren.tv/news/v-mire/948072-voennye-rf-dostavili-gumanitarnuiu-pomoshch-personalu-chernobylskoi-aes; Denis Karlovskii, "Okkupanty planirovali sniat' feik s gumpomoshch'iu personalu ChAĖS," *Ukraïns'ka pravda*, March 7, 2022, www.pravda.com.ua/rus/news/2022/03/7/7329196/; "'Izvestiia' na informatsionnoi voine Rossii protiv Ukrainy," Tsentr zhurnalistskikh rassledovanii, May 27, 2022, https://investigator.org.ua/publication/243372/.

3. Maksim Kamenev, "Rebiata, vy ser'ezno? Vy ponimaete kuda vy edete? Istoriia rossiiskoi okkupatsii Chernobyl'skoi atomnoi stantsii i zony otchuzhdeniia," *Graty*, June 9, 2022, https://graty.me/rebyata-vy-serezno-vy-ponimaete-kuda-vy-edete-istoriya-rossijskoj-okkupaczii-chernobylskoj-atomnoj-stanczii-i-zony-otchuzhdeniya/; "Chornobyl' pid chas viiny. Okupanty mohly sprovokuvaty novu trahediiu," 4:00; Nataliia Pavlenko, "Okupatsiia ChAES: rosiiany v Rudomu lisi ïly, spaly, a zi stantsiї vkraly navit' servizy," *Pereiaslav.City*, September 3, 2022, https://pereiaslav.city/articles/234076/okupaciya-chaes-rosiyani-v-rudomu-lisi-ili-spali-a-zi-stancii-vkrali-navit-servizi; Olga Osipova, "Ia ostalsia na rabochem meste. Ia ne imeyu prava ego pokidat'," *Meduza*, April 1, 2022, https://meduza.io/feature/2022/04/01/ya-ostalsya-na-rabochem-meste-ya-ne-imeyu-prava-ego-pokidat; interview with Oleksii Shelestii, The Reckoning Project, 2022.

4. Osipova, "Ia ostalsia na rabochem meste"; "Rosiiany perevdiahnulysia u formu spivrobitnykiv ChAES i otrymaly humanitarku–radnytsia mera Slavutycha," *Hromads'ke radio*, March 6, 2022, https://hromadske.radio/news/2022/03/06/rosiianyperevdiahnulysia-u-formu-spivrobitnykiv-chaes-i-otrymaly-humanitarku-radnytsia-mera-slavutycha.

5. Pavlenko, "Okupatsiia ChAES"; Dmytro Fionik, "Apokalipsys ne s'ohodni," *Liga.net*, July 23, 2022, https://projects.liga.net/apocalypse-is-not-today/.

6. Osipova, "Ia ostalsia na rabochem meste."

7. Osipova, "Ia ostalsia na rabochem meste"; "Oni iskali preslovutye ameri-kanskie laboratorii; rabotnik ChAĖS ob okkupatsii"; www.youtube.com/watch?v=XtofZSCrPUA, 0:40.

8. Fionik, "Apokalipsys ne s'ohodni."

9. "Chornobyl 22," 3:44.

10. Interview with Valerii Semenov, The Reckoning Project, 2022.

11. Osipova, "Ia ostalsia na rabochem meste"; Chornobyl NPP. Chronicle of Occu-pation. Part 2: Straining, www.youtube.com/watch?v=snPYoevNBMY; Pavlenko, "Okupatsiia ChAES."

12. Interview with Valerii Semenov, The Reckoning Project, 2022; interview with Serhii Dediukhin, The Reckoning Project, 2022.

13. Interview with Valentyn Heiko, The Reckoning Project, 2022.

14. "Oni iskali preslovutye amerikanskie laboratorii; rabotnik ChAĖS ob okkupatsii," 5:53.

15. Pavlenko, "Okupatsiia ChAES."

16. Interview with Valerii Semenov, The Reckoning Project, 2022.

17. Interview with Serhii Dediukhin, The Reckoning Project, 2022.

18. Fionik, "Apokalipsys ne s'ohodni."

19. Pavlenko, "Okupatsiia ChAES."

20. "Oni iskali preslovutye amerikanskie laboratorii; rabotnik ChAĖS ob okkupatsii"; "Chornobyl' pid chas viiny. Okupanty mohly sprovokuvaty novu trahediiu," 4:00; Pavlenko, "Okupatsiia ChAES."

21. Oleg Gorodkov, "Kak buriaty chitali Oruella i ukrali trusy u dneprovskikh stalk-erov na ChAĖS," *Kust*, May 12, 2022, https://kustdnipro.com/ru/kak-buryaty-chytaly-oruella-y-ukraly-trusy-u-dneprovskyh-stalkerov-na-chaes/.

22. Interview with Oleksandr Skyrda, The Reckoning Project, 2022.

23. Interview with Oleksandr Skyrda, The Reckoning Project, 2022.

24. Interview with Ievhen Markevych, The Reckoning Project, 2022; interview with Leonid Struk, The Reckoning Project, 2022.

25. Interview with Oleksandr Skyrda, The Reckoning Project, 2022.

26. Interview with Oleksandr Skyrda, The Reckoning Project, 2022; interview with Liudmyla Besedina, The Reckoning Project, 2022.

27. Interview with Liudmyla Besedina, The Reckoning Project, 2022; interview with Leonid Struk, The Reckoning Project, 2022.

28. Interview with Liudmyla Besedina, The Reckoning Project, 2022; interview with Leonid Struk, The Reckoning Project, 2022; interview with Viktor Yatsuk, The Reckoning Project, 2022.

29. Interview with Leonid Struk, The Reckoning Project, 2022.

30. Interview with Leonid Struk, The Reckoning Project, 2022.

31. Interview with Leonid Struk, The Reckoning Project, 2022.

32. Interview with Leonid Struk, The Reckoning Project, 2022.

9. Shadow of Fukushima

1. Olga Osipova, "Ia ostalsia na rabochem meste. Ia ne imeyu prava ego pokidat'," *Meduza*, April 1, 2022, https://meduza.io/feature/2022/04/01/ya-ostalsya-na-rabochem-meste-ya-ne-imeyu-prava-ego-pokidat; Chornobyl NPP, "Chronicle

of Occupation. Part 2: Straining," www.youtube.com/watch?v=snPYoevNBMY, 2:00.

2. Chornobyl NPP. Chronicle of Occupation. Part 2: Straining.

3. Osipova, "Ia ostalsia na rabochem meste"; Chornobyl NPP. Chronicle of Occupation. Part 2: Straining.

4. "Chernobyl New Safe Confinement (NSC), Ukraine," *Power Technology,* March 8, 2022; "KhOIaT-1—khranilishche otrabotannogo iadernogo topliva," *Chernobyl Zone,* April 3, 2021, www.chernobylzone.com.ua/infobase/spent-nuclear-fuel -store.html; "Promezhutochnoe khranilishche iadernogo topliva 'sukhogo tipa' (KhOIaT-2)," April 13, 2023, Chernobyl'skaia AĖS, https://chnpp.gov.ua/ru/183 -proekty/realizuemye-proekty/435-2-ru435; "Ukraine's centralised used fuel storage facility 'ready,'" *World Nuclear News,* April 21, 2022.

5. Osipova, "Ia ostalsia na rabochem meste."

6. "Chornobyl Zone 'Storage Facilities' or Why ISF Is Not a Repository"; "Promezhutochnoe khranilishche otrabotavshego topliva 'sukhogo tipa' (KhOIaT-2)"; Chornobyl NPP. Chronicle of Occupation. Part 2: Straining, 10:55.

7. Chornobyl NPP. Chronicle of Occupation. Part 2: Straining, 10:55.

8. Osipova, "Ia ostalsia na rabochem meste"; Chornobyl NPP. Chronicle of Occupation. Part 2: Straining, 11:50.

9. Chornobyl NPP. Chronicle of Occupation. Part 2: Straining, 8:13; "Chem grozit otkliuchenie ėlektrichestva na Chernobyl'skoi AĖS?" *BBC News Russian Service,* March 10, 2022, www.bbc.com/russian/features-60691216.

10. Ian Sale, "Ukraine war: Chernobyl radiation fears as minister calls for Russia to allow for urgent repairs," *Sky News,* March 9, 2022, https://news.sky.com/story/ ukraine-war-chernobyl-radiation-fears-as-minister-calls-for-russia-to-allow-for -urgent-repairs-12561615.

11. "Update 17 - IAEA Director General Statement on Situation in Ukraine," IAEA, March 10, 2022.

12. @BalthasarLinda, Twitter, March 9, 2022, https://twitter.com/BalthasarLinda1/ status/1501701367907426306.

13. Iogita Limaie, "Chernobyl' vo vremia russkogo vtorzheniia: 'My vorovali u rossiian toplivo, chtoby ne dopustit' katastrofu,'" *BBC News Russian Service,* April 9, 2022, www.bbc.com/russian/news-61046931.

14. Derzhavna inspektsiia iadernoho rehuliuvannia Ukraïny, Facebook page, March 11, 2022, www.facebook.com/profile.php?id=100064837892613.

15. "Update 17 - IAEA Director General Statement on Situation in Ukraine," IAEA, March 10, 2022; Adela Suliman, Annabelle Chapman, and David L. Stern, "Russian official says Belarus restored power to Chernobyl site, but IAEA awaits confirmation," *Washington Post,* March 10, 2022.

16. "Ukrainskie natsionalisty atakovali ėlektrosnabzhenie Chernobyl'skoi AĖS," *Izvestiia,* March 9, 2022, https://iz.ru/1302810/2022-03-09/vsu-nanesli-udar-po -pitaiushchim-chernobylskuiu-aes-liniiam-elektroperedachi.

17. Chornobyl NPP. Chronicle of Occupation. Part 2: Straining, 10:55; "Chem grozit otkliuchenie ėlektrichestva na Chernobyl'skoi AĖS?"; Derzhavna inspektsiia iadernoho rehuliuvannia Ukraïny, Facebook page, March 9, 2022, www.facebook .com/profile.php?id=100064837892613; "ChAES znestrumlena. Ukraïns'ki

enerhetyky vedut' perehovory z viis'kovymy RF," *BBC News*, Ukraine, March 9, 2022, www.bbc.com/ukrainian/news-60679062.

18. "Minoborony RF soglasilos' na proezd ukrainskoi remontnoi brigady v raion ChAÈS," *Interfax*, March 10, 2022, www.interfax.ru/world/827495.

19. https://www.facebook.com/dazv.gov.ua?__cft__%5b0%5d=AZW0SNcL8CzI4Z ob_hCsSgkvjoMoxvP1rkYVrfmLti2MCUO5cT-eYRZ4yWNxtLEIITl4jbdt_pgW eT1OnuZRUzbtKU3guSnFbVfIKhFeD11g7wNA3apmVCr3UeeyVz1Q1ARCYo smrYD8CRzBxPJw50ja2NxUP9YLtX85UQvPb756jA&__tn__=-UC%2CP-R; Derzhavne ahentstvo Ukraïny z upravlinnia Zonoiu vidchuzhennia, Facebook page, March 11 and 13, 2022, www.facebook.com/dazv.gov.ua; interview with Valerii Semenov, The Reckoning Project, 2022.

20. Interview with Valerii Semenov, The Reckoning Project, 2022; "Okupanty znovu poshkodyly liniiu na ChAES, iaku naperedodni vidremontuvalo 'Ukrenerho,'" *Ekonomichna pravda*, March 14, 2022, www.epravda.com.ua/ news/2022/03/14/683986/; "Update 21 - IAEA Director General Statement on Situation in Ukraine," IAEA, March 14, 2022.

21. "RF prorabotala s Belorus'iu vopros ènergosnabzheniia Chernobyl'skoi AÈS ot belorusskoi ènergosistemy," *BelTA*, March 9, 2022, www.belta.by/society/ view/rf-prorabotala-s-belarusjju-vopros-energosnabzhenija-chernobylskoj-aes-ot -belorusskoj-energosistemy-489231-2022/; "Èlektroènergiia na Chernobyl'skuiu AÈS idet iz Belorussii," *Sputnik News*, March 10, 2022, https://lt.sputniknews .ru/20220310/elektroenergiya-na-chernobylskuyu-aes-idet-iz-belorussii -22044620.html.

22. "Putin poblagodaril Lukashenko za vosstanovlenie èlektrosnabzheniia Cher-nobyl'skoi AÈS," TASS, March 11, 2022, https://tass.ru/ekonomika/14040429; "Lukashenko orders Belarusian specialists to ensure power supply to Chernobyl plant—BelTA," Reuters, March 10, 2022, www.reuters.com/world/europe/ lukashenko-orders-belarusian-specialists-ensure-power-supply-chernobyl-plant -2022-03-10/.

23. Interview with Valerii Semenov, The Reckoning Project, 2022; Dmytro Fionik, "Apokalipsys ne s'ohodni," *Liga.net*, July 23, 2022, https://projects.liga.net/ apocalypse-is-not-today/; "ChAES Okupatsiia," *Novyny* ChAES, April 26, 2022, 2–6, chrome-extension://efaidnbmnnnibpcajpcglclefindmkaj/https://chnpp.gov .ua/images/pdf/2022-04-26_1.pdf; Chornobyl NPP. Chronicle of Occupation. Part 2: Straining, 8:28.

24. Chornobyl NPP. Chronicle of Occupation. Part 2: Straining, 8:28; Fionik, "Apoka-lipsys ne s'ohodni"; "ChAES Okupatsiia."

25. Chornobyl NPP. Chronicle of Occupation. Part 2: Straining.

26. Chornobyl NPP. Chronicle of Occupation. Part 2: Straining; Osipova, "Ia ostalsia na rabochem meste."

27. Osipova, "Ia ostalsia na rabochem meste"; Chornobyl NPP. Chronicle of Occupa-tion. Part 2: Straining, 4:22.

28. Chornobyl NPP. Chronicle of Occupation. Part 2: Straining, 6:12; Fionik, "Apokalipsys ne s'ohodni"; "ChAES Okupatsiia."

29. Chornobyl NPP. Chronicle of Occupation. Part 2: Straining, 12:35.

30. Interview with Valerii Semenov, The Reckoning Project, 2022.

31. Fionik, "Apokalipsys ne s'ohodni"; Chornobyl NPP. Chronicle of Occupation. Part 2: Straining, 14:39.

32. Interview with Oleksii Shelestii, The Reckoning Project, 2022.

33. Chornobyl NPP. Chronicle of Occupation. Part 2: Straining,14:39; Fionik, "Apokalipsys ne s'ohodni"; "ChAES Okupatsiia."

34. Derzhavna inspektsiia iadernoho rehuliuvannia Ukraïny, Facebook page, March 16, 2022, www.facebook.com/profile.php?id=100064837892613; "Update 22 - IAEA Director General Statement on Situation in Ukraine," IAEA, March 15, 2022.

10. Volunteers

1. Joe Parkinson and Drew Hinshaw, "Inside Chernobyl, 200 Exhausted Staff Toil Round the Clock at Russian Gunpoint," *Wall Street Journal*, March 15, 2022.

2. Parkinson and Hinshaw, "Inside Chernobyl."

3. Interview with Valerii Semenov, The Reckoning Project, 2022; interview with Oleksandr Kalishuk, The Reckoning Project, 2022.

4. Nataliia Pavlenko, "Okupatsiia ChAES: rosiiany v Rudomu lisi ïly, spaly, a zi stantsiï vkraly navit' servizy," *Pereiaslav.City*, September 3, 2022, https://pereiaslav.city/articles/234076/okupaciya-chaes-rosiyani-v-rudomu-lisi-ili-spali-a-zi-stancii-vkrali-navit-servizi; Olga Osipova, "Ia ostalsia na rabochem meste. Ia ne imeyu prava ego pokidat'," *Meduza*, April 1, 2022, https://meduza.io/feature/2022/04/01/ya-ostalsya-na-rabochem-meste-ya-ne-imeyu-prava-ego-pokidat.

5. Chornobyl NPP. Chronicle of Occupation. Part 2: Straining, www.youtube.com/watch?v=snPYoevNBMY.

6. Maksim Kamenev, "Rebiata, vy ser'ezno? Vy ponimaete kuda vy edete? Istoriia rossiiskoi okkupatsii Chernobyl'skoi atomnoi stantsii i zony otchuzhdeniia," *Graty*, June 9, 2022, https://graty.me/rebyata-vy-serezno-vy-ponimaete-kuda-vy-edete-istoriya-rossijskoj-okkupaczii-chernobylskoj-atomnoj-stanczii-i-zony-otchuzhdeniya; Chornobyl NPP. Chronicle of Occupation. Part 4: De-Occupation, www.youtube.com/watch?v=JvkFOoPgoSs.

7. Chornobyl NPP. Chronicle of Occupation. Part 4: De-Occupation.

8. Chernobyl NPP. ChNPP Under Occupation: Interview of Witnesses, www.youtube.com/watch?v=To6-4RepTuY.

9. Iuliia Mamoilenko, "Situatsiia na granitse s Belorus'iu snova opasnaia—interv'iu s nachal'nikom Chernobyl'skoi zony," *Segodnia*, July 7, 2022, www.segodnya.ua/ua/strana/intervyu/maroderily-35-dney-ne-ostalos-ni-odnih-ucelevshih-dverey-v-kakom-sostoyanii-chernobyl-posle-deokkupacii-1629307.html; Chornobyl NPP. Chronicle of Occupation. Part 4: De-Occupation.

10. Chornobyl NPP. Chronicle of Occupation. Part 2: Straining; Kamenev, "Rebiata, vy ser'ezno?"

11. Interview with Oleksii Shelestii, The Reckoning Project, 2022; interview with Oleksandr Kalishuk, The Reckoning Project, 2022; interview with Vitalii Popov, The Reckoning Project, 2022.

12. Pavlenko, "Okupatsiia ChAES"; Chornobyl NPP. Chronicle of Occupation. Part 2: Straining; Chornobyl NPP. Chronicle of Occupation. Part 3: Resistance,

www.youtube.com/watch?v=ZJkS1UUZUlk&t=20s; "Heneral maior Oleksii Rtyshchev," *InformNapalm*, September 18, 2022, https://informnapalm.org/osintbees/2022/09/18/heneral-maior-oleksii-rtyshchev/.

13. Interview with Oleksandr Kalishuk, The Reckoning Project, 2022.

14. Kamenev, "Rebiata, vy ser'ezno?"; Chornobyl NPP. Chronicle of Occupation. Part 2: Straining.

15. Chornobyl NPP. Chronicle of Occupation. Part 2: Straining.

16. Chornobyl NPP. Chronicle of Occupation. Part 2: Straining.

17. Kamenev, "Rebiata, vy ser'ezno?"; Chornobyl NPP. Chronicle of Occupation. Part 2: Straining; "25 khodok na samorobnomu chovni: dvoie rybalok z Mniova perevezly 160 spivrobitnykiv Chornobyl's'koï AES," *Suspil'ne. Novyny*, May 2, 2022, https://suspilne.media/235054-25-hodok-na-samorobnomu-covni-dvoe-ribalok-z-mnova-perevezli-160-spivrobitnikiv-cornobilskoi-aes/.

18. "25 khodok na samorobnomu chovni."

19. Kamenev, "Rebiata, vy ser'ezno?"; Chornobyl NPP. Chronicle of Occupation. Part 2: Straining; "25 khodok na samorobnomu chovni."

20. "25 khodok na samorobnomu chovni"; Kamenev, "Rebiata, vy ser'ezno?"; Chornobyl NPP. Chronicle of Occupation. Part 2: Straining.

21. Chornobyl NPP. Chronicle of Occupation. Part 2: Straining.

22. Chernobyl NPP. ChNPP Under Occupation: Interview of Witnesses; Dmytro Fionik, "Apokalipsys ne s'ohodni," *Liga.net*, July 23, 2022, https://projects.liga.net/apocalypse-is-not-today/; Kamenev, "Rebiata, vy ser'ezno?"

23. Chornobyl NPP. Chronicle of Occupation. Part 2: Straining.

24. Chernobyl NPP. ChNPP Under Occupation: Interview of Witnesses; Fionik, "Apokalipsys ne s'ohodni"; Kamenev, "Rebiata, vy ser'ezno?"

25. Chornobyl NPP. Chronicle of Occupation. Part 2: Straining.

26. Chornobyl NPP. Chronicle of Occupation. Part 4: De-Occupation.

27. Chornobyl NPP. Chronicle of Occupation. Part 2: Straining; Mamoilenko, "Situatsiia na granitse s Belorus'iu snova opasnaia."

28. Fionik, "Apokalipsys ne s'ohodni"; "ChAES Okupatsiia," *Novyny ChAES*, April 26, 2022, chrome-extension://efaidnbmnnnibpcajpcglclefindmkaj/https://chnpp.gov.ua/images/pdf/2022-04-26_1.pdf.

29. Chornobyl NPP. Chronicle of Occupation. Part 3: Resistance; "Heneral maior Oleksii Rtyshchev"; Kamenev, "Rebiata, vy ser'ezno?"; Chornobyl NPP. Chronicle of Occupation. Part 4: De-Occupation.

30. Chernobyl NPP. ChNPP Under Occupation: Interview of Witnesses; Yuliia Surzhykova, "Chornobyl': pro okupatsiiu, vandalizm ta pohrabuvannia stantsiï—ochyma ïï spivrobitnykiv," *Suspil'ne Novyny*, June 23, 2022, https://suspilne.media/253335-cornobil-pro-okupaciu-vandalizm-ta-pograbuvanna-stancii-ocima-ii-spivrobitnikiv/.

31. Surzhykova, "Chornobyl': pro okupatsiiu, vandalizm ta pohrabuvannia stantsiï—ochyma ïï spivrobitnykiv."

32. Andrew Carey, Kostan Nechyporenko, and Jack Guy, "Russia destroys Chernobyl radiation monitoring lab, says Ukraine," CNN, March 23, 2022; Vitalii Nikulin, "Neumelaia postanovka: kadry iz 'razgrablennoi voennymi RF' po versii SMI SShA laboratorii v Chernobyle," *TV Zvezda. Novosti*, March 26, 2022, https://tvzvezda.ru/news/2022326543-Uqx07.html.

33. Nikulin, "Neumelaia postanovka."

34. "Zona povyshennoi bezopasnosti: rosgvardeitsy okhraniaiut Chernobyl'skuiu AĖS ot ukrainskikh diversantov," *NTV Novosti*, March 26, 2022, www.ntv.ru/novosti/2699047/.

35. Chernobyl NPP. ChNPP Under Occupation: Interview of Witnesses.

36. Chernobyl NPP. ChNPP Under Occupation: Interview of Witnesses.

37. Chernobyl NPP. ChNPP Under Occupation: Interview of Witnesses; Kamenev, "Rebiata, vy ser'ezno?"; "Nachal'nyk zminy AES: okupanty obitsialy ne chipaty Slavutych," *Ukraïns'ka enerhetyka*, April 20, 2022, https://ua-energy.org/uk/posts/nachalnyk-zminy-chaes-okupanty-obitsialy-ne-chipaty-slavutych.

38. Interview with Vitalii Popov, The Reckoning Project, 2022.

11. The Battle for Slavutych

1. Chornobyl NPP. Chronicle of Occupation. Part 2: Straining, www.youtube.com/watch?v=snPYoevNBMY.

2. "Persha vydacha humanitarnoï dopomohy u Slavutychi," *TV MediaDim Slavutych*, March 20, 2022, www.facebook.com/watch/?v=482092276729605.

3. Chornobyl NPP. Chronicle of Occupation. Part 2: Straining.

4. Chornobyl NPP. Chronicle of Occupation. Part 2: Straining.

5. Nataliya Gumenyuk, "Atomnyky taki sami, iak i inshi. My tezh boïmosia bezgluzdykh liudei"—mer Slavutycha," *Suspil'ne Novyny*, September 7, 2022, https://suspilne.media/279175-atomniki-taki-sami-ak-j-insi-mi-tez-boimosa-bezgluzdih-ludej-mer-slavutica/.

6. Gumenyuk, "Atomnyky taki sami, iak i inshi."

7. "Informatsiia do slavutchan vid mis'koho holovy na 9:00, 25.02.2022," *TV MediaDim Slavutych*, February 25, 2022.

8. "Informatsiia dlia slavutchan vid mis'koho holovy na 9:00 27.02. 2022," *TV MediaDim Slavutych*, February 27, 2022, www.facebook.com/watch/?v=703373987327665.

9. "Informatsiia dlia slavutchan vid mis'koho holovy na 9:00 27.02. 2022."

10. "Holos zirok," *TV MediaDim Slavutych*, February 27, 2022, www.facebook.com/100063654212599/videos/324303465935601; "Samoe strashnoe utro v zhizni. Rossiia napala na Ukrainu," *Meduza*, February 24, 2022, https://web.archive.org/web/20220302211306/https://meduza.io/feature/2022/02/24/samoe-strashnoe-utro-v-zhizni; "Ivan Dorn," *VokrugTV*, www.vokrug.tv/person/show/ivandron/.

11. Gumenyuk, "Atomnyky taki sami, iak i inshi."

12. "Aktual'ne interv'iu z dyrektorom KP DEU Serhiiem Shershenem," *TV MediaDim Slavutych*, February 19, 2022, www.facebook.com/100063654212599/videos/951716492376489.

13. Chornobyl NPP. Chronicle of Occupation. Part 3: Resistance, www.youtube.com/watch?v=ZJkS1UUZUlk&t=20s.

14. Chornobyl NPP. Chronicle of Occupation. Part 3: Resistance.

15. Chornobyl NPP. Chronicle of Occupation. Part 3: Resistance.

16. Chornobyl NPP. Chronicle of Occupation. Part 3: Resistance; Gumenyuk, "Atomnyky taki sami, iak i inshi."

17. Vasyl' Chepurnyi, "U Chernihovi tretii den' nema elektryky, vody, tepla. Oku-

panty tsilespriamovano stvoriuiut' humanitarnu katastrofu," *Ukraïns'kyi Reporter*, March 26, 2022, https://ukrreporter.com.ua/war/u-chernigovi-tretij -tyzhden-nema-elektryky-vody-tepla-okupanty-tsilespryamovano-stvoryuyut -gumanitarnu-katastrofu.html; Iryna Synel'nyk, "35 dniv okupatsiï: iak druzhyna viis'kovoho peredavala ZSU koordynaty voroha," *UNIAN*, April 15, 2022, www.unian.ua/war/mihaylo-kocyubinske-na-chernigivshchini-provelo-35-dniv-v -okupaciji-yak-vizhivali-miscevi-reportazh-novini-vtorgnennya-rosiji-v-ukrajinu -11787579.html.

18. Chornobyl NPP. Chronicle of Occupation. Part 3: Resistance.

19. "Pidsumky dnia vid 21.03.2022 vid mis'koho holovy Slavutycha Iu. Fomicheva," *TV MediaDim Slavutych*, March 21, 2022, www.facebook.com/100063654212599/ videos/1143359783147731; Gumenyuk, "Atomnyky taki sami, iak i inshi."

20. Vadym Ivkin, "Tochka vidliku abo try doby, pro iaki ne kozhen slavutchanyn znaie," *Slavutych.cn.ua*, October 14, 2022, https://slavutich.cn.ua/news/centr_ uvagu/20203-tochka-vidliku-abo-tri-dobi-pro-jaki-ne-kozhen-slavutchanin-znae .html; Chornobyl NPP. Chronicle of Occupation. Part 3: Resistance.

21. Ivkin, "Tochka vidliku abo try doby, pro iaki ne kozhen slavutchanyn znaie."

22. Ivkin, "Tochka vidliku abo try doby, pro iaki ne kozhen slavutchanyn znaie"; Chornobyl NPP. Chronicle of Occupation. Part 3: Resistance.

23. "Pidsumky dnia vid 23.03.2022 vid mis'koho holovy Slavutycha Iu. Fomicheva," *TV MediaDim Slavutych*, March 23, 2022, www.youtube.com/ watch?v=iBAnjNEThCY; Maksim Tsaruk, "Vrag riadom s nami": mėr Slavuticha rasskazal o situatsii v gorode," *Zerkalo nedeli*, March 23, 2022, https://zn.ua/ UKRAINE/vrah-rjadom-s-nami-mer-slavuticha-rasskazal-o-situatsii-v-horode .html.

24. Ivkin, "Tochka vidliku abo try doby, pro iaki ne kozhen slavutchanyn znaie"; Chornobyl NPP. Chronicle of Occupation. Part 3: Resistance.

25. Ivkin, "Tochka vidliku abo try doby, pro iaki ne kozhen slavutchanyn znaie."

26. "Ukrainskie spetssluzhby sobrali dannye podrazdelenii RF dlia fiksatsii prestuplenii v Kievskoi oblasti," *RBK Ukraina*, April 3, 2022, https://news.rbc.ua/ rus/war-in-ukraine/ukrainskie-spetssluzhby-sobrali-dannye-podrazdeleniy -1649009887.html; "SBU nazvala rosiis'koho komandyra, chyï pidlehli katuvaly i hrabuvaly v seli Andriïvka na Chernihivshchyni," *Sudovyi Reporter*, January 13, 2023, https://sudreporter.org/sbu-nazvala-rosijskogo-komandyra-chyyi -pidlegli-katuvaly-i-grabuvaly-v-seli-andriyivka-na-chernigivshhyni/; Sluzhba bezpeky Ukraïny, "Povidomlennia pro pidozru u vyvchenni kryminal'nykh pravoporushen'," Chernihiv, January 13, 2023, file:///C:/Users/sep773/Downloads/ pidozra_Abgarjan_A.S._Ukr.pdf.

27. Dmytro Fionik, "Apokalipsys ne s'ohodni," *Liga.net*, July 23, 2022, https://projects .liga.net/apocalypse-is-not-today/; Chornobyl NPP. Chronicle of Occupation. Part 3: Resistance.

28. Chornobyl NPP. Chronicle of Occupation. Part 3: Resistance.

29. Chornobyl NPP. Chronicle of Occupation. Part 3: Resistance; Fionik, "Apokalipsys ne s'ohodni"; Ivkin, "Tochka vidliku abo try doby, pro iaki ne kozhen slavutchanyn znaie."

30. Gumenyuk, "Atomnyky taki sami, iak i inshi."

31. Fionik, "Apokalipsys ne s'ohodni"; Gumenyuk, "Atomnyky taki sami, iak i inshi."
32. Fionik, "Apokalipsys ne s'ohodni"; Gumenyuk, "Atomnyky taki sami, iak i inshi."
33. Fionik, "Apokalipsys ne s'ohodni."
34. Fionik, "Apokalipsys ne s'ohodni"; Gumenyuk, "Atomnyky taki sami, iak i inshi."
35. Fionik, "Apokalipsys ne s'ohodni."
36. Fionik, "Apokalipsys ne s'ohodni"; Gumenyuk, "Atomnyky taki sami, iak i inshi."
37. Gumenyuk, "Atomnyky taki sami, iak i inshi"; "Vony pryishly: deputaty Slavutyts'koï mis'koï rady VIII sklykannia," Kyivvlada, November 13, 2020, https://kievvlast.com.ua/text/voni-projshli-deputati-slavutitskoi-miskoi-radi-viii-sklikannya; Chornobyl NPP. Chronicle of Occupation. Part 3: Resistance; "Slavutych tse Ukraïna," TV MediaDim Slavutych, March 26, 2022, www.facebook.com/watch/?v=5433830673342770.
38. Chornobyl NPP. Chronicle of Occupation. Part 3: Resistance; "Slavutych tse Ukraïna"; Gumenyuk, "Atomnyky taki sami, iak i inshi."
39. Fionik, "Apokalipsys ne s'ohodni"; "U Slavutychi sviashchennyk pishov do skupchennia okupantiv i skazav, shcho pro nykh dumaie," RISU: Relihiino-informatsiina sluzhba Ukraïny, March 30, 2022, https://risu.ua/u-slavutichi-svyashchenik-pishov-do-skupchennya-okupantiv-i-skazav-shcho-pro-nih-dumaye_n127766.
40. Fionik, "Apokalipsys ne s'ohodni"; "U Slavutychi sviashchennyk pishov do skupchennia okupantiv."
41. Gumenyuk, "Atomnyky taki sami, iak i inshi"; Fionik, "Apokalipsys ne s'ohodni"; "U Slavutychi sviashchennyk pishov do skupchennia okupantiv."
42. Chornobyl NPP. Chronicle of Occupation. Part 3: Resistance; "Slavutych tse Ukraïna"; Gumenyuk, "Atomnyky taki sami, iak i inshi."
43. "Slavutich pod polnym kontrolem voennykh RF. Ëfir ot 28.03.2022 (11:30), "60 minut," Rossiia 1, March 28, 2022, https://smotrim.ru/video/2395919; "Rosiis'ki okupanty zalyshyly Slavutych," Interfax-Ukraina, March 28, 2022, https://web.archive.org/web/20220328091801/https://ua.interfax.com.ua/news/general/818575.html; "U Slavutychi v boiu z okupantamy zahynuly troie biitsiv teroborony," Informator.ua, March 28, 2022, https://informator.ua/uk/u-slavutichi-v-boyu-z-okupantami-zaginuli-troye-biyciv-teroboroni; Fionik, "Apokalipsys ne s'ohodni."
44. Sluzhba bezpeky Ukraïny, "Povidomlennia pro pidozru u vyvchenni kryminal'nykh pravoporushen'," Chernihiv, January 13, 2023.
45. Gumenyuk, "Atomnyky taki sami, iak i inshi"; Dariia Durova, "Rosiiany, shcho vtekly s ChAES, zabraly iz soboiu zakhoplenykh u polon natshvardiitsiv," Obozrevatel', March 31, 2022, https://web.archive.org/web/20220403212520/https://news.obozrevatel.com/ukr/vojna-v-ukraine/rosiyani-scho-vtekli-z-chaes-zabrali-iz-soboyu-zahoplenih-u-polon-natsgvardijtsiv.htm.

12. Liberation

1. Maksim Kamenev, "Rebiata, vy ser'ezno? Vy ponimaete kuda vy edete? Istoriia rossiiskoi okkupatsii Chernobyl'skoi atomnoi stantsii i zony otchuzhdeniia," Graty, June 9, 2022, https://graty.me/rebyata-vy-serezno-vy-ponimaete-kuda-vy-edete-istoriya-rossijskoj-okkupaczii-chernobylskoj-atomnoj-stanczii-i-zony

-otchuzhdeniya; Chornobyl NPP. Chronicle of Occupation. Part 2: Straining, www.youtube.com/watch?v=JvkFOoPgoSs.

2. Chornobyl NPP. Chronicle of Occupation. Part 2: Straining.

3. Chornobyl NPP. Chronicle of Occupation. Part 2: Straining.

4. Chornobyl NPP. Chronicle of Occupation. Part 2: Straining; "Occupation of the Chornobyl nuclear power plant: What does the station look like after the Russians," *Ukrainian Witness*, www.youtube.com/watch?v=XtofZSCrPUA.

5. Vira Kasiian, "Okupanty pishly z ChAES i pidpysaly 'Akt priema i peredachi okhrany' stantsiï (dokument)," *Livyi Bereh*, March 31, 2022, https://lb.ua/society/2022/03/31/511788_okupanti_pishli_iz_chaes_i_pidpisali.html; "Muliukin, Nikolai Nikolaevich," *Mirotvorets*, https://myrotvorets.center/criminal/mulyukin-nikolaj-nikolaevich/.

6. Kasiian, "Okupanty pishly z ChAES i pidpysaly 'Akt priema i peredachi okhrany' stantsiï"; Chornobyl NPP. Chronicle of Occupation. Part 2: Straining; "Occupation of the Chornobyl nuclear power plant: What does the station look like after the Russians."

7. Kasiian, "Okupanty pishly z ChAES i pidpysaly 'Akt priema i peredachi okhrany' stantsiï."

8. "Occupation of the Chornobyl nuclear power plant: What does the station look like after the Russians"; Aleksandr Emelianenkov, "Chernye byli pro Ryzhii les: rossiiskikh voennykh shel'muiut Chernobylem," *RG.RU*, April 7, 2022, https://rg.ru/2022/04/07/chernye-byli-pro-ryzhij-les-rossijskih-voennyh-shelmuiut-chernobylem.html; interview with Valentyn Heiko, The Reckoning Project, 2022; Chornobyl NPP. Chronicle of Occupation. Part 2: Straining; ChNPP Under Occupation: Interview of Witnesses, www.youtube.com/watch?v=To6-4RepTuY; Yuliia Surzhykova, "Chornobyl': pro okupatsiiu, vandalizm ta pohrabuvannia stantsiï – ochyma ïi spivrobitnykiv," *Suspi'lne Novyny*, June 23, 2022, https://suspilne.media/253335-cornobil-pro-okupaciu-vandalizm-ta-pograbuvanna-stancii-ocima-ii-spivrobitnikiv/.

9. Chornobyl NPP. Chronicle of Occupation. Part 2: Straining; ChNPP Under Occupation: Interview of Witnesses; "Aftermath of ChNPP occupation by Russian army," www.youtube.com/watch?v=WDnIB3cKUF4.

10. "Rik vyzvolennia: Kyïvshchyna," Ukraïns'kyi instytut natsional'noï pam'iati, https://uinp.gov.ua/informaciyni-materialy/vyzvoleni-regiony-materialy-do-richnyci-deokupaciyi/rik-vyzvolennya-kyyivshchyny; "'Tse ne vidvedennia, a naslidky vyhnannia': Zelens'kyi pro vidkhid rosiis'kykh viisk z napriamkiv Kyieva ta Chernihova," TSN, March 30, 2022, https://tsn.ua/politika/ce-ne-vidvedennya-a-naslidki-vignannya-zelenskiy-pro-vidhid-rosiyskih-viysk-z-napryamkiv-kiyeva-ta-chernigova-2024986.html.

11. Nebi Qena and Yuras Karmanau, "Moscow says it will curb assault on Kyiv, Chernihiv; Russian troops seen withdrawing," *Times of Israel*, March 29, 2022.

12. Chornobyl NPP. Chronicle of Occupation. Part 2: Straining; ChNPP Under Occupation: Interview of Witnesses; Aftermath of ChNPP Occupation by Russian Army."

13. "Chornobyl NPP. Chronicle of Occupation. Part 2: Straining; Iryna Balachuk, "U Zoni vidchuzhennia pomityly vorozhyi tank: rukhavsia do Chornobylia," *Ukraïns'ka pravda*, April 1, 2022, www.pravda.com.ua/news/2022/04/1/7336314/.

14. Chornobyl NPP. Chronicle of Occupation. Part 2: Straining; ChNPP Under Occupation: Interview of Witnesses.

15. Chornobyl NPP. Chronicle of Occupation. Part 2: Straining.

16. "Oni iskali preslovutye amerikanskie laboratorii: rabotnik ChAÈS ob okkupatsii," *Telekanal ICTV*, www.youtube.com/watch?v=D-THwUDkiUE&t=182s 13:50; Chornobyl NPP. Chronicle of Occupation. Part 2: Straining.

17. "Oni iskali preslovutye amerikanskie laboratorii," 13:50; Chornobyl NPP. Chronicle of Occupation. Part 2: Straining.

18. Violetta Orlova, "VSU vziali pod kontrol' raion Pripiati i uchastok granitsy s Belorus'iu," *UNIAN*, April 3, 2022, www.unian.net/war/vsu-vzyali-pod-kontrol -rayon-pripyati-i-uchastok-granicy-s-belarusyu-foto-novosti-vtorzheniya-rossii-na -ukrainu-11771092.html.

19. Interview with Oleksandr Skyrda, The Reckoning Project, 2022.

20. Malachy Browne, David Botti, and Haley Willis, "Satellite images show bodies lay in Bucha for weeks, despite Russian claims," *New York Times*, April 4, 2022.

21. Kostia Andreikovets, "At least 458 Ukrainians died in the Bucha community as a result of the actions of the Russians," *Babel*, August 8, 2022, https://babel.ua/en/ news/82626-at-least-458-ukrainians-died-in-the-bucha-community-as-a-result -of-the-actions-of-the-russians; "The situation of human rights in Ukraine in the context of the armed attack by the Russian Federation, 24 February to 15 May 2022," United Nations Human Rights, Office of High Commissioner, Country Reports, June 29, 2022; "Rik vyzvolennia: Kyïvshchyna."

22. Occupation of the Chornobyl nuclear power plant: What does the station look like after the Russians."

23. Violetta Orlova, "Okkupanty obokrali muzei 'Zvezda Polyn' v Chernobyle: zabrali televizory, a ostavili musor," *UNIAN*, April 27, 2022, www.unian.net/ russianworld/okkupanty-obokrali-muzey-zvezda-polyn-v-chernobyle-zabrali -televizory-a-ostavili-musor-novosti-rossii-11803254.html.

24. "Aftermath of ChNPP Occupation by Russian Army"; Yuliia Mamoilenko, "Sytuatsiia na kordoni z Bilorusiieiu znovu nebezpechna – interv'iu z nachal'nykom Chornobyl's'koï zony," *S'ohodni*, July 7, 2022, www.segodnya.ua/ua/strana/ intervyu/maroderily-35-dney-ne-ostalos-ni-odnih-ucelevshih-dverey-v-kakom -sostoyanii-chernobyl-posle-deokkupacii-1629307.html.

25. Natalie Colarossi, "Russian Troops Took Highly Radioactive 'Souvenirs' from Chernobyl: Ukraine," *Newsweek*, April 10, 2022; Max Bearak and Serhiy Morgunov, "In Chernobyl's delicate nuclear labs, Russians looted safety systems," *Washington Post*, June 2, 2022.

26. "Rashysty rozhrabovuiut' Chornobyl'. Detali," *Galinfo*, March 16, 2022, https:// galinfo.com.ua/news/rashysty_rozgrabovuyut_chornobyl_detali_382458.html; Maryna Tkachuk, "Pozhezhnyk z okupovanoho Chornobylia: My pyly vodu z Pryp'iati, ale ne braly podachok vid rosiian," *Novynarnia*, May 31, 2022, https:// novynarnia.com/2022/05/31/my-pyly-vodu-z-prypyati/.

27. Shimon Briman, "How Russia Tried to Destroy Yitzhak Rabin's Family Village in Ukraine," *Haaretz*, April 10, 2023.

28. Kamenev, "Rebiata, vy ser'ezno?"

29. Kamenev, "Rebiata, vy ser'ezno?"; Oleksandr Syrota's Facebook page, March

24, 2022, www.facebook.com/aes.planca/posts/pfbid0GQh3R7gv5LtFLLM2mjL 3uG2KiB2BeH8gvCHrgQpJRM9796h16nm9hcmX9WBK2dDFl; "Unprotected Russian soldiers disturbed radioactive dust in Chernobyl's 'Red Forest,' workers say," *Reuters*, March 29, 2022.

30. "Pidtverdzheno smert' pershoho rosiis'koho okupȧnta vid radiatsiï v Chorno-byli," *Kyiv24News*, April 1, 2022, https://kyiv24.news/news/pidtverdzheno-smert -pershogo-rosijskogo-okupanta-vid-radiacziyi-v-chornobyli; Denys Karlovs'kyi, "Okupanty, iaki ryly okopy v lisakh na ChAES zasluhovuiut' na premiiu Darvina—Vereshchuk," *Ukraïns'ka pravda*, March 31, 2022, www.pravda.com .ua/news/2022/03/31/7336167/.

31. "Enerhoatom: pidtverdylasia informatsiia pro okopy, iaki rashysty ryly priamo v Rudomu lisi," *Ukraïns'ki natsional'ni novyny*, March 31, 2022, www.unn.com .ua/uk/news/1970500-energoatom-pidtverdilasya-informatsiya-pro-okopi-yaki -rashisti-rili-pryamo-v-rudomu-lisi; Stephen Mulvey, "Chernobyl's continuing hazards," *BBC News*, April 25, 2006.

32. Eliza Mackintosh, Sebastian Shukla, and Sarah-Grace Mankarious, "Inside the hospitals that concealed Russian casualties," *CNN Special Report*, October 25, 2022; Dmitrii Zhogov, "Mirnyi atom na voine: "svetilis' li rossiiane v Zone, kak zhivetsia vozle Iuzhnoukrainskoi AÈS i grozit li Ukraine vtoroi Chernobyl'?" *Dums'ka*, September 30, 2022, https://dumskaya.net/news/mirnyy-atom-na -voyne-svetilis-li-rossiyane-v-che-169151/ua/.

33. "Okopy v Rudomu lisi," *Ukrinform TV*, www.youtube.com/watch?v=JM10N2 Hi7v8; "Nebezpechni okopy," *Espreso.TV*, www.youtube.com/watch?v=8_J34 -lt2Io; "Health Effects of the Chernobyl Accident," Canadian Nuclear Safety Commission, March 2022, https://nuclearsafety.gc.ca/eng/resources/health/ health-effects-chernobyl-accident.cfm#:~:text=Among%20the%20600%20 workers%20onsite,rest%20of%20the%20exposed%20workers; "'Russians have left, but Chernobyl will never leave them': Life under occupation at Chernobyl," *France24*, www.youtube.com/watch?v=xAJhmi2BQl4.

34. "Rosiiskomu polkovnyku politsii natshvardii zahroshuie do 12 rokiv v'iaznytsi," *Zmina*, May 30, 2022, https://zmina.info/news/rosijskomu-polkovnyku-policziyi -naczgvardiyi-zagrozhuye-do-12-rokiv-vyaznyczi-za-sylove-zahoplennya-ta -rozgrabuvannya-chaes.

35. "Pravookhorontsi rozkryly osobu rosiis'koho henerala, shcho keruvav zakhoplenniam i hrabunkom ChAES," *5 Kanal*, May 25, 2022, www.5.ua/ suspilstvo/pravookhorontsi-rozkryly-osobu-rosiiskoho-henerala-shcho-keruvav -zakhoplenniam-i-hrabunkom-chaes-278179.html.

36. Jack Watling, Oleksandr V. Danylyuk, and Nick Reynolds, *Preliminary Lessons from Russia's Unconventional Operations During the Russo-Ukrainian War, Febru-ary 2022–February 2023*, Royal United Services Institute, 2023, 6, https://static .rusi.org/202303-SR-Unconventional-Operations-Russo-Ukrainian-War-web -final.pdf.pdf; Valentyna Romanenko, "SBU zaiavila, chto nardep Derkach zaver-bovan rossiiskoi razvedkoi," *Ukraïns'ka pravda*, June 24, 2022, www.pravda.com .ua/rus/news/2022/06/24/7354412/; "Deputata Andriia Derkacha oholosheno u rozshuk," *Radio Svoboda*, September 16, 2022, www.radiosvoboda.org/a/news -derkach-nabu-rozshuk/32036494.html.

37. Alina Dubovs'ka, "Na Rivnenshchyni zatrymaly posadovtsia Enerhoatomu za pidozroiu u derzhzradi," *Suspilne Novyny*, March 24, 2022.

38. Oleksiy Yarmolenko, "The Prosecutor General's Office made public the details of the case of the ex-head of the Crimean SSU Kulinich. He was recruited by the FSB, and his accomplice was the ex-deputy secretary of the National Security Council," *Babel*, July 23, 2022; Aliona Mazurenko, "Eks-heneral SBU Naumov, i akyi dopomih rosiianam zakhopyty ChAES, mozhe otrymaty prytulok u RF—ZMI," *Ukraïns'ka pravda*, August 30, 2022, www.pravda.com.ua/news/2022/08/30/7365305/; https://vlasti.net/ru/news/305214; Igor Petrovskikh, "Poka odnogo 'chernobyl'skogo' moshennika izuchaet GBR, ego podel'nik Naumov poluchaet dolzhnosti i nagrady v SBU," *Antikor*, October 15, 2019, https://antikor.com.ua/ru/articles/334692-poka_odnogo_chernobyljskogo_moshennika_izuchaet_gbr_ego_podeljnik_naumov_poluchaet_dolhnosti_i_nagrady_v_sbu.

39. "Chornobyl' foreva: iak odyn z kerivnykiv SBU Andrii Naumov zarobliaie na zoni vidchuzhennia," *Poligraf*, August 18, 2020, https://polygraf.net/chornobyl-foreva-iak-odyn-z-kerivnykiv-sbu-andrii-naumov-zarobliaie-na-zoni-vidchuzhennia.

40. Mykhailo Senchenko, "Chornobyl' foreva: iak odyn z kerivnykiv SBU Andrii Naumov zarobliaie na Zoni vidchuzhennia," *Antikor*, August 18, 2020, https://antikor.com.ua/articles/401961-chornobilj_foreva_jak_odin_z_kerivnikiv_sbu_andrij_naumov_zarobljaje_na_zoni_vidchuhennja; https://www.pravda.com.ua/news/2022/05/18/7347003/; Mari Saito and Maria Tsvetkova, "The Enemy Within," Reuters, July 28, 2022; Gergana Krasteva, "Putin infiltrated Chernobyl 'with Russian spies' before easy invasion," *Metro*, July 31, 2022.

41. Saito and Tsvetkova, "The Enemy Within."

42. Ihor Berezhans'kyi, "Vberehly svit vid novoï trahediï: Zelens'kyi nahorodyv spivrobitnykiv ChAES, iaki pratsiuvaly v umovakh okupatsiï," TSN, April 27, 2022, https://tsn.ua/ukrayina/vbereshli-svit-vid-novoyi-tragediyi-zelenskiy-nagorodiv-spivrobitnikiv-chaes-yaki-pracyuvali-v-umovah-okupaciyi-2047237.html; "Novyi obmin polonenymy. Zvil'neni zakhysnyky Chornobylia i Mariuopolia," *BBC News Ukraine*, January 8, 2023, www.bbc.com/ukrainian/news-64203928; "Chornobyl 22"; "Iak vdalosia utrymaty stabilnist pid chas okuoatsii ChAES?" *Telekanal Rada*, March 25, 2023, www.youtube.com/watch?v=DVBOY1ow2dA.

43. Petro Didula, "Okupovana rosiianamy Chornobyl's'ka zona ta okopy u Rudomu lisi – pershyi u sviti pryklad mizhnarodnoho iadernoho teroryzmu,—Iaroslav Yemelianenko," Ukraïns'kyi katolyts'kyi universytet, *Novyny*, July 25, 2022, https://ucu.edu.ua/news/okupovana-rosiyanamy-chornobylska-zona-ta-okopy-v-rudomu-lisi-pershyj-u-sviti-pryklad-mizhnarodnogo-yadernogo-teroryzmu-yaroslav-yemelyanenko/.

44. Didula, "Okupovana rosiianamy Chornobyl's'ka zona ta okopy u Rudomu lisi."

45. Didula, "Okupovana rosiianamy Chornobyl's'ka zona ta okopy u Rudomu lisi."

Epilogue

1. Volodymyr Kostyrin, "Zelens'kyi vruchyv derzhavni nahorody pratsivnykam ChAES: vberehly svit vid novoï katastrofy," *RBK Ukraïna*, April 27, 2022, www.rbc.ua/ukr/news/zelenskiy-vruchil-gosudarstvennye-nagrady-1651010613

.html; https://chnpp.gov.ua/ru/about/labour-glory-ru/gosudarstvennye-nagrady
-ukrainy.

2. Serhii Plokhy, "Chornobyl: A Tombstone of the Reckless Empire," Harvard Ukrainian Research Institute, April 21, 2016; Peter Kaiser, "IAEA Chief Visits Chernobyl Accident Site, Calls for Strengthened Nuclear Safety," International Atomic
Energy Agency, *News*, April 20, 2011.

3. "Heightened security fears on Chernobyl disaster anniversary," United Nations,
UN News, April 26, 2022.

4. Francois Murphy, "IAEA board passes resolution calling on Russia to leave
Zaporizhzhia," Reuters, September 15, 2022; Hanna Arhirova, "Ukraine nuclear
workers recount abuse, threats from Russians," AP News, October 5, 2022.

5. Julian Borger, "Ukraine: Cooling pond at Zaporizhzhia plant at risk after dam collapse – report," *The Guardian*, June 8, 2022; "IAEA's Grossi 'learned a lot' from
Zaporizhzhia visit," *World Nuclear News*, June 16, 2023.

6. George M. Moore, "How international law applies to attacks on nuclear and associated facilities in Ukraine," *Bulletin of the Atomic Scientists*, March 6, 2022.

INDEX